SPINOZA

ALSO AVAILABLE FROM BLOOMSBURY

Philosophy for Non-Philosophers, Louis Althusser
Being and Event, Alain Badiou
Conditions, Alain Badiou
Infinite Thought, Alain Badiou
Logics of Worlds, Alain Badiou
Theoretical Writings, Alain Badiou
Theory of the Subject, Alain Badiou
From Communism to Capitalism, Michel Henry
Seeing the Invisible, Michel Henry
Lines of Flight, Félix Guattari
After Finitude, Quentin Meillassoux
Time for Revolution, Antonio Negri
The Five Senses, Michel Serres
Statues, Michel Serres
Rome, Michel Serres
Geometry, Michel Serres
Art and Fear, Paul Virilio
Negative Horizon, Paul Virilio
Althusser's Lesson, Jacques Rancière
Dissensus, Jacques Rancière
Politics of Aesthetics, Jacques Rancière
The Lost Thread, Jacques Rancière

SPINOZA

The Ethics of an Outlaw

Ivan Segré

Translated by David Broder

Bloomsbury Academic
An imprint of Bloomsbury Publishing Plc

B L O O M S B U R Y
LONDON • OXFORD • NEW YORK • NEW DELHI • SYDNEY

Bloomsbury Academic

An imprint of Bloomsbury Publishing Plc

50 Bedford Square
London
WC1B 3DP
UK

1385 Broadway
New York
NY 10018
USA

www.bloomsbury.com

BLOOMSBURY and the Diana logo are trademarks of Bloomsbury Publishing Plc

First published in French as *Le manteau de Spinoza*, La Fabrique 2014

© Ivan Segré, 2014

Copyright to the English edition © Bloomsbury Publishing Plc, 2017

David Broder has asserted his right under the Copyright, Designs and Patents Act, 1988, to be identified as Translator of this work.

All rights reserved. No part of this publication may be reproduced or transmitted in any form or by any means, electronic or mechanical, including photocopying, recording, or any information storage or retrieval system, without prior permission in writing from the publishers.

No responsibility for loss caused to any individual or organization acting on or refraining from action as a result of the material in this publication can be accepted by Bloomsbury or the author.

British Library Cataloguing-in-Publication Data
A catalogue record for this book is available from the British Library.

ISBN: HB: 9781472596437
PB: 9781350016613
ePDF: 9781472596451
ePub: 9781472596444

Library of Congress Cataloging-in-Publication Data
A catalogue record for this book is available from the Library of Congress.

Typeset by Fakenham Prepress Solutions, Fakenham, Norfolk NR21 8NN
Printed and bound in India

CONTENTS

Translator's Note vii
Prologue viii

PART ONE THE PHILOSOPHER, ELECTION AND HATRED. SPINOZA AND THE 'BOURGEOIS' THEORISTS 1

Introduction 3

1 Discourse on Method 11

2 The Song of the Sign 23

3 Kingship 35

4 On Contradiction 47

PART TWO SPINOZA'S BIBLE 59

Introduction 61

5 The *At Judaei* Manifesto 71

6 A 'Christ' without the Passion 81

7 The Origin of the Law 95

8 True Otherness 109

9 The Masquerade 121

10 The Tree of Knowledge 133

Epilogue 155
Apologue: The Spectre's Manifesto 159
Notes 161
Index 183

TRANSLATOR'S NOTE

This book, in your hands, was first published by *La Fabrique* in Paris in 2014. Its original title was *Le manteau de Spinoza: Pour une éthique hors la loi* ('Spinoza's Coat: For An Outlaw Ethics'). Ivan Segré explains this reference, absent from the title of the English edition, in his Epilogue. The hole in Spinoza's coat was a lasting mark of an attempt on the philosopher's life. More than that, it symbolized the bourgeois hatred for the act of knowledge. This is precisely the hatred aroused by Spinoza's 'outlaw ethics': the subject of this book.

*

Throughout the present translation we cite Spinoza's *Theoretical-Political Treatise* (*Tractatus Theologico-Politicus*, *TTP*) from the 2007 Cambridge University Press version, edited by Jonathan Israel and translated by Michael Silverthorne and Jonathan Israel. However, we will also refer to a series of French translations that Segré references and indeed compares, including Charles Appuhn's translation – *Traité théologico-politique* (Paris: Garnier, 1965) – as well as other versions by Madeleine Francès and Robert Misrahi (Paris: Gallimard, 1954) and Jacqueline Lagrée and Pierre-François Moreau (Paris: PUF, 1999).

David Broder, Rome, May 2016

PROLOGUE

Spinoza had a hole in his coat. Someone tried to stab him and his coat bore the mark of the attack. It became 'Spinoza's coat'.

In the Hebrew Bible, the clothing covering up man's nudity has a history. It starts with Adam and Eve. After they fell into sin, they discovered that they were naked and they sewed together a loincloth made of fig leaves. The story continues with Noah. Having arrived off the Ark, Noah planted a vineyard, got drunk and let his guard down as he fell asleep naked in his tent. *Ham*, meaning 'heat' in Hebrew – the bad son, the wicked man – discovered his father naked in the tent and went to tell his brothers about it. (According to one Talmud scholar, the wording implies that he raped his father; another says that *Ham* raped *and* castrated him.) *Shem* – 'name' in Hebrew – together with his other brother *Yaphet* – 'beauty' – got a robe and went into the tent facing backward in order to cover up their father's nudity: man's nudity. This is the garment that Jacob later gives to Joseph. It is the bloodied tunic that Jacob's sons bring back to their father after selling their brother as a slave.

The Law is a sleeping, naked signifier. The wine is the hidden meaning, the secret; the tent is a study hall. And there are two practices of exegesis. One corresponds to *Ham*, the 'heat'; and then there is another that corresponds to *Shem*, the 'name'. When *Yaphet* associates with *Ham*, sophistication makes a pact with violence; when he associates with *Shem*, it is the idea that regulates sophistication.

Jean-Claude Milner, a theorist of the name 'Jew', wrote the following in a book dedicated to May 1968:

> Will anyone dare say out loud that the only true event of the twentieth century was the return of the name 'Jew'? With its corollary: the disappearance of the name 'worker'. (…) The conclusion? When we exalt the name 'worker' we are necessarily engaging in a denial: leaving aside the cradle of infantile regression, we have but one purpose, namely to deny what *is* in order to explain what *is not*.[1]

Let's take Milner's conclusion as a hypothesis. Let's say that 'the return of the name "Jew"', such as the *bourgeois* theorists conceive it, has a certain function, namely to forbid *our* modernity. So on the one hand, there is rationalist philosophy, and revolutionary politics on the other. Or, to put that another way, the return of the name 'Jew' has its corollary in the disappearance of the name 'worker'. Of course we need to re-establish some missing links in order to bring this correlation into view. The first of these links is a text of St Paul's. In his *Letter to the Ephesians*, where he addresses the reconciliation of the Jews and the pagans 'by the Cross', we read

> For he is our peace, who hath made both one, and hath broken down the middle wall of partition between us; Having abolished in his flesh the enmity, even the law of commandments contained in ordinances; for to make in himself of twain one new man, so making peace; And that he might reconcile both unto God in one body by the cross, having slain the enmity thereby.[2]

In their notes, the authors of the *Traduction œcuménique de la bible* [TOB; 1975–6, 'Ecumenical Translation of the Bible'] explain that 'this Law of commandments and ordinances' is the 'Law of Moses, which made the Jews a privileged people, separating them from the pagans. Jesus did away with this law, fulfilling it once and for all by his Cross.' Christ did away with the 'partition' of enmity by fulfilling the Law through his loving sacrifice. That is the Christian argument; that is 'the mystery of the blood of Christ'. The crucifixion fulfilled the Law of Moses as symbolized through circumcision, and thus did away with the 'partition' that *prevents* humanity by dividing humanity. If the name 'Jew' is a cause of hatred, that is because it erects an obstacle to the advent of an egalitarian universality; because it *forbids* it.

Let's now introduce the second link in the chain. It is an extract from Marx and Engels's *The German Ideology*:

> If power is taken as the basis of right, as Hobbes, etc., do, then right, law, etc., are merely the symptom, the expression of other relations upon which state power rests. The material life of individuals, which by no means depends merely on their "will", their mode of production and form of intercourse, which mutually determine each other — this is the real basis of the state and remains so at all the stages at which division of labour and private property are still necessary, quite independently of the will of individuals. These actual relations are in no way created by the state power; on the contrary they are the power creating it. The individuals who rule in these conditions — leaving aside the fact that

their power must assume the form of the state — have to give their will, which is determined by these definite conditions, a universal expression as the will of the state, as law, an expression whose content is always determined by the relations of this class, as the civil and criminal law demonstrates in the clearest possible way.[3]

In analysing the power relations, class relations and inegalitarian 'base' that together determine the Law, Marx and Engels desacralize and ultimately pull it apart. They then go on to herald the 'kingship'[4] of the names 'worker', 'proletarian' and 'communist': the names of *another* law immanent to the emancipation process and the revolutionary becoming.

Milner concludes that the 'return of the name "Jew"' has its 'corollary' in the 'disappearance of the name "worker"'. This is logically coherent, if the name 'Jew' does indeed symbolize the 'partition' effected by the Law; if through circumcision the Jew embodies this barrier. So the return of the name 'Jew' forbids the revolutionary becoming of the name 'worker', or at the very least sets up a barrier to its royalty.

But others give the name 'Jew' a different meaning, because they understand it differently. In 1979 Claude Birman – a young disciple of Jean Zacklad's – wrote a preface for Verdier's edition of Maimonides's *Guide for the Perplexed*, in which he explained that

> The God of Israel is defined as the god who 'brought [the Jews] out of Egypt' (*Exodus* 20:1–2); that is to say, the god who liberates from oppression and delivers from servitude. The four-letter Name (YHWH) is the name of a liberating god: and this is not just an add-on, as if it were one of his 'qualities' among others; rather, this god is *essentially* liberating. Such a god is incompatible with any other (*Exodus* 20:3–6) in the measure that the ultimate meaning of the creation is absolute freedom. And the Revelation's role is to enlighten processes of liberation, such that they might aptly discern, in the course of the world, what this freedom does and does not entail (Ex. 20:7).

So there are two schools of thought on the subject of the name 'Jew'. They are not only antagonistic, but *antinomic*. On the one hand, there are the *bourgeois* theorists of the name 'Jew'. They purport to forbid the revolutionary becoming of the name 'worker' in the name of the Law and the 'partition'. On the other hand, there are the *worker* theorists of the name 'Jew'. They claim that this name refers not to the subject of a Law, but to the subject who knows a god who leads the Jews 'out of Egypt', and that the law of the name 'Jew' – 'incompatible with any other' – is to live according to the guidance of this knowledge.

The new French edition of the *Guide for the Perplexed*, also from Éditions Verdier, has been relieved of Claude Birman's preface. And simultaneous to this, Verdier is publishing Jean-Claude Milner's works regarding the name 'Jew'. So a page has turned since 1979. But the texts – both ancient and modern – remain, and we have learned how to read them. That demands the patient study of a forgotten art: the Hebrew art of exegesis. 'Bourgeois' theorists make a pretence of doing so; let's now examine their pretentions.

PART ONE

THE PHILOSOPHER, ELECTION AND HATRED. SPINOZA AND THE 'BOURGEOIS' THEORISTS

Why, look you now, how unworthy a thing you make of me! You would play upon me, you would seem to know my stops, you would pluck out the heart of my mystery, you would sound me from my lowest note to the top of my compass; and there is much music, excellent voice, in this little organ, yet cannot you make it speak. 'Sblood, do you think I am easier to be played on than a pipe? Call me what instrument you will, though you can fret me, you cannot play upon me.

WILLIAM SHAKESPEARE, *HAMLET*, III, 2

PART ONE

THE PHILOSOPHER,
ELECTION
AND HATRED:
SPINOZA AND
THE BOURGEOIS
THEORISTS

INTRODUCTION

Spinoza was excommunicated in 1656 when he was twenty-four years old. The *Herem* pronounced against him was symptomatic: the order of reason is heterogeneous to what serves as tradition and this provokes a police-type reaction. In 1670 he brought out his *Theological-Political Treatise* (*TTP*), in which he argued that 'the freedom to philosophize may not only be allowed without danger to piety and the stability of the republic but cannot be refused without destroying the peace of the republic and piety itself'.[1] If Descartes established the rationalist framework of our modernity, it was Spinoza who drew out its ethical and political conclusions.

His consistent Cartesianism haunted the theorists of the *ancien régime*. A few months after the *TTP* was published – without the author's name and under the cover of a made-up German publisher – it was banned. In a November 1671 letter to Arnauld, Leibniz denounced the manner in which the Cartesian sect purported to make *tabula rasa* of scholasticism. In passing, he referred to Spinoza (albeit without mentioning his name) as the 'author of a horrible book on the freedom of philosophizing'. From its first appearance, the book had horrified many learned minds and Leibniz was a cautious type. Georges Friedmann dedicated his *Leibniz et Spinoza* 'to the memory of Marc Bloch and Jean Cavaillès', 'just and learned men who died in 1944 in service of freedom and a better city'. Referring to the circles in which Spinoza moved, he reviewed the reactions to the *TTP*:

> Thomasius's *Programma adversus anonymum*, Rappolt's *Oratorio contra naturalistas*, the writings of Dürr, a professor at Altorf, of Miegus, a professor at Heidelberg, and of Johannes Melchior, a preacher in Frech, near Bonn, were cutting, impassioned pamphlets, and Leibniz noted as much when he congratulated his teacher Thomasius of 'having treated this intolerably licentious libel as it deserved'. In a July 1670 letter the philologist Franz Burman condemned this 'most extremely pestilential

(*pestilentissimus*) book, fat with all sorts of evils, to the anger of the Gods and men'. And as we have seen, writing to Leibniz J. G. Graevius used the same superlative to attack a work 'that leaves a window wide open to atheism' at the same time as categorically denouncing 'the Jew Spinoza, chased out of the Synagogue for his monstrous opinions' as its author. Philippe van Limborch – while himself being the head of the Arminians in Holland – agreed with these judgments to the letter, showing no less zeal: as he wrote in a 1671 letter to a friend whom he supplied with a copy of the *Treatise*, 'I do not remember having ever read a more pestilential (*pestilentiorem*) book. It mocks the prophets and apostles. For him, there have never been any miracles and there could not be any. There is a *fatum*, by which God himself is bound; and yet he describes God in such a way as to seem entirely to banish him from existence. I wanted to submit to you the erudition defecated (*defoecata*) and the critique ground-out by this man, so that you might know what monsters our Holland produces (*quae monstra producat Batavia nostra*). People of this kind do not only attack this or that belief, but the very soul of religion. This book is not to be shown to just anyone, but only to the learned, whose mind is well-trained in distinguishing good from bad'. Around the same time, Sinold, writing to Leibniz, suggested to him that 'according to some, such an author is not to be refuted, but crushed'.[2]

The hatred of Spinoza is connected to this sort of reaction, which is in a sense its origin. So what should we think of those enlightened, learned thinkers relaying the same judgement as Thomasius, Miegus, Graevius, Diafoirus, etc. three centuries later? What should we think of Hermann Cohen, Leo Strauss, Emmanuel Levinas, Benny Lévy, or indeed of Jean-Claude Milner? What is this 'cause of the Jews' – which they consider so self-evident that they can claim that Spinoza betrayed it? In his 1915 work, *Spinoza on State and Religion, Judaism and Christianity*, Hermann Cohen concludes that 'Spinoza remains the real accuser of Judaism in the eyes of the Christian world'.[3] The accuser or informer is a lamentably renowned figure in Jewish history. Such was the deed of the Jewish converts to Christianity who, seeking to demonstrate their sincerity in their new faith, thought it opportune to denounce their former coreligionists to the authorities and thus contributed to their persecution.

In the commentary that he dedicated to Cohen's text a few years later (in 1924), Leo Strauss was more measured, but felt the need to recognize that the excommunication was well-founded: 'As to a "human" assessment of Spinoza's coldness and alienness toward Judaism, this would presuppose an assessment of the conduct of the Jews toward him: not an assessment of the ban of excommunication (against which, naturally, nothing can be objected) but, rather, of the expressions of private attitudes that were presumably not above criticism to the same extent as the ban of excommunication [*Herem*] itself'.[4] When he returned to this same theme in 1965 his judgement was still just as measured, but it was also more decisive. He began by relating Hermann Cohen's accusations: 'Spinoza remains up to the present day the accuser *par excellence* of Judaism before an anti-Jewish world; the disposition of his mind and heart toward Jews and Judaism were "anti-natural"; he committed a "humanly incomprehensible act of treachery"; he was possessed by an "evil demon"'. Then, Strauss expounds his own personal judgement: 'Our case against Spinoza is in certain regards stronger than Cohen thought. One may doubt whether Spinoza's action is truly humanly incomprehensible or devilish, but one must grant that it is amazingly unscrupulous.'[5] Emmanuel Levinas's judgement was no friendlier. In a 1955 article entitled 'Le cas Spinoza', he justified his precursors' arguments:

> We are entirely of the same view as our late, admirable friend Jacob Gordin: that Spinoza was guilty of betrayal. In the history of ideas, he subordinated the truth of Judaism to the New Testament revelation ... Thus we immediately see the nefarious role that Spinoza played in the decomposition of the Jewish intelligentsia, even if for its representatives – as for Spinoza himself – Christianity was only a penultimate truth, and even if the adoration of God, in spirit and in truth, must still surmount Christianity.[6]

Hermann Cohen, Leo Strauss, Jacob Gordin, Emmanuel Levinas ... the accusation of 'treachery' levelled against Spinoza marks out a sort of intellectual genealogy. And it was Benny Lévy – in a certain sense, the last-born – who was the most radical in this regard. In *Le Meurtre du pasteur* (2002) he wrote:

> Come on then, moderns, one more push, we must finish with Moses once and for all; we need the murder of the shepherd, in the right and proper form. This is the extremely modern programme of the final solution.

And in the immediately subsequent part of his book, devoted to Spinoza, he continued: 'The extremely modern programme begins with Spinoza (and ends with Freud).'[7] Finally, in his 2013 work *Le Sage trompeur*,[8]

Jean-Claude Milner himself took over the case against the philosopher. He summarized his argument by adopting the judgement that Léon Poliakov had pronounced in his *Histoire de l'antisémitisme*:

> His anti-Jewish polemic opened the way for the rationalist or secular anti-Semitism of modern times, perhaps the most dangerous that there is. It was this that allowed Hermann Cohen to emphasise Spinoza's 'devilish irony'.[9]

This is a faithful account of Jean-Claude Milner's conclusion, at least, if not his argumentation. This is, moreover, the close-held conviction common to all of them, the seal of the *union sacrée* against Spinoza – namely, that his ethical rationalism is not *innocent*. We propose to analyse a textbook case of the bill of indictment against him.

Jean-Claude Milner's *Le Sage trompeur* – subtitled 'Free arguments on Spinoza and the Jews. Short reading guide I' – first took the form of a lecture, which he gave in the context of the seminars held by the Institut d'études lévinassiennes. Three of his other books also originated in seminars held by this Institute: *Les Penchants criminels de l'Europe démocratique* (2003); *Le Juif de savoir* (2005); and *L'Arrogance du présent* (2009).[10] *Le Sage trompeur* is the fourth book in a series that Milner has termed his 'works concerning the name "Jew"'.[11] Let's briefly summarize Milner's doctrine. For Spinoza, the name 'Jew' is an obstacle. That is why he strove to get rid of it. In order to do so, he proceeded methodically and without hatred: he rationalized the disappearance of the name 'Jew' and indeed provided a programme for it. That is Spinoza's singularity. We are mistaken when we think that his ethics' goal is human freedom. They have a more determinate aim, seeking to emancipate Europe from what is holding it back: the name 'Jew'. That is what results from Milner's methodical reading of a Spinoza text. After all, he himself also proceeds methodically: he picks out a passage from the *TTP*, he sets it up as a 'Manifesto', names it *Hodie Judaei* ('Today the Jews', in reference to its first words), and maintaining that this is where Spinoza expounded his political doctrine on the name 'Jew', subjects the text to his analytical scrutiny. And at the end of his investigation, he unravels its doctrine – not as it appears to the ordinary person, but as it ought to be understood by an educated reader. His principle is a simple one: the educated reader is the reader who is able to read Spinoza's text as Spinoza himself wished it to be read. And according to Milner, Spinoza wanted his educated readers to read it as follows:

> if the political authorities are concerned with the freedom and well-being of the governed, they should take to heart the need to remove the

term 'Jew' from everyday language. In this perspective, it is superfluous to distinguish between those who conduct themselves as Jews, within an established religious community, and those who persist in calling themselves Jews even without conducting themselves as Jews. This is not a matter of a race, but of a name. It is not a matter of putting anyone to death, but of achieving – without any bloodletting – a situation in which no one calls themselves a Jew. This sage would pride himself on his respect for the measures taken to this end. He would pride himself even more on anticipating these measures. And above all on theorising them.[12]

Milner cites the *Hodie Judaei* manifesto that concludes the *TTP*'s third chapter, using Charles Appuhn's translation:[13]

Thus the Jews today have absolutely nothing that they can attribute to themselves but not to other peoples. As for their being dispersed and stateless for so many years, it is not at all surprising that, after separating themselves from all the nations in this way, they brought the resentment of all men upon themselves, not only because of their external rites which are contrary to the rites of other nations, but also by the sign of circumcision which they zealously maintain. But experience has shown that it is the resentment of the gentiles to a large extent that preserves them. When the king of Spain at one time compelled the Jews to accept the religion of his kingdom or go into exile, a large number of Jews converted to the Catholic faith. All those who accepted it were granted the privileges of native Spaniards and were considered worthy of all positions of dignity. Hence they immediately integrated with the Spanish, so that in a short time there were no remnants of them left and no memory of them. But quite the opposite happened to those whom the king of Portugal compelled to convert to the religion of his kingdom. For though they submitted to this faith, they continued to live apart from all men, doubtless because he declared them unworthy of all higher positions. Furthermore, I think that the sign of circumcision has such great importance as almost to persuade me that this thing alone will preserve their nation for ever, and in fact, were it not that the principles of their religion weaken their courage, I would believe unreservedly that at some time, given an opportunity, since all things are changeable, they might re-establish their state, and God will choose them again. We also have an excellent example of this among the Chinese, who likewise zealously retain a kind of topknot on their heads, by which they distinguish themselves from all other men, and have preserved themselves in this distinctive manner for many thousands of years, so that they far surpass all nations in antiquity. Nor have they always had their own state. They have lost it and then recovered it, and without doubt will recover it again, when the Tartars become demoralized through luxury and idleness.[14]

At the end of a hundred-odd pages of learned analyses, Milner concludes that what we have here is a political doctrine whose unmentionable yet determined goal is the disappearance of the name 'Jew'. The reason is this name's own culpability:

> Effectively – and it is the most general of Spinoza's indecent theories, from which all the others derive – the Jews are responsible and at fault for the resentment that they attract.[15]

In this view, Spinoza is the theorist of the fault that attaches to the Jews on account of the fact they are Jews – whether they 'remain attached to the principles of the Jewish religion' or not. The principle is that 'the name alone suffices to set the resentment machine in motion'.[16] And since the name 'Jew' is the cause of resentment, it must disappear in order for the resentment to stop, as the effect cannot cease until its cause has disappeared. That, according to Milner, is the order of Spinoza's reasoning. At the end of his *Le Sage trompeur*, he concludes:

> A name must disappear without leaving any traces. The same demand that was once reserved to those who could bear the name Jew – either on their own account, or via one of their parents or grand-parents – is now extended to everyone. Casting off family genealogies, modern Jewish apostasy has become a duty for all who can speak. Each and every one of them, whatever their own memories, can and must arrive at the total oblivion of this single name. The docile lovers of erudition assure us that the universal will easily win through, along with peace on earth. Taking the name Jew for the most powerful factor in driving the troubles that history has produced, they suppose that with its abolition the resentment in everyone's hearts will be extinguished. Overflowing in their intellectual love for humanity, these impassioned types show their impatience. They get worked up about such an ancient name being so slow to fall into disuse. They despair, yet are ever-hopeful. The *Hodie Judaei* manifesto should reassure them, for it shall reign. At the price of a metamorphosis. A rigorous, difficult text will become like an opinion aerosol. If Spinoza was long praised by people who did not understand

him, he will soon be perfectly well understood even by those who have not read him. Intoxicated by the smell of the perfect persecution, the Spinozists will press on as a crowd through the lanes of a welcoming, densely-populated park. Except that they will not know that they are Spinozists.[17]

Spinoza sought to distinguish between the 'learned' man guided by reason and the common man – the man of the 'crowd' (vulgus) dominated by inadequate ideas, by passions. But Milner tells us that this pretence was a misleading one: the future would show that the philosopher's political wisdom was the same as the crowd's. How do we get from a learned text to the drunkenness of the crowd? 'At the price of a metamorphosis'. The *Hodie Judaei* manifesto, a text by a learned man addressed to other learned men, will reign – if it doesn't already – in the manner of an 'opinion aerosol'. The 'metamorphosis' is only possible because Spinoza ultimately did nothing more than articulate the passion of the common man in an erudite manner – and indeed, secretly so. An exemplary philosopher, he would have known better than anyone how to set out a programme for the disappearance of the name 'Jew', such that the universal could easily win through.

*

According to Milner the *Hodie Judaei* marked Spinoza's break with the Jews. It was the argument for his conversion – in spirit – to Christianity, and the political expression of his *ressentiment*.[18] So let's examine the text under indictment. As against Jean-Claude Milner's 'short reading guide' relaying the original curse levelled against the philosopher, let's instead propose another practice of exegesis that can give voice to Spinoza's blessing – תקון – (*tikkun*).

1 THE DISCOURSE ON METHOD

Jean-Claude Milner argues that there is a passage of Spinoza's *TTP* outlining in broad terms a policy that could 'make the word Jew disappear from everyday language'.[1] He claims that the return of the name 'Jew' has the corollary of the disappearance of the name 'worker' and that Spinoza is setting out a programme for the disappearance of the name 'Jew'. This link is very useful to us insofar as it shows what connects Spinoza to the name 'worker'. We will not concede without serious examination the claim that Spinoza set out a programme for the disappearance of the name 'Jew', but we will however, accept that his ethical rationalism is not unrelated to the becoming of the name 'worker'. At the beginning of the *Hodie Judaei* manifesto, there is some discussion of the 'resentment of all men' (*omnium odium*) that the Jews bring upon themselves by living separately, attached to particular rites. This is also evocative of a famous formulation in Tacitus's work regarding the people who were deemed guilty of hating the human race. In his *Annals* the Roman historian describes the persecution of the early Christians under Nero in 64 AD. After the Great Fire of Rome opinion was turning against the accused Nero, who thus sought a means of diverting the people's anger.

> But neither human help, nor imperial munificence, nor all the modes of placating Heaven, could stifle scandal or dispel the belief that the fire had taken place by order. Therefore, to scotch the rumour, Nero substituted as culprits, and punished with the utmost refinements of cruelty, a class of men, loathed for their vices, whom the crowd styled Christians. Christus, the founder of the name, had undergone the death penalty in the reign of Tiberius, by sentence of the procurator Pontius Pilatus, and the pernicious superstition was checked for a moment, only to break

out once more, not merely in Judaea, the home of the disease, but in the capital itself, where all things horrible or shameful in the world collect and find a vogue. First, then, the confessed members of the sect were arrested; next, on their disclosures, vast numbers were convicted, not so much on the count of arson as for hatred of the human race [*multitudo ingens haud proinde in crimine incendii quam odio humani generis conuicti sunt*]. And derision accompanied their end ... in spite of a guilt which had earned the most exemplary punishment, there arose a sentiment of pity, due to the impression that they were being sacrificed not for the welfare of the state but to the ferocity of a single man.[2]

Tacitus used the formulation '*odio humani generis*' ('hatred of the human race') to characterize the Christians' crime. They had been accused of introducing 'pernicious superstition' ('*exitiabilis superstitio*') to Rome. Nero had them persecuted with the greatest cruelty. The historian concludes that this spectacle ended up earning them pity, even if they were guilty (*sontes*), because it was understood that they were not being persecuted for the sake of the public good (*utilitate publica*). Spinoza had a copy of Tacitus's works, as would any erudite reader of his. So we need to compare the two texts. If Milner's reconstruction of Spinoza's doctrine is accurate, it should follow the same pattern as Tacitus's text, apart from modifying its terms and its conclusion. Here the persecution is not the work of a tyrant, but of a 'free republic'; the persecuted are not the early Christians, but the last Jews; and there is no question of compassion, since the whole point of the persecution is public welfare.

In order to understand the secret logic of this inversion we have to turn to another text contemporary to Tacitus's, namely the Letter to the Ephesians: 'For He Himself is our peace, who made both groups into one and broke down the barrier of the dividing wall, by abolishing in His flesh the enmity, which is the Law of commandments contained in ordinances.'[3] According to Milner, Spinoza adopted the pattern of Tacitus's text but inverted its conclusions by ordering it in different terms: for whereas the Christians were innocent, the Jews are guilty.

For the author of *Le Sage trompeur*, it is very important to demonstrate that this is indeed Spinoza's secret doctrine, in order to justify a doctrine of his own. The most coherent of the bourgeois theorists of the name 'Jew', Milner's doctrine, is the following: *what the theorist of the name 'worker' conceives in terms of a common good is, in the last analysis, nothing other than a rationalized form of the persecution of the Jews.*

*

Le Sage trompeur is subtitled 'Short reading guide I'. So it is the first volume of a how-to-read – and in this case that means learning how to read Spinoza. Evidently, his reading is all the more masterly the more distant the propositions he brings to light are from Spinoza's own explicit meaning. Distractedly reading the *Hodie Judaei* manifesto, and even reading it attentively, it is not apparent that Spinoza thinks any kind of political authority must 'make the word "Jew" disappear from everyday language'. Moreover, there is far too much discussion of Jews, Hebrews and the Hebrew language in the *TTP* for a read of the short passage at the end of Chapter III to establish a hypothesis of this order. And yet this is where Spinoza supposedly teaches his lessons on the 'perfect persecution' of the Jews. At least that is what an erudite reader like Milner takes from it.

The principle of an expert reading consists of moving from the text's manifest meaning to a hidden one. There are things that Spinoza says explicitly, but also things that he does not say and which the reader must understand for himself. Milner brings into play the decisive consideration that there are anomalies in the explicit meaning of the *Hodie Judaei*. He concludes from this that Spinoza is employing a particular method in his writing. And if there is a method in his writing, there must be a corresponding method for reading it: 'I have chosen to base myself on the reading method elaborated by Leo Strauss'.[4] On these bases, Milner proceeds methodically to reconstruct a hidden meaning, and at the end of his enquiry he believes that he has unravelled the philosopher's secret doctrine: that a political authority must persecute the Jews, but without hatred, in order for the persecution to be 'perfect'.

Let's concede to Milner, that the extract under consideration is a 'manifesto' where Spinoza expounds the policy he recommends with regard to the Jews and that he uses a certain art in his writing. The last stage of the argumentation is the decisive one, because it means that we have to be able to reconstruct Spinoza's hidden meaning in order to be able to read the text in question. The difficulty that such an exercise raises is that the hypothesis of a hidden meaning introduces the possibility of saying … anything. It introduces the possibility of making the text say what you really want it to say, since effectively – and by definition – the hidden meaning is not explicitly formulated therein. So we need some fool-proof check. I propose setting down the following interpretative rule: the implicit meaning does not contradict the explicit meaning; it internalizes it.

If Spinoza uses a certain art in his writing in the *TTP*, based on implicit meaning, this is not because his argument is unsayable. Rather, it is because he fears being heard by those who might be angered by what he says, on account of their own stupidity. Spinoza does not have to trick such people in order to avoid them hearing him, but merely to say nothing explicitly, so that only the reader who is capable of understanding for himself will hear him. Spinoza is principally addressing himself to this latter reader, and that is why he uses this method in his writing. Is this Milner's understanding? In titling his book *Le Sage trompeur* ('The deceptive sage'), Milner seems to be declaring from the outset that he is imputing to Spinoza the will to deceive and not a certain art in his writing. Of course, he denies that this is what he is saying:

> All the same, his central motive was not the will to deceive. Indeed, I will remind the reader of my position: yes, Spinoza wrote untruths on Spain; no, he did not set out to deceive, because he principally addressed himself to those who were capable of rectifying them; yes, he accepted – as collateral damage – that the ignorant would be deceived.[5]

The meaning of the book's title is thus considerably altered: Spinoza 'did not set out to deceive'. Formulated in these terms, his argument may not contradict proposition 72 of Book IV of the *Ethics*: 'Homo liber nunquam dolo malo, sed semper cum fide agit' ('The free man never acts deceitfully, but always with good faith').[6] It seems that Milner does not want to contradict this principle but to produce a surprising interpretation of it; namely, that Spinoza considered deception legitimate so long as it only deceived the ignorant. Is Milner's exegesis an admissible one? How should we interpret '*cum fide*', 'with good faith', as opposed to '*dolo malo*', 'deceitfully'? Let's answer: an honest art of writing does not have to deceive the ignorant even as 'collateral damage', for it rests on the idea that there is no ignorance, in the last analysis, other than the passion of ignorance.

The *Hodie Judaei* manifesto appears at the end of the *TTP*'s third chapter, which is entitled 'On the vocation of the Hebrews, and whether the prophetic gift was peculiar to them'. Here Spinoza examines the Hebrews' 'chosen' status. He explains that their particular 'election' relates to the laws that govern their state, and he thus concludes that once their state has been destroyed their 'election' is no more. Their 'election' pertains to Hebrews as a nation and not as individuals, and in a certain sense this is a universal distinguishing principle. Each nation, as a sovereign nation, lives under a political regime and laws that are its own, and in this sense we can say that each sovereign nation is 'chosen'. Nonetheless, in the past there was also an 'election' particular to the Hebrews:

> nations are distinguished one from another only by the [form of] society and laws in which they live and under which they are governed.

> The Hebrew people, accordingly, was chosen by God above others not for its understanding or for its qualities of mind, but owing to the form of its society and the good fortune, over so many years, with which it shaped and preserved its state.[7]

However, others have not understood 'election' in this sense. At the end of the third chapter Spinoza sets out to refute the arguments of those who define it in terms of salvation, as if the Hebrews' 'chosenness' were the unconditional promise of a particular and exclusive alliance with God, due to last for eternity:

> It remains only to respond to some arguments by which certain people seek to persuade themselves that the election of the Jews was not temporal and applicable only to their commonwealth, but eternal. We see (they say) that, after the loss of their state, the Jews were scattered everywhere for so many years and separated from all nations, and yet they still survived, as no other nation has. The sacred books, we see also, seem to teach in many places that God has chosen the Jews for himself for ever, and therefore although they have lost their state, they still remain the chosen of God.[8]

Those who insist that the Jews' 'election' was not 'temporal and applicable only to their commonwealth, but eternal' have two arguments attesting – they claim – to the fact that this 'election' is permanent and not conditional on the existence of a sovereign state. The first is an argument of an historical order: the Jews as a people survived the destruction of their state as well as being scattered across the nations, and the conservation of their people can only be explained by their 'chosen' status. The second is an argument of an exegetic order: the Biblical texts relating to 'election' describe it as permanent. These two arguments are interlinked: it is because their election is permanent (as in the Biblical or exegetic argument) that the Jews have preserved their existence as a nation, even though they were exiled across various different nations (the historical argument). Spinoza concludes his third chapter by refuting these two arguments, each of which he examines separately. He begins by refuting the exegetic argument, and then moves on to the historical argument. Milner sets up the refutation of this second argument as Spinoza's 'manifesto'. Its first sentence is the conclusion of what went before. Spinoza comes to establish that Scripture conceives the particular 'election' of the Jews as 'temporal and applicable only to their commonwealth' and thus concludes, that given that their state has ceased to exist, they have ceased to be 'chosen'. In consequence:

the Jews today have absolutely nothing that they can attribute to themselves but not to other peoples.[9]

Spinoza then comes to refute the second argument, of a historical order. How can we explain the fact that the Jews preserved their national existence across so many centuries? He answers that the Jews' particularism kept them separate from the gentiles, and that this separation attracted the gentiles' resentment against them. Indeed 'it is the resentment of the gentiles to a large extent that preserves [the Jews]'.

At this stage in our analysis, we could concede Milner's point that Spinoza considers the Jews 'responsible' for the resentment that they arouse, if by that we mean that they attract resentment through their 'religious' attachment to particular rites.[10] But Milner adds 'and at fault'. But Spinoza does not say that the Jews are 'at fault' for the resentment they arouse. He portrays a causal chain in which the Jews' attachment to their rites provokes resentment, and this resentment preserves them as a nation. What is the *implicit* meaning of Spinoza's argument? Are the Jews 'at fault' for the hatred that they provoke, or, conversely, are the gentiles at fault for resenting the Jews? The answer seems a simple one, if we hold firm to proposition 45 of Book IV of the *Ethics*. Indeed, here Spinoza teaches that 'Hatred can never be good' and in the *scholium* he explains: 'here and in what follows, by hatred I mean only hatred toward men'.[11] If we accept that Spinoza saw Jews as men then it follows that the gentiles' hatred toward the Jews could 'never be right'.

But let's return to the incriminated text. The explanation for the preservation of the Jews, Spinoza makes clear, is the gentiles' resentment toward them; and in order to justify his analysis, he immediately invokes 'experience': namely, the fact that the forced conversion of the Jews in Spain and in Portugal produced exactly opposite results. In Spain, where the Jews 'were granted the privileges of native Spaniards and were considered worthy of all positions of dignity', 'they immediately integrated with the Spanish, so that in a short time there were no remnants of them left and no memory of them'; in Portugal, conversely, they continued to resent the Jews, and that is what preserved the Jews, as a persecuted group. 'Experience' confirmed Spinoza's reading, making it evident. For it was now evident that the Jews are not mainly resented because they live separately; rather, they live separately mainly because they are resented. The Spanish 'experience' bore witness to this, because the Jews stopped living separately after they stopped being resented; as did the Portuguese 'experience', because there they 'continued to live apart from all men, doubtless *because* [the king of Portugal] *declared them unworthy of all higher positions*'.

The first paragraph of the *Hodie Judaei* therefore rests on the following argumentation: the gentiles' resentment toward the Jews led to their persecution, particularly in excluding them from higher positions for being Jewish (or of Jewish origin, if they were converts); thus the resentment toward the Jews produced their separateness; and it was precisely their separateness that preserved their condition as a nation apart; thus the resentment against the Jews preserved the Jews. QED.

A corollary proposition follows from this: the policy regarding the Jews that Spinoza recommends in his *Hodie Judaei* manifesto consists of giving them access to higher posts – in other words, of not resenting them. For it is wrong to resent the Jews; and this was where the theological-political authorities in Portugal erred, unlike in Spain. That is the explicit meaning of the text in question. But we might ask: if in both the Spanish and Portuguese cases the Jews were compelled to convert to Christianity, is this therefore a presupposition of the policy that Spinoza is recommending? The *Hodie Judaei* manifesto gives no explicit answer to this question. Spinoza employed a certain method in his writing, which Leo Strauss termed the art of writing under persecution. This method relies on the reader's capacity to understand for himself what has gone unsaid. Let's turn back to the manifesto's opening words: 'Thus the Jews today have absolutely nothing that they can attribute to themselves but not to other peoples.' The explicit meaning is that the Jews' particular 'election' ceased with their loss of sovereignty, and that nothing else distinguishes them from other peoples, including as regards understanding and virtue. If they are not 'above' other nations in this regard, nor are they 'below' them. Seemliness requires the art of understatement; but whoever can see the literal meaning can also feel its spirit. For Spinoza, the watchword that should govern the republicans' (essentially meaning, the Christians') policy toward the Jews was, 'Oh come on, now, I don't hate you at all!' He formulates the basis for this in §7 of his Preface to the *TTP*:

> It may indeed be the highest secret of monarchical government and utterly essential to it, to keep men deceived, and to disguise the fear that sways them with the specious name of religion, so that they will fight for their servitude as if they were fighting for their own deliverance, and will not think it humiliating but supremely glorious to spill their blood and sacrifice their lives for the glorification of a single man. But in a free republic (*respublica*), on the other hand, nothing that can be devised or attempted will be less successful. For it is completely contrary to the common liberty to shackle the free judgment of the individual with prejudices or constraints of any kind. Alleged subversion for ostensibly

religious reasons undoubtedly arises only because laws are enacted about doctrinal matters, and beliefs are subjected to prosecution and condemnation as if they were crimes, and those who support and subscribe to these condemned beliefs are sacrificed not for the common welfare but to the hatred and cruelty of their enemies.[12]

Here, we can hear the echo of Tacitus's text; but we will remain focused on Spinoza's explicit meaning, namely that 'it is completely contrary to the common liberty to shackle the free judgment of the individual with prejudices or constraints of any kind'. So we would be contradicting ourselves if we maintained that Spinoza saw the Jews' conversion to another religion as the *sine qua non* condition of their access to higher posts. We know Milner's answer to this objection: that the explicit meaning is misleading. His argument is the following: the Spanish 'experience' that Spinoza introduces is an untruth, designed to deceive the 'ignorant'.

The main difficulty that the *Hodie Judaei* manifesto poses is Spinoza's recourse to an untruth that he invokes as an 'experience':

> But experience has shown that it is the resentment of the gentiles to a large extent that preserves them.

What then follows is an invocation of the Spanish 'experience'. But it is not true that once the Jews of Spain converted they shared in all 'the privileges of native Spaniards', or that they 'immediately integrated with the Spanish, such that in a short time there were no remnants of them left and no memory of them'. The *limpieza de sangre*, which excluded Spaniards with Jewish ancestry from higher posts and the Inquisition, which persecuted the practice of the Jewish religion, tell us that the opposite was true. Did Spinoza intentionally resort to an untruth disguised as 'experience'? This is how Milner justifies his 'method for reading' Spinoza:

> I have chosen to base myself on the method for reading Spinoza that was elaborated by Leo Strauss. In fact, I am relying on an extremely restricted version of this method. Conscious that I am not doing justice to the full breadth of Strauss's endeavour, and also conscious that the hypothesis of a 'forgotten art of writing' raises serious objections, I will make minimal reference to it: 'If a master of the art of writing commits such blunders as would shame an intelligent highschool boy, it is reasonable to assume that they are intentional'. At most, I will engage to eliminate the subjective element still preserved within this rule. For who can determine what would shame an intelligent highschool

boy? I will stick to objective blunders: paralogisms, untruths, hidden allusions, etc.[13]

So what we need to do, here, is to interpret Spinoza's recourse to an untruth whose function is to confirm his analysis. We should begin by remarking that while it is not true that Spain's theological-political authorities stopped persecuting the Jews after they converted – and nor is it true that they were so integrated among the Spaniards that there was no longer any trace of them – it does not follow from this that Spinoza's reasoning is itself false: for if the Spanish authorities had stopped persecuting the Jews, then they would have been integrated among the Spaniards. The untruth that Spinoza invokes in the guise of 'experience' leaves his reasoning intact, even after we have established the truth: it neither validates nor invalidates it. However, the question remains; why resort to an untruth? One of two things must be the case: either Spinoza was ignorant of the realities in Spain or else he did understand them. If he did not know, the debate is over; if he did, then the recourse to an untruth must have been deliberate. Let's follow what Milner says on this point: Spinoza knows that he is invoking a false 'experience' and in consequence he also knows that a number of his readers know that. He suspects that while some of them will object, other more circumspect ones will immediately understand that even his reasoning would remain valid even if the historical truth were put back in place. These latter will then ask: is the author ignorant of the facts, or does he want to articulate his reasoning around a fiction? Having arrived that far, they have two possible methods for analysing Spinoza's invocation of the Spanish 'experience': either our own one, which I would term a 'literal' method in the sense that it proceeds from the explicit meaning toward the implicit one; or else Jean-Claude Milner's method, which I would characterize as 'expeditious'. His analysis is as follows: Spinoza saw the Jews' conversion to Islam as the solution to the 'Jewish' problem, and his manoeuvre consists of praising the Ottoman Empire's policy with regard to converts under the guise of discussing Catholic Spain. This is a minimal rule of caution, surely an illustration of the philosopher's motto *caute*, 'cautiously':

> It is true that even the most elementary caution demanded that Spinoza could not express himself openly. The Turks were seen as the mortal enemies of Christendom. Conversion to Islam was considered the least excusable thing a civilised man could do. The noun 'renegade' has retained its pejorative connotation into our own time; and that is because it still bears the marks of its old usage, the only one the *Académie française*'s dictionary used until the mid-nineteenth century.

A renegade was a Christian taken prisoner by the Turks who won his freedom by becoming a Muslim.[14]

Milner portrays Spinoza's programme as being defined by the example of the Ottoman Empire and the false Jewish messiah Sabbatai Zevi's[15] conversion to Islam. For Milner, although Spinoza disguises this under the mask of Catholic Spain, his programme was indeed, the Jews' conversion to Islam, such that their name would forever disappear from human memory. For any professor of philosophy, this is a fat piece of nonsense: the Amsterdam philosopher's plan was not a matter of converting Jews to Islam, but of converting men to liberty.

In order to decide between these two interpretations, we need to determine whether Spinoza thought that the political authorities should compel the Jews to convert to another religion. When we read the philosopher's preface to the *TTP*, we see that he explicitly opposed the use of compulsion in matters of judgement. If we stick to the explicit meaning of the *Hodie Judaei* manifesto, he says nothing of compulsion, except insofar as he relates the forced conversion of the Jews by invoking the Spanish 'experience'. (In fact, this is the only non-fictional element of the 'experience' in question). What should we conclude from this?

If the solution that Spinoza advocated consisted of converting the Jews to Islam, as Milner argues, it would follow that he was setting out a programme for forcibly converting the Jews to Islam, on the Spanish model – but with the nuance that it was in fact the Turks who had been clever enough to apply the policy that Spinoza instead imputed to Spain. That is to say, the policy of giving the Jews access to higher posts once they have converted, such that the Jews and even the memory of their name will disappear. The fictional 'experience' is, then, the happy synthesis of the Spanish experience – namely its element of forced conversion – and the Turkish experience – namely its element of assimilating the converted. All the same, his use of this disguise can only be justified in terms of obeying a rule of caution. Milner thus argues that in the Europe of the seventeenth century, praise for the Ottoman Empire – and what is more, praise for conversion to Islam, even by Jews – could not be explicit.

Let's venture another hypothesis: that when Spinoza invoked Spain, he did so because the forced conversion of the Jews contradicted the republican principle that he expounded right from his Preface: 'everyone is permitted to worship God according to his own mind'.[16] That, at least, is the contradiction that must strike the reader.

Let's continue with our reading method, which proceeds from the explicit meaning toward the implicit one. By hating the Jews, the gentiles set them apart. The Spanish 'experience' is an untruth, because it is absurd: the conversion of the Jews was forced upon them under pain of expulsion; they were invariably suspected of secretly remaining Jews and thus they continued to be resented, persecuted and set apart. Thus, they were preserved in their condition as a separate nation, as the historically attested Portuguese case bears witness.

Spinoza here, introduces a Spanish 'experience' that was not only non-existent, but could not have existed in this – illogical – form; for compulsion in matters of religion did not allow the Jews to mix into the Spanish nation. Conversely, if we radicalize the fictitious character of the Spanish 'experience', getting rid of what still remains of its attachment to historical reality, namely hatred (the forced conversion of the Jews of Spain, under pain of compulsion), it is not absurd. It now instead becomes an 'experience' guided by the idea: in a free republic, the Jews' access to higher posts must not be conditional on their conversion, '[f]or it is completely contrary to the common liberty to shackle the free judgment of the individual with prejudices or constraints of any kind'[17] – just as a man's 'election' relates not to ethnic or confessional belonging, but to understanding and virtue.

2 THE SONG OF THE SIGN[1]

What was Spinoza's purpose, here? Milner thinks that we can conclude that the philosopher's aim was the disappearance of the Jews, effacing even the memory of their existence – as indicated by his invocation of the Spanish 'experience'. If it is resentment that preserves the Jews – and in Spinoza's judgement, hatred among men is a bad thing – then doesn't it follow that he judges what preserves the Jews a bad thing – and, by consequence, that he judges the preservation of the Jews a bad thing? Such is Milner's reasoning.

Yet, the disappearance of the name 'Jew' was not one of the aims of Spinoza's policy; it was, at most, its likely consequence, for it is hatred that preserves Jews' condition as a separate nation and not their particular rituals. It so happens in the order of nature, that in the absence of a Jewish state, only the gentiles' resentment could preserve the Jews for so long and not their 'election'; if the persecution stopped, the Jews would become so mixed in among the nations that soon little would remain of them – not even the memory. That, at least, is what the Spanish 'experience' proves – even if it is imaginary …

Does this mean that Spinoza imagined the disappearance of the name 'Jew'? Does it mean that he desired that? Let's go back to the explicit meaning of the *Hodie Judaei* manifesto. The 'election' particular to the Jews relates to the laws of their state, their national sovereignty; it ceases as soon as their state is destroyed. Having established that much, we have to account for the fact that the Jews nonetheless preserved 'their condition as a nation'. The answer is that 'it is the resentment of the gentiles to a large extent that preserves' the Jews. 'Experience' had confirmed this chain of cause and effect: as soon as the persecution stopped, the Jews no longer preserved their condition as a separate nation, but mixed in among the country's inhabitants – so much so that nothing was left of them, even the memory of their existence. It is here that Spinoza turns back to the 'sign of circumcision'.

> I think that the sign of circumcision has such great importance as almost to persuade me that this thing alone will preserve their nation for ever[2]

Spinoza's explanation, confirmed by the Spanish 'experience', appears in between two separate references to the 'sign of circumcision'. In the first case, he emphasizes the importance of a sign distinguishing the Jews from other nations; in the second case, he concludes that it 'has such great importance' that 'this thing alone' could 'preserve their nation for ever'.

This necessarily poses the reader the following problem. On the one hand, Spinoza is arguing that it is resentment that preserves the Jews as a separate nation, but as soon as this resentment ceases, they will no longer continue to be Jews, not even in the memory. On the other hand, he is arguing that the 'sign of circumcision' could 'preserve their nation forever'. However, if the sign of circumcision is of 'such great importance', it follows that even after the persecution has ceased, and even after they have been given access to higher posts and are considered equal to others, the Jews will remain in the condition of a nation. So we are far from nothing remaining of them, even the memory. The judgement Spinoza passes on the sign of circumcision in the second paragraph refutes his explanation in the first. This is a good moment to recall Leo Strauss's interpretative rule, which Jean-Claude Milner also proposes to employ: 'If a master in the art of writing makes such blunders as would shame an intelligent highschool boy, it is reasonable to assume that they are intentional.' If the manifest contradiction between the disappearance of the Jews – evidenced by Spinoza's invocation of the Spanish 'experience' – and the value that he attributes to the 'sign of circumcision' is intentional, then we really must be in the presence of a certain art of writing.

The explicit meaning of the first paragraph of the *Hodie Judaei* manifesto is that the Jews conserve their condition as a separate nation on account of the other nations' hatred toward them, and that, in consequence, they will cease to be preserved as such as soon as the hatred stops – as the Spanish 'experience' confirms. And Spinoza advocates an end to the persecution of the Jews, in particular by ceasing to exclude them from higher posts. Does that mean that he is setting out a programme for their disappearance? If the goal Spinoza is pursuing is the disappearance of the name 'Jew', then the value that he attributes to the sign of circumcision 'in this affair' reduces to nothing his policy's very *raison d'être*. After all, he judges 'this thing alone' capable of 'preserv[ing] their nation for ever', whether or not the Jews are hated. If, conversely, his goal is to conquer hatred, to secure a decisive victory against it, then the value that he attributes to the sign of circumcision is the secret pivot of his demonstration. For if the sign of circumcision is capable of preserving the Jewish nation's existence forever, it follows that what is at issue in the *Hodie Judaei* manifesto is not the disappearance of the name 'Jew', but the disappearance of hatred, even as the name 'Jew' is perpetuated. That is, moreover, basic logic, because only if the hatred ceases *while* the name 'Jew' endures could we conclude that the hatred *of which the Jews are the object* has been defeated. However, Milner imputes the opposite reasoning to Spinoza:

> If the correct policy were followed unfailingly everywhere, and if the offending name and the memory of the people who bore it were effaced for ever, then our sage would have to greet this as the advent of human happiness. For their disappearance would effectively mean that hatred had lost a decisive battle[3]

According to Milner, Spinoza concluded that the name 'Jew' is in itself a vehicle for hatred, as if it were doomed to be hated. So the philosopher would thus be identifying the name 'Jew' with a sort of *negative* 'election'; hence the reasoning Milner ascribes to him: if the name 'Jew' is a cause of hatred – and it is – then the disappearance of hatred requires the disappearance of the name 'Jew', since the disappearance of the effect requires the disappearance of its cause.

Such reasoning would, however, seem absurd to any intelligent high school boy. Wouldn't persecuting the Jews to the point of their name forever disappearing itself be a policy of hatred – in which case, the disappearance of the name 'Jew' would mean hatred winning, and not losing, a 'decisive battle'?

Milner does not claim to have cut loose from the principle of non-contradiction. So he introduces a nuance, regarding the distinction between an 'imperfect 'persecution and a 'perfect' one; and a persecution is 'perfect' if it owes nothing to hatred. Here, 'perfect persecution' is the solution – that is, the solution to the problem posed by the name 'Jew': 'To use deliberately anachronistic language, only a policy that is resolutely unfettered by anti-Semitism can succeed in abolishing the Jews – both their existence and the memory of them.'[4] The policy that Spinoza advocates is capable of overcoming the partial setback of Nazism. Nonetheless, Milner recognizes that there is a 'limit'. It is 'only one limit, however, albeit one that is of the utmost importance to us moderns: no massacres allowed'.[5] Spinoza was no Nazi: 'Let's give him his due. When he remained cautious, he was not only thinking about his own safety; he was also thinking about the safety of the Jews, those crystallisers of hatred. He wanted them to stop causing harm, but not at the price of debasing those who pursued them.'[6] We still have to resolve the contradiction between a policy seeking 'to make the word *Jew* disappear from everyday language' and a 'sign of circumcision', Spinoza considered to have 'such great importance' as to 'preserve their nation for ever'. That is where the Ottoman Empire comes into question – and the educated reader will have recognized it, under the mask of Catholic Spain:

> For the Turks were known for their practise of circumcision; better, they made it into a requirement, which converting Christians had to submit to. In converting to Islam, Sabbatai Zevi brought together two demands that were considered irreconcilable: he preserved circumcision while abandoning the principles of the Jewish religion. The meaning of circumcision was thus altered[7]

The value that Spinoza attributes to the 'sign of circumcision' no longer stands in contradiction with the goal being pursued. Rather, it specifies the means for achieving it: the word 'Jew' will disappear from everyday language when the Jews convert to Islam. For while the sign of circumcision will 'preserve their nation for ever', they will exist as Turks. We will still hear talk of Turks, but not of Jews.

So is it right to say – as Milner understands it – that Spinoza thinks that the name 'Jew' has to disappear in order for hatred to be defeated? Or are we instead right in understanding him as saying that hatred must disappear (and not the name 'Jew')?

*

Spinoza explains that the Jews could forever be conserved in the condition of a nation thanks to the 'sign of circumcision', even though they are dispersed and no longer form a state. This introduces the possibility of them one day re-establishing their state (*imperium*):

> were it not that the principles of their religion weaken their courage, I would believe unreservedly that at some time, given an opportunity, since all things are changeable, they might reestablish their state, and God will choose them again.[8]

'Were it not that the principles of their religion weaken their courage', Spinoza could make this possibility a conviction or even a certainty. So long as the Jews imagine that they are 'chosen' by God even as they live dispersed and submissive among the nations, they put the re-establishment of their state in doubt, for this means that they do not consider their 'election' conditional on sovereignty. The two arguments on 'election' that Spinoza proposes to refute at the end of chapter III – the exegetic (Biblical) argument and the historical one – exemplify the principles that weaken the Jews' courage. It is because the Jews believe that their 'election' relates to their rites and not to their sovereignty that they run the risk of not re-establishing their state. As we have seen, Spinoza distinguishes between two different meanings of the word 'election' – one related to understanding and virtue, and the other to 'the state and the other good things in this life' – and it is in this second sense that Scripture ascribes a national 'election' to the Hebrews. So if they re-establish their state, 'God will choose them anew'. Various different commentators have seen this as bearing the doctrine of a political Zionism. So it is important to emphasize that Spinoza's remark concerning the possible re-establishment of the Hebrews' state is inscribed within a reasoning that articulates two propositions, namely:

1 The political authorities must judge their citizens' religious or ethnic identity irrelevant to their free access to all higher posts. In other words, there is an *incontrovertible principle* that all people are equal in relation to understanding and virtue.

2 The political authorities must not set the disappearance of the collective's particular constituent ethnic and religious identities as a condition of this principle. Its application must not be dependent on one or another of them being the majority or minority. Rather it must be applied unconditionally, since the various particularisms of ethnic or religious identity are on principle irrelevant to the public good.

It is on these two conditions, that the policy of hatred will cease and together with this, the collective's power to act will grow.

Continuing his reflection on the 'sign of circumcision', Spinoza brings up a 'remarkable example' that he has found among the Chinese. This is the conclusion of *Hodie Judaei* (as Milner seeks to delimit it, as a 'manifesto'). Upon a first approach, the explicit meaning of Spinoza's concluding argumentation seems obvious, telling us that the 'remarkable example' of the Chinese confirms what he says about the Jews – namely, that the 'sign of circumcision' can ensure their existence as a nation for eternity and that it is thus probable that they will re-establish their empire and God will elect them anew.

Nonetheless, we cannot fail to note that the 'remarkable example' of the Chinese has exactly the same function as the Spanish 'experience'. Since we know that the Spanish 'experience' is fictitious, we must immediately question the veracity of the 'remarkable example' of the Chinese.

All should be aware that the Chinese 'have preserved themselves in this distinctive manner for many thousands of years, so that they far surpass all nations in antiquity' and that they even built a wall on account of the invasions they suffered in the past. So the topknot endures. This is the basis upon which Spinoza constructs the analogy between the Chinese and Jewish cases: circumcision is to the Jews what the 'kind of topknot on their heads, by which they distinguish themselves from all other men' is to the Chinese. Since the reader of the *TTP* could not be expected to know as much about China as he would about Spain, Spinoza confers the same function on the two examples and situates them at the same place in his work. The attentive reader should deduce from this that they were conceived in the same way: just as the Spanish 'experience' that Spinoza relates has both some truth to it (the forced conversion of the Jews) and also some falsehood (the absence of persecution and the disappearance of the name 'Jew'), there is similarly both true and false in the Chinese example. But the falsehood here, alone, concerns the 'kind of topknot on their heads, by which they distinguish themselves from all other men'.

Spinoza relates the 'remarkable example' of the Chinese in order to provide experiential proof of his reasoning regarding the Jews. Yet, the analogy between the Chinese and the Jews is built on an untruth: the topknot is not a distinctive sign that the Chinese 'conserve very religiously', but a distinctive sign of the Tartars imposed on the Chinese as a sign of their submission. Milner quite reasonably establishes that Spinoza must have been aware of this, since the only documentary source available to him – a book by the Jesuit priest Martino Martini – is clear on this point. If his distortion of historical truth was intentional, then here once again he was employing a certain art of writing. Milner concludes that the analogy, based on an untruth, is a decoy: Spinoza did not intend to establish a correspondence between the Chinese nation, which probably would liberate itself from the Tartar occupier, and the Jewish nation. Any correspondence that does exist would have to be reconstituted and Milner maintains that it should be reconstituted as follows:

> Spinoza foresaw that the Chinese would win. In the interpretation that I have proposed, he linked their reconquest to their abandonment of Christianity. This much emerges from a comparison with Martini ... Just as the Chinese renounced the debilitating religion of the pontiffs,

so, too, in the eyes of the world, had Sabbatai Zevi renounced a feminising Judaism[9]

The problem is that the analogy reconstituted by Milner is no better-founded than the one Spinoza makes explicitly. If the one is founded on an untruth concerning the Chinese topknot, the other is founded on an untruth concerning Judaism – for Judaism is not to the Jews what the 'debilitating religion of the pontiffs' is to the Chinese. Having begun with these rather fragile foundations, Milner nonetheless proceeds in reconstructing a hidden meaning in Spinoza:

> After analysing the Chinese example, I noted that Spinoza articulates two positions to one another: that circumcision would allow the Jews their reconquest, and that the principles of the Jewish religion are an obstacle to their reconquest. This is flagrantly contradictory, since circumcision is part of the Jewish religion. That is, unless Spinoza had in mind some real example where the Jews kept circumcision while renouncing their religion. Sabbatai Zevi offered exactly the example he required. After all, the Turks were known for practising circumcision … In converting to Islam, Sabbatai Zevi met both of the two requirements that had been considered irreconcilable, keeping circumcision while abandoning the principles of the Jewish religion … Spinoza points out the path to follow: imitating Sabbatai Zevi. More precisely: imitating his apostasy and not his messianism. Such an apparently anodyne proposal becomes clearer in passing. He refers to the election of the Jews immediately after their state is reconstituted: 'God will elect them anew'. We should not shy away from interpreting this as follows: the Jews will again become a chosen people if and only if they convert to Islam.[10]

Milner brings into relief a contradiction between what the 'sign of circumcision' allows and what 'the principles of [the Jews'] religion' prohibit: while the former makes it probable that the Jews' state will be re-established, the latter make it improbable. Yet, 'circumcision is part of the Jewish religion'. In order to resolve this contradiction, he invokes the false messiah Sabbatai Zevi. However, he omits to mention that whereas the 'sign of circumcision' concerns the flesh, the 'principles of their religion' concern the heart, weakening the Jews' courage. Circumcision is the inscription of the letter in the flesh of the speaking body; as applied to the heart, it is the understanding of the letter, its spirit. The 'sign of circumcision' can ensure the eternal existence of the Jewish nation, because like the letter it cannot be effaced. But it is still necessary also to understand the letter, or else it will exist only as a cadaver denuded of spirit. Thus the 'sign of circumcision' is not one of the 'principles of their religion' but its letter, which is beyond these principles' understanding. That is precisely what Spinoza works to demonstrate as he refutes the exegesis of those who ascribe 'election' a meaning that he says it does not have.

Milner resolves what he identifies as an insurmountable contradiction by invoking the false messiah. But what would make the Jews apply *en masse* the programme that Milner ascribes to Spinoza – 'imitating Sabbatai Zevi'? By any logic, the path to follow would be that of expelling the Jews from Europe and convincing the Turks to convert them to Islam. Yet Milner also evokes the 'possibility of their abandoning [Judaism] without compulsion'.[11] At this level of analysis, things remain rather enigmatic. Did Milner's Spinoza imagine that the Jews would follow Sabbatai Zevi's example *en masse*, like the Chinese liberating themselves from the 'debilitating religion of the pontiffs'? If we do concede that Spinoza was as ignorant as Milner says, we would thus have to conclude that he sincerely believed that the Jews of Spain had melted into the nation, and that the topknot was a distinctive sign that the Chinese 'conserved very religiously'.

Milner concludes: 'We should not shy away from interpreting this as follows: the Jews will again become a chosen people, if and only if they convert to Islam.'[12] In vain would we object that 'election' is a clear and distinct concept in Spinoza, meaning either a nation's sovereignty – for instance, the Netherlands freeing itself of the Spanish yoke – or the ethics of a free man – for instance, Spinoza's own – and that it is thus contradictory to conclude that in his writing 'election' could mean a more or less forced conversion to one or another religion. We already know what Milner's answer is to this objection: that Spinoza's explicit meaning is deceptive.

But let's get back to Spinoza's explicit meaning. He ventures a remarkable analogy: the 'sign of circumcision' is to the Jews what the topknot is to the Chinese. Spinoza employs the Latin word *comma* for 'topknot'. Lagrée and Moreau translate this as 'topknot', Appuhn as 'type of tail' and Misrahi as 'lock in the form of a tail'. The Latin word *comma* designates a 'division of a period', 'cæsura in verse', or 'mark of punctuation' (Lewis/Short, *A Latin Dictionary*). In one note, Milner remarks:

> Martini [the Jesuit who had written on China] rightly speaks of a tail, a *cauda*. By contrast, we can gauge the extent of Spinoza's displacement operation in choosing a typographical metaphor (*comma*) rather than an anatomical one (*cauda*).[13]

Certainly, this displacement is not an innocent one. Yet, it is far from certain that it is best characterized in terms of its 'extent'. In passing from an anatomical metaphor to a typographical one, Spinoza is passing from the body to writing. The Chinese topknot, braid or pigtail nonetheless retains its form. And we do not need to identify a historical untruth in order to understand that this is a rather shaky analogy: if Spinoza 'attributes such value to the sign of circumcision, in this affair', that is evidently because it cannot be effaced, since it would be impossible to cut off this sign without thereby cutting off the … Conversely, the Chinese 'pigtail' could be cut off without harm, for it is a braid of hair. Effacing one and the other 'sign' does not have the same significance. Therefore, 'in this affair' the Chinese topknot cannot correspond to the 'sign of circumcision'. Finally there's the *coup de grâce*: consulting the Jesuit Martino Martini's book, it turns out that the Chinese topknot was a sign of submission to the Tartar occupier and had been imposed upon the Chinese. Does this mean that nothing is left of the analogy between the Jews and the Chinese?

The analogy between Jewish circumcision and the Chinese topknot is certainly a shaky one, but it is explicit. And we have to start out from the explicit meaning – not to dispel it, but to understand it. To put that another way, we have to move from the topknot to the sign of circumcision in a way that will allow us to grasp the passage from the Latin *cauda* (the anatomical metaphor for the 'tail') to the Latin *comma* (the typographical metaphor for the *cæsura* in verse). Once we establish that the 'remarkable example' of the Chinese has no function other than to evoke the Jews' future by way of analogy, then the explicit argument reveals its implicit meaning: if the 'Holy Land', the object of the Crusades, was now under Turkish domination and within range of Catholic Spain, then tomorrow the Jews may well re-establish their state 'as soon as the [Turks'] courage began to be weakened by a life of languish and luxury'. The Jews would then achieve their own *reconquista*. The circumcision, a sign of submission and disgrace, would again be a sign of 'election'.

*

The *Hodie Judaei* manifesto is §12 of Chapter III of the *TTP*. In his introduction, Milner justifies his decision to separate out this particular text: '§12 is attached to the beginning of §11 … Nonetheless, as a methodological choice I will treat the cited extract, §12, as an autonomous manifesto, which we can separate from the chapter in which it appears'.[14] Let's concede to Milner that Spinoza's refutation of the historical argument is 'separable' from his refutation of the exegetic (Biblical) argument.

However, it is rather more dubious to separate 'the cited extract' from the last paragraph of Chapter III (§13) immediately following it. Let's look at it again:

> A last point: if anyone wants to insist that the Jews have been chosen for this or any other reason by God for ever, I will not argue with him, if he will accept that this election, whether temporal or eternal, in so far as it is merely peculiar to the Jews, regards only their polity and their material interests (since this is all that can distinguish one nation from another), and that no people is distinguished from another with regard to understanding and true virtue, and hence in these spheres God does not choose one nation above any other.[15]

In separating the *Hodie Judaei* manifesto from its conclusion, Milner is not isolating it, but amputating it. And he is not only amputating one of its limbs, but its heart: namely, that 'no people is distinguished from another with regard to understanding and true virtue, and hence in these spheres God does not choose one nation above any other'.

Principally basing himself on the fact that Spinoza resorted to two untruths regarding the Chinese topknot and the happy assimilation of the Jews of Spain, Milner concludes that his explicit meaning must be deceptive. Having established that much, he takes the liberty of making some 'free arguments on Spinoza and the Jews'. Let's take the liberty of elaborating our own argument on the basis of Spinoza's explicit meaning. What is an experience? In the *TTP*, Spinoza explains that 'since all of Scripture was revealed for the benefit of a whole people in the first place and, ultimately, for the entire human race', 'whoever ... wants to be understood by everybody', 'must substantiate his points by experience alone and thoroughly adapt his arguments and the definitions of his teaching to the capacity of the common people'.[16] The philosopher expounds his teaching through the following order of reasoning: because Scripture is addressed to the common people, it must be substantiated by 'experience alone'. But if we are to draw a lesson from 'experience alone' we still need to be able to interpret it, since we have to understand a proof in order to know it. Having established that much, let's turn back to the *Hodie Judaei* manifesto.

Spinoza explains that there are 'certain people' who defend the thesis of an eternal 'election' by arguing from experience. The experience in question is the astonishing preservation of the Jews across the course of history, in spite of their dispersed and stateless existence. In refuting this argument – an argument of a historical order – Spinoza advances a line of reasoning that he twice claims has 'experiential' proof. Yet, the Spanish 'experience' and, after that, the 'remarkable example' of the Chinese, are both built on untruths. So a Jewish experience, a Spanish experience and a Chinese experience are articulated around the theme of 'election'. In this picture the singularity of the Jewish experience is that it is not fictional. After all, it is not built on an untruth: the persistence of dispersed Jewish communities is a proven historical fact.

However, it is possible to take a historically proven experience and not learn any truth from it, just as it is possible to take a fiction and not learn anything false from that. This seems to be the philosopher's teaching: experience does not teach us any truth by itself, unless it is guided by the idea. Thus those who contradicted Spinoza were drawing false arguments from a historically proven experience, whereas the philosophical reader was able to draw true lessons from a fictitious one. So the question is posed: does the Bible's value owe to its narration of historically proven miraculous experiences, or the fact that its essentially fictitious narratives are guided by ideas?

Thus, appears the guiding thread that links the Jewish, the Spanish and the Chinese experiences and which ultimately arrives at a hidden teaching of Spinoza's. Indeed, this is one of those teachings to which he accorded the greatest value: *the uncircumcised man is the man who believes in the truth of an experience but without the idea.*

3 KINGSHIP

For Milner, Spinoza's ethics is an 'ethics of indecency'.[1] This formulation is no value judgement, but a translation of Spinoza's own motto – 'cautiously' (*caute*). Milner connects this to the formula that we find in Baldassare Castiglione's *The Book of the Courtier*, '*si non caste, tamen caute*' ('If not chastely, at least cautiously').[2] The Archbishop of Hamburg Adalbert of Bremen had pronounced these words in the late eleventh century, in reference to priestly celibacy. Milner chooses to translate *non caste* as 'indecency'. The philosopher expounds his thinking cautiously (*caute*) because it is indecent (*non caste*). We can only recognize this if we are able to identify his decoys:

> I will seek to identify the decoys that Spinoza devised out of caution; I will unpack them in order to bring to light which propositions he accorded value. These can be recognised on account of their indecent character. Since for Spinoza indecency consists of contradicting the common morality, in the best of cases his secret propositions will continue to shock us. If they do not shock us, then we have to think what might have aroused scandal in the Netherlands of the seventeenth century.[3]

Milner defines an interpretative protocol: first we have to find the 'decoys devised out of caution', then we have to pull them apart in order to bring to light the teachings that the philosopher wanted to hide from the view of the indiscrete. Ultimately 'indecency' is the criterion allowing us to check whether we have indeed brought the philosopher's teaching to light – that is, whether it 'contradicts the common morality'. So if we claim to have discovered the 'propositions he accorded value', but they would not have contradicted the common morality of seventeenth-century Europe, then we must be on the wrong track. Conversely, Milner continues, 'in the best of cases' the philosopher's indecent propositions 'will continue to shock *us*' (my emphasis). The author evidently presupposes the existence of an 'us' composed of him and his reader, linked by a common morality. This seems to contradict a prior remark of his warning the reader:

> If this or that result of my investigation awakens some passion in me, I will keep quiet about it. I will take the liberty of referring the interested reader to my other works concerning the name 'Jew'. They will be able to determine by cross-reference what favourable or unfavourable judgment I carry, deep down, with regard to certain of Spinoza's theses.[4]

The analyst proceeds with the cold objectivity of a clinician: he exposes Spinoza's doctrine, bringing it to light as best he can, but holding back from passing judgement. He will not say anything about what he thinks 'deep down' and nor will he give voice to his 'passion'. Nonetheless, it may well be that when he brings an 'us' into play he is taking care to reassure his reader: they have a common morality. Halfway along, having been able to identify a certain number of decoys devised out of caution, Milner can bring to light the first of the propositions to which Spinoza accorded value:

> A thesis is insinuated without being uttered (*caute*). We could legitimately characterise it as indecent (*non caste*). And summarise it as follows: *It is possible for a political authority to make all trace of the Jews disappear, on condition that its decision owes nothing to hatred.* Thus he determines the ideal type of what we could call the *perfect persecution*.[5]

Has Milner observed his own interpretative protocol? Apparently so, because we have a rule of caution: 'a thesis is insinuated without being uttered' – and once this thesis has been brought to light, it does indeed prove to be indecent. At least, 'we could legitimately characterise it as indecent'. But this is a strange formulation. Could we equally legitimately *not* characterize it as indecent? Let's pose the question in more precise terms: the 'thesis' thus brought to light is certainly indecent relative to today's common morality, but is it indecent relative to the morality prevalent in the seventeenth-century Netherlands or Europe more broadly? Let's concede to Milner that 'mak[ing] all trace of the Jews disappear' has not belonged to the common morality in Europe, since … 1945. But before that? Milner answers, 'We could legitimately characterise it as indecent'. Hence, in recommending the 'perfect persecution' of the Jews, Spinoza so contradicted the common morality of seventeenth-century Europe that he had to resort to decoys. However, Milner should know that in seventeenth-century Europe it was writing the name 'Jew' – rather than effacing it – that contradicted the common morality. And we could legitimately suppose that an educated reader of his would also know that.

So when it comes to the ignorance that Milner seems to share with his reader, we are faced with the following alternative: either it is not deliberate, or else it is deliberate, in which case it must be read using a certain interpretative method.

Let's try to get a clearer view of things. Indecency is tolerable if it is possible to keep it hidden from view. The ecclesiastical authorities of the eleventh century were well-aware that the priests' chastity was relative; hence they tolerated a certain libertinism – despite its indecency – on the express condition that it was hidden from view. Spinoza's motto – *caute* – hints at the formula that the archbishop of Hamburg pronounced with regard to priestly celibacy at the end of the eleventh century: *si non caste, tamen caute*. If this comparison with Spinoza's motto holds, then there must be some analogy with priestly celibacy – in other words, the theological-political authorities must have had a norm of not persecuting the Jews, or at least of not persecuting them to the point of 'making the word *Jew* disappear from everyday language'. If that were so, the Spinoza 'thesis' brought to light by Milner – namely, that it is desirable and '*possible for a political authority to make all trace of the Jews disappear*' – would indeed have proven indecent. The problem with this is that the analogy does not hold: in the Europe of the seventeenth century, it was writing the name 'Jew' that was *non caste*, rather than effacing it. (Moreover, the motto in question, '*si non caste, tamen caute*', *literally* brings us back to writing about the 'sign of circumcision', rather than effacing it.) Conversely, Milner argues that this analogy does hold: that in the Europe of the seventeenth century it was highly indecent to set out a programme for effacing the name 'Jew'. Or more precisely, that the indecency consisted of effacing the name 'Jew' and not of writing it. The programme for eradicating the name 'Jew' was born with Spinoza: it had not gone before him. Nonetheless, Spinoza's 'final solution' is distinct from the Nazi one, as it rules out mass murder. It is a 'perfect persecution' that consists of making the Jews disappear, but without any 'individual' being put to death except in exceptional, legal circumstances:

> Perhaps Spinoza would not have objected to a death sentence pronounced against an individual, within legal forms; but he ruled out mass murders in advance[6]

The solution is to compel the Jews to convert to Islam. Only the lives of the recalcitrant will be under threat. That is Spinoza's programme as revealed by the learned reader Milner. This programme's indecency could not lie in its advocacy of the expulsion of the Jews or their forced conversion, since neither contradicted the common morality of the Europe of the seventeenth century. Milner thus concludes, that its indecency lay in its advocacy of 'conversion to Islam', which 'was considered the least excusable thing a civilised man could do'.[7] But in the Europe of that time, was the Jew a 'civilised man' or rather – in the best of cases – a tolerated man? And if a 'renegade was a Christian taken prisoner by the Turks who won his freedom by becoming a Muslim',[8] does it follow that it was indecent for a Jew to become a Muslim? Certainly, in Christendom the Jew was expected to become a Christian. But Milner's conclusion is that Europe's theological-political authorities would have considered a programme seeking the conversion of the Jews to Islam so indecent that Spinoza had to disguise it beyond all recognition. And this, in a brief passage of a book – the *TTP* – that was in any case eminently scandalous, given that the philosopher here explicitly challenged all religious dogmas whether Jewish, Christian or Muslim. Such a conclusion is not just naivety, nonsense or flimflam: it is a schoolboy prank.

We know Leo Strauss's rule: 'if a master of the art of writing commits such blunders as would shame an intelligent highschool boy, it is reasonable to assume that they are intentional'. Given that Milner says that he has adopted this rule as his own, we could conclude that his blunder is intentional – in other words, that he has devised a decoy. And if we are not to be duped by this decoy then we have to be able to pick it apart. All in all, this is a very simple task: where Milner writes the name 'Jew' we should read the name 'Spinoza'. That is how we get the propositions to which Milner accords value. Let's take an example: 'We thus again get back to the same thesis; in a free republic, the persecution [of Spinoza] is all the more necessary than elsewhere, because it is the just punishment for an unpardonable crime'. And we have to re-read Milner's whole book like that. But if the philosopher's 'unpardonable crime' was not that of setting out a programme for the 'perfect persecution' of the Jews – which is only a decoy – then what was it? Let's proceed with our investigation.

*

To reconstruct the argumentation in which the *Hodie Judaei* manifesto is inserted we have to turn back to the beginning of the eleventh paragraph of *TTP*'s third chapter. Here, Spinoza undertakes to refute 'certain people' on the subject of 'election'. Firstly, he refutes their exegesis of the Bible (§11) and then he refutes these same people's interpretation of the historical preservation of the Jews (§12). Who are these 'certain people' whom Spinoza seeks to refute? Later he goes on to name them, or at least the most important ones: it is 'especially' the Pharisees who having 'frequently cited' 'other passages' from the Bible, teach that the 'election' of the Hebrews is immutable and not relative to their sovereignty. Who are 'the Pharisees'? This word first occurs in the second chapter of the *TTP*. Spinoza explains that the purpose of the Biblical prophecies is to convince, which is the reason why they are formulated in a metaphorical language. They are meant to strike the imagination and not to produce 'universal [reasons] intended to convince everybody'. He then gives examples drawn from the Hebrew Bible, but also the Gospels:

> Nor should we think any differently about the reasons with which Christ convicts the Pharisees of obstinacy and ignorance and exhorts his disciples to the true life: for clearly, he adapted his arguments to the beliefs and principles of those individuals. For instance, when he said to the Pharisees (see Matthew 12.26), 'and if Satan casts out Satan, he is divided against himself; how then will his kingdom stand', he meant only to sway the Pharisees on the basis of their own notions and not to teach men that demons exist or that there is some sort of realm of demons.[9]

This is the first time that the Pharisees appear in the *TTP*. Spinoza mentions them because Christ addressed them in Matthew 12.26. And Spinoza himself also addresses them in his third chapter, seeking to prove their obstinacy and ignorance on the subject of 'election'. Lagrée and Moreau's notes referring to the first occurrence of the word 'Pharisee', explain that 'Spinoza uses this to designate both one of the Jewish sects, opposed to the Sadducees, and the representatives of the rabbinical tradition'.[10] Here, he is using 'Pharisees' to designate both those whom Jesus addressed and those whom he is himself addressing. Could we, then, identify the one discourse with the other: the discourse of Christ addressing the 'Pharisees' and that of the anonymous author of the *TTP*? Did Spinoza mean 'only to sway the Pharisees on the basis of their own notions'? We could possibly argue as much, albeit with one essential qualification: Spinoza was also addressing the wise man and thus his text did articulate 'universal [reasons] intended to convince everybody'. He wrote in the language of learned Europe: Latin. Was this the language of 'universal [reasons] intended to convince everybody'? Was the Latin of learned Europe the language of the programme of making the name 'Jew' disappear? We have to refer back to the original text in order to see what does not appear in the French[11] translations of the *TTP*: the Hebrew letter of the Bible. Spinoza cites the verses in Hebrew before providing a Latin translation of them. Still today, learned Europeans who want to be well-versed in Scripture have to be able to read Hebrew. Neither Latin nor Greek will suffice. The Renaissance and then the Reformation kept alive the Hebrew letter with the *veritas hebraica*, just as Jerome did when he undertook to return to the Hebrew original rather than translate the Greek version (the *Septuagint*). They kept alive a knowledge with which Spinoza was intimately acquainted. He knew the Bible verses to the letter from childhood. And he brought out the full significance of the Hebrew-signifier-shaped hole in the language of educated Europe, drawing out even its very most indecent political consequences: the possibility of the re-establishment of a state for the Jews in the 'Holy Land'. But if the re-establishment of their state evidenced their 'election', it was still necessary to understand the meaning that this notion took on in the Bible. That is why the *Hodie Judaei* manifesto cannot be separated from what precedes it, namely Spinoza's examination of the 'Pharisees'' exegetic or Biblical argument. This latter, is principally based on two prophetic texts, one by the prophet Jeremiah and a second one by the prophet Ezekiel. We will cite the relevant verses from the *King James* version:

> Thus saith the Lord, which giveth the sun for a light by day, and the ordinances of the moon and of the stars for a light by night, which divideth the sea when the waves thereof roar; The Lord of hosts is his name:

> If those ordinances depart from before me, saith the LORD, then the seed of Israel also shall cease from being a nation before me for ever.

> Thus saith the Lord; If heaven above can be measured, and the foundations of the earth searched out beneath, I will also cast off all the seed of Israel for all that they have done, saith the Lord.[12]

> And that which cometh into your mind shall not be at all, that ye say, We will be as the heathen, as the families of the countries, to serve wood and stone.

> As I live, saith the Lord God, surely with a mighty hand, and with a stretched out arm, and with fury poured out, will I rule over you[13]

According to Spinoza 'the Pharisees' commented on Jeremiah's verses in the following terms: 'the prophet testifies that the seed of Israel will remain the people of God for ever and goes so far as to compare them with the fixed order of the heavens and of nature'.[14] This is the same idea as the one they say governs the verses from Ezekiel. If this were the case the 'election' of the Jews would be immutable, in the image of 'the fixed order of the heavens and nature' – for 'election' would then exclusively depend on the 'seed of Israel'. To put that another way, it would exclusively (or at least, essentially) be a matter of an alliance between God and a particular nation (seed). This is the interpretation that Spinoza wants to refute, for his doctrine holds that 'God did not elect the Hebrew nation absolutely and for ever'.[15] Firstly, he objects that Moses made a comparison between the Hebrews and the Canaanites: just as these latter were chased out of the land of Canaan or even perished on account of their behaviour, so, too, would the Hebrews be chased out or perish if they behaved badly. He cites two verses in support of this argument, Leviticus 18.27-28 and Deuteronomy 8.19-20, quoting this latter verse first in Hebrew and then in Latin. On this basis, he provides a quite different reading of the Prophets:

> If therefore the prophets announced to them a new and eternal covenant of God, a covenant of knowledge, love and grace, it is easy to show that it was promised only to the pious. For in the same chapter of Ezekiel which we have just cited, it is expressly stated that God will separate from them the rebels and backsliders, and at Zephaniah 3.12-13 that God will take the arrogant from their midst and conserve the poor.[16]

When Spinoza speaks of the 'new and eternal covenant', he is alluding to the verses from Jeremiah immediately prior to those that the 'Pharisees' quote in support of their doctrine. Jeremiah 31.31-34 does indeed speak of a 'new covenant':

> But this shall be the covenant that I will make with the house of Israel; after those days, saith the Lord, I will put my law in their inward parts, and write it in their hearts; and will be their God, and they shall be my people.[17]

We have reached a dividing-line. These verses were the stakes of a sharp theological dispute between 'Pharisees' and Christians: was this a new covenant with the Jewish nation or a new covenant with another Israel, the Christian one, *versus Israel*? The 'Pharisees' emphasized the subsequent verses in Jeremiah, where they read that the Biblical God's covenant with Israel is an alliance with the 'seed of Israel' and that it is as immutable as 'the fixed order of the heavens and nature'. Spinoza wanted to refute them.

Does that make his exegesis a Christian one? From the verses in Jeremiah, Ezekiel and Zephaniah the philosopher concludes that:

> Since this election is made solely on the basis of true virtue, it is unthinkable that it has been promised only to pious Jews, to the exclusion of other pious people. Rather we must accept that the true gentile prophets, who, as we have shown, existed in all nations, also promised the same election to the faithful of their peoples and offered them its consolation. That this eternal covenant of God, the covenant of knowledge and of love, is universal.[18]

Spinoza teaches that the 'election' in question, depends not on a 'seed' or religious conversion, but 'understanding' and 'true virtue'. Consequently, just as election 'has been promised only to pious Jews' to the exclusion of the impious, so too, will pious gentiles be chosen. In Spinoza's Bible exegesis, 'understanding' and 'true virtue' take the place that 'the seed of Israel' does in the 'Pharisees'' exegesis. To translate that into a different language, we could say that the emancipatory, universal and egalitarian idea takes this place instead of a national myth. Is this an 'unpardonable crime'?

*

Milner says that he is inspired by Leo Strauss's interpretative method, but he is a disciple far more gifted and insightful than his master. Doubtless disorientated by his misuse of his own method, Leo Strauss concludes that in the *TTP* Spinoza is expounding on the one hand an 'assimilationist solution' to the 'Jewish problem' and on the other hand a 'Zionist solution'. He writes, with regard to the first solution:

> the liberal society with a view to which Spinoza has composed the Treatise is then a society of which Jews and Christians can be equally members, of which Jews and Christians can be equal members. For such a society he wished to provide ... The former suggestion and the general purpose of the Theologico-political Treatise are obviously connected: freedom of philosophy requires, or seems to require, a liberal state, and a liberal state is a state which is not as such either Christian or Jewish.[19]

Meanwhile he identifies the 'Zionist solution' in the second paragraph of the *Hodie Judaei* manifesto, crediting Spinoza with being the first to formulate its principle:

As far as I know, this is the oldest suggestion of a purely political solution to the Jewish problem: the substitution of a purely political solution for the miracle of redemption toward which men can only contribute, if at all, through a life of piety. This is the first inkling of unqualifiedly political Zionism.[20]

Jean-Claude Milner's judgement on this is evidently an unremitting one: that Leo Strauss is confusingly naive. For Milner, Strauss's interpretation of the *Hodie Judaei* manifesto is a sort of 'collateral damage' of Spinoza's acceptance that the ignorant would be deceived. Strauss did not understand that the explicit meaning is deceptive: he was not able to rectify, correct and recompose Spinoza's argumentation, such as to make the text offer up its secret doctrine – the programme neither for a 'Zionist solution' or an 'assimilationist' one, but for the Jews' conversion to Islam. It's true: Leo Strauss went much too far in explaining that Spinoza wished for the establishment of a 'liberal state' – 'a state that is not, as such, either Christian or Jewish'. These lines written in 1965 have become extremely subversive on account of the State of Israel's enduring military occupation of the totality of historical Palestine. We immediately get a measure of the threat that this represents: for if Spinoza's 'liberal' policy were applied to Israel/Palestine, this would suffice to realizing the equality of everyone in the 'Holy Land', by means other than an improbable partition. So a ban has to be slapped on Leo Strauss's interpretation. That is why Milner characterizes him as ignorant.

We now have the answer to the enigma *Le Sage trompeur* posed us with: the question of how Spinoza could have envisaged the *en masse* conversion of the Jews to Islam, such that the word *Jew* would disappear from everyday language even despite the persistence of the sign of circumcision persisting. The answer is certainly an anachronistic one; but then again, Spinoza was a visionary. For the term *Jewish state* to disappear from everyday language, it would suffice to apply today in Israel/Palestine the 'liberal' policy that Spinoza recommended in the Europe of yesteryear. It would suffice for there to be a common state from the river Jordan to the sea.

We know the argument used by the authorities who today govern the 'Holy Land': a joint state in Israel–Palestine – a common state for all of its inhabitants, be they Jews, Christians or Muslims – would ultimately mean the conversion of a 'Jewish' state into an 'Islamic' state.[21] This is the argument that governs Jean-Claude Milner's *Court traité de lecture*. Under the trappings of scholarship, Milner is relaying the nationalist consensus that emanates from the Israeli state apparatus – hence his claim to have succeeded in exposing Spinoza's secret doctrine:

> The Jews would be in a position to reconstruct a state if they succeeded in doing what was impossible in Europe in the seventeenth century: circumcision, without Judaism. But this impossibility is possible in Islam. So conversion to Islam is the only apostasy allowing the re-establishment of Jewish state power in the one region of the world where this power has ever existed ... Quite clearly, this would require things changing. To put that another way, it would require the Ottoman Empire accepting the existence of a Jewish state under its authority, albeit a Jewish state all of whose citizens – without exception – publicly renounced the Jewish religion and converted to Islam. Well, in human affairs things are always changing: what is improbable today is possible tomorrow. For Spinoza, following the example of Sabbatai Zevi was the way ahead for the rebuilders of a Jewish state, on condition that they abandon what he considered a phoney messianism[22]

So according to Milner, Spinoza's 'liberal' policy was not what we might think: it did not seek to establish a state that was neither – as such – Christian or Jewish or Muslim, but instead to convert a 'Jewish' state into an 'Islamic' state. And this doctrine has a name: the 'perfect persecution' of the Jews. The conclusion? That whoever asserts the idea of a common good is an 'anti-Semite', making a masked advance.

Let's get back to Spinoza. The *Hodie Judaei* manifesto is situated at the junction between a text by Paul and a text by Tacitus. According to the Roman historian, it was the Christians who introduced hatred for the human race to Rome, whereas according to the apostle Christ delivered humanity from hatred by accomplishing the Law through his flesh – through the crucifixion. The Roman historian's judgement on the first Christians is the same as the judgement that the first Christians passed on the Jews. But Nero was no Christ: he did not abolish hatred through his flesh, but absolved his own hatred through the flesh of others. Tacitus was himself aware of this: for while he did not see the Christians as republicans, tyranny was nonetheless the enemy of the public interest. The cruel persecutions of which they were victims touched Tacitus, kindling his empathy. His compassion was the minimal expression of a resistance against tyranny; better, it was all that remained of republican sentiment in Rome.

For his part, Spinoza took things one step further – a philosopher's step, a prophet's step. Tacitus implicitly tied the future of the public interest to the fortunes of the persecuted. But a compassion not guided by the idea is ambivalent and cannot endure. To rationalize compassion with the persecuted is to reaffirm the idea of a common good. Beyond substituting the 'Jews' for the early 'Christians', Spinoza replaces compassion with the idea.

And his idea is the following: if 'election' is relative to 'understanding and true virtue' and 'virtue is nothing else but action in accordance with laws of one's own nature', then it is in itself the affirmation of a common good, because no nation has been made different from any other in this regard.[23] Is this the programme of a 'perfect persecution' or a way of keeping alive the ancient Hebrew tradition?

Leo Strauss understood the first aspect of the *Hodie Judaei* manifesto, namely that Spinoza was fighting for a 'liberal state' – 'a state that is not, as such, Christian or Jewish'. But there is also the second aspect that Strauss calls the 'Zionist solution'. Yet, Spinoza was a rational thinker and the two aspects are inseparable: if the Jews could not recover their status as sovereign men in Europe they would recover it by re-establishing their state in the 'Holy Land', thus realizing the political ideal of the Bible. This was the ideal that the *TTP* sought to restore, but which monarchist and counter-revolutionary Europe sought to suppress. Since their state would be founded on an *idea* of the common good, it would not as such be Jewish, Christian, Turkish, or Chinese – for in the last instance, these names are irrelevant to understanding and true virtue.

4 ON CONTRADICTION

In Chapter XX of the *TTP* Spinoza shows 'that in a free state everyone is allowed to think what they wish and to say what they think',[1] with a few exceptions. For in a state there are also 'seditious' views, which are thus to be condemned:

> It is those views which, simply by being put forward, dissolve the agreement by which each person surrenders their right to act according to their own judgment. For example, it is seditious for anyone to hold that a sovereign power does not have an autonomous right or that one should not keep a promise or that everyone should live according to their own judgment, and other views of this kind which are directly contrary to the aforesaid agreement.[2]

Spinoza gives three examples of seditious views. Milner argues that each of them corresponds to a determinate group of men: the first to 'Roman Catholics, who submit the civil powers to the power of the Pope' and the third to those men 'who do not accept their singular caprice being restrained by any universal rule': the 'atheists', understood 'in the sense that Spinoza absolutely refused to be one'.[3] What remains to be identified is the group of men attached to the second seditious opinion: namely 'that no one has to keep their promises'.

The problem is that Spinoza himself says that a promise can be broken. He formulates this thesis in Chapter XVI of the *TTP*. In order to resolve this apparent contradiction, Milner explains that for Spinoza a promise can legitimately be broken if it proves unreasonable, but must not be broken arbitrarily 'upon the whim of interest', for example in order 'to acquire honours and riches'.[4] The second seditious opinion should thus be understood as one in which 'The reason for going against one's word is not on the terrain of a rational judgement of an objective situation, but that of an enslaving passion'.[5] Having established this much, Milner can identify the group of seditious men to whom Spinoza was implicitly referring:

> If there does exist a group founded, as a group, on such principles, it should be recognised as follows: its members collectively proclaim that they are not constrained by promises. It happens that this group can be identified; it has long been denounced on this basis.[6]

That is to say, the Jews, who 'each year during Yom Kippur recite the Kol Nidre', the prayer cancelling the vows and promises pronounced at the start of the day of pardoning. The breaking of the covenant is not motivated by a rational judgement on an objective situation and is thus an example of the second seditious opinion. Milner explains 'The *Kol Nidre* was known by all outside of Judaism in the seventeenth century, and very widely understood as an authorisation not to keep their promises.' In support of this argument, he cites Johannes Buxtof, the famous Protestant Hebraist whose comments on the *Kol Nidre* warned his readers: 'see what the Jew's word can be worth, especially when it is addressed to a Christian'.[7] So it would be beside the point to object that the *Kol Nidre* prayer does not free a Jew of promises he has made to his neighbour, but only of those that he has made to himself.[8] The question is how the *Kol Nidre* was 'very widely understood' 'in the seventeenth century'. And so when Spinoza condemns the opinion that 'no one has to keep their promises', he is implicitly referring to the Jews, because that is how a reader of Buxtof's would understand it. Milner concludes with regard to this seditious opinion that Spinoza supposedly ascribes to the Jews:

> It touches on the very fundaments of humanity, as distinct from animality. If we observe that a certain human group constitutes itself by suspending its vows and promises, and if this suspension is pronounced on a fixed date in the course of a certain religious ceremony regardless of whether objective circumstances have changed, then this group has corrupted man's relation with his own word. More seriously, it has made this corruption a religious principle and a rite of belonging. Humanity as a whole is fundamentally disposed to hate the members of this group, because they dissolve the very thing that is most human about it. It is fundamentally disposed to hate the members of this group with the greatest intensity, because they dissolve the very thing that is most human about humanity. Here lies the primary cause of Jewish separateness and the universal hatred toward the Jews … In the last analysis, it appears that the name Jew is ultimately the decisive cause.

Not for circumstantial reasons, but for structural ones. It attacks the very name of mankind. There is but one inevitable solution: to efface the name Jew from languages and memories. That must be the aim of any persecution claiming to represent a policy. This is Spinoza's Good News; this is his indecent Gospel, the *continuo basso* accompanying his very cautious Credo.[9]

For Milner, it is essential to reach the conclusion that Spinoza did not consider the Jews to be men, or at least that he judged that the Jew had 'corrupted man's relation with his own word'. This allows Milner to reappraise the proposition in the *Ethics*, IV, 45, with regard to hatred never being a good thing – 'here and in what follows, by hatred I mean only hatred toward men' – as only applying to those men who have not corrupted man's relation with his own word: meaning, not the Jews. If the Jews or the name 'Jew' incarnate hatred of the human race, then hating them is to hate hatred and is thus a sort of love for the human race. 'In the last analysis', it thus appears that Spinoza's doctrine is a 'Gospel', albeit one that he had to hide in the Europe of the seventeenth century for fear of being persecuted. Milner stretches this ambiguity as far as he can. Yet, he and his reader both well know that the programme here being ascribed to Spinoza only became indecent after 1945, or more exactly after Auschwitz had become the name of evil (over the 1960s and 1970s) and anti-Judaism a view condemned by the common morality. This is so anachronistic as to constitute a flagrant untruth.

To finish, let's examine the last argument of *Le Sage trompeur*. Is it true that the second seditious opinion that Spinoza mentions in the final chapter of the *TTP* must be about Jews, because they recite the *Kol Nidre* every year? Milner explains that the average seventeenth-century reader would have understood it as such (and that Spinoza could not have been unaware of this). Milner thus takes the following approach: the question is not how the author of the *TTP* understood things, but how a reader *governed by a certain anti-Jewish prejudice* understood them; and on that basis we should conclude that this was also how Spinoza understood them. In other words, while Spinoza certainly was aware that the *Kol Nidre* prayer did not disavow a man's promises to his neighbour, he was also aware that outside of Judaism, anti-Jewish prejudice determined how it was interpreted – meaning, that it was the untruth that prevailed.

Let's apply Milner's approach to his own text, given two or three centuries' distance. We are in the twenty-third century and for whatever reason, some ideologue wants to make out that the famous *bourgeois* theorist of the name 'Jew' was an anti-Semite. He explains that at the beginning of the twenty-first century the average reader in France and in Europe was influenced by an anti-Jewish prejudice, which could take the form of truly criminal leanings. He then cites long extracts from Milner's text, that explain that the persecution that Spinoza advocated was 'perfect' because it did not resort to mass murder. Since Milner knew that his reader, governed by a violent anti-Jewish prejudice, would have understood this as praise for Spinoza, then he must himself have seen the 'perfect persecution of the Jews' as 'Good News'. And it's been proven: a deceptive animal bites its own tail. That is its distinctive sign.

*

Let's return to our own method for reading Spinoza. How did he interpret the second seditious opinion? To put that another way, how should a normal reader trying to read and understand the text in front of him understand this problem? After all, that is the reader whom Spinoza is addressing – not the reader governed by prejudices. Like Milner, Spinoza is establishing a covenant with a certain type of reader, as he tells us in his book's preface:

> I believe the main points are well enough known to philosophers [i.e. those capable of rational reasoning]. As for others, I am not particularly eager to recommend this treatise to them, for I have no reason to expect that it could please them in any way. I know how obstinately those prejudices stick in the mind that the heart has embraced in the form of piety. I know that it is as impossible to rid the common people of superstition as it is to rid them of fear. I know that the constancy of the common people is obstinacy, and that they are not governed by reason but swayed by impulse in approving or finding fault. I do not therefore invite the common people and those who are afflicted with the same feelings as they are [i.e. who think theologically], to read these things. I would wish them to ignore the book altogether rather than make a nuisance of themselves by interpreting it perversely, as they do with everything[10]

How should a reader of the *TTP*, as described by Spinoza – if not a philosopher, at least an honest man – understand the second seditious opinion, 'that no one has to keep his promises'? Evidently this brings up a contradiction, since in Chapter XVI Spinoza states in equally explicit terms, that a promise is not binding on whoever utters it. He explains that it is 'a universal law of human nature that no one neglects anything that they deem good unless they hope for a greater good or fear a greater loss, and no one puts up with anything bad except to avoid something worse or because he hopes for something better.'[11] Indeed, 'of two good things every single person will choose the one which he himself judges to be the greater good, and of two bad things he will choose that which he deems to be less bad'. 'This law is so firmly inscribed in human nature', Spinoza continues, 'that it may be included among the eternal truths that no one can fail to know.'[12] He then concludes:

> It necessarily follows that no one will promise without deception to give up his right to all things, and absolutely no one will keep his promises except from fear of a greater ill or hope of a greater good ... We conclude from this that any agreement can have force only if it is in our interest, and when it is not in our interest, the agreement fails and remains void. For this reason, we also conclude that it is foolish to call for someone else to keep faith with oneself, in perpetuity, if at the same time one does not try to ensure that violating the agreement will result in greater loss than gain for the violator. This principle should play the most important role in the formation of a state[13]

Spinoza's doctrine is explicit: the agreement does not have force because some transcendent Law compels the keeping of promises, but because it is in our interest; and 'when it is not in our interest, the agreement fails and remains void'. Milner explains that the 'group' whose unity is based on the second seditious opinion, has 'corrupted man's relation with his own word'. Judging by Chapter XVI of the *TTP* the 'group' in question is none other than humanity itself, such as Spinoza conceives it. Milner does not ignore the apparent contradiction, but resolves it by distinguishing between two categories of breaking one's word: one kind is legitimate because it is founded on a 'rational judgment', whereas the other kind is illegitimate because it is founded on an 'enslaving passion'. But that's taking things a little too fast. If we stick to Spinoza's explicit meaning, an agreement's only legitimacy and only guarantee reside in the fact that 'violating the agreement will result in greater loss than gain for the violator'. For this is the 'universal law of human nature':

> Since I am obliged by natural right to choose the lesser of two evils, I have a sovereign right to break the bond of such an agreement and render what was said to be unsaid. This, I say, is allowed by natural right, whether I see it by true and certain reason or whether it is out of mere belief that I appear to grasp that I was wrong to make the promise. For

whether I discern things truly or falsely, it is the greater harm that I shall fear and, by nature's design, strive by every means to avoid[14]

Breaking the agreement is *legitimate* as soon as one of its parties considers that a greater good, or a lesser evil, will result from breaking it. This is true no matter whether the agreement is broken based on rational judgement, or a false reasoning, opinion or passion, and no matter whether the person breaking the agreement is seeing things 'truly or falsely'. This is a 'universal law of human nature' that no human can ever free himself from, by definition, since he is himself part of this nature. So how should we understand what Spinoza says in Chapter XX judging it 'seditious' for anyone to stipulate that 'no one has to keep his promises'? When he has himself explained in Chapter XVI that no one is *legitimately* obliged to keep his promises when he judges – for right or wrong – that it is preferable for him to break them? Leo Strauss writes of the contradictions peppering the *TTP*:

> The sound rule for reading the *Treatise* is, that in case of a contradiction, the statement most opposed to what Spinoza considered the vulgar view has to be regarded as expressing his serious view; nay, that even a necessary implication of a heterodox character has to take precedence over a contradictory statement that is never explicitly contradicted by Spinoza. In other words, if the final theses of the individual chapters of the *Treatise* (as distinguished from the almost constantly repeated accommodations) are not consistent with each other, we are led by the observation of this fact and our ensuing reflection to a consistent view that is no longer explicitly stated, but clearly presupposed, by Spinoza; and we have to recognize this view as his serious view, or as the secret par excellence of the *Treatise*. Only by following this rule of reading can we understand Spinoza's thought exactly as he himself understood it and avoid the danger of becoming or remaining the dupes of his accommodations.[15]

Leo Strauss wanted to establish 'the sound rule for reading the *Treatise*', which would save us from 'becoming or remaining ... dupes'. When there is a contradiction, we have to be able to decide between two incompatible claims. The rule in such a case is that 'the statement most opposed to what Spinoza considered the vulgar view has to be regarded as expressing his serious view'. What is the 'vulgar view' in our example? Does the ordinary man think it legitimate or illegitimate not to keep his promises? We know that the common morality considers it illegitimate. Thus, the claim that expresses Spinoza's 'serious view' is the one contradicting this, namely that we do not have to keep our promises. So following Leo Strauss's method for reading Spinoza, the group of men to whom the second seditious opinion attaches is not the Jews, but the Spinozists.

While himself making use of the 'reading method elaborated by Leo Strauss' Milner nonetheless follows a different line of path. Starting out from the principle that Spinoza deliberately contradicts himself, he concludes that the explicit meaning is deceptive – that it is literally *senseless*. Having made short shrift of the explicit meaning he proposes to freely expound his own reasoning. Indeed, Strauss's interpretative rule allows this: 'even a necessary implication of a heterodox character has to take precedence over a contradictory statement that is never explicitly contradicted by Spinoza'. Milner has built his doctrine on this: it is right to contradict an explicit claim of Spinoza's, even when he himself never did so, if a 'necessary implication of a heterodox character' demands it. All that remains is to freely expound upon the 'heterodox nature' of persecuting the Jews, the piccolo flute or cardiologists, and you can make Spinoza say absolutely whatever you like. Let's take a textbook example: Spinoza explicitly states that the rule in a republic is that 'everyone's judgment is free and unshackled [and] each may worship God as his conscience dictates'. Yet, Milner explains that Spinoza wants to convert the Jews to Islam. How is this possible? Let's apply Strauss's rule: if we judge the perfect persecution of the Jews 'heterodox' in nature, and moreover judge it a 'necessary implication' of the second seditious opinion cited by Spinoza in Chapter XX of the *TTP*, then we are at liberty to contradict all of Spinoza's explicit claims, including the one asserting 'everyone's ... free and unshackled' judgement to 'worship God as his conscience dictates'. Having established such rules for interpretation we can freely develop our reasoning *ad libidum*.

So there is reason to distrust Strauss's 'sound rule', just as there is reason to distrust any rule that claims to *transcend* the thing that it is the rule for. Indeed, we know where that leads: free rein to the enthusiasms of the police. But for rules we would do better to refer back to Spinoza himself, whose *Treatise of the Improvement of the Understanding* elaborates two rules that are of the very highest importance to us. The first is a rule of caution that he has set himself:

> To speak in a manner intelligible to the multitude, and to comply with every general custom that does not hinder the attainment of our purpose. For we can gain from the multitude no small advantages, provided that we strive to accommodate ourselves to its understanding

as far as possible: moreover, we shall in this way gain a friendly audience for the reception of the truth.[16]

The second rule concerns 'the nature of the method for finding out the truth'. Spinoza maintains that 'for proving the truth, and for valid reasoning, we need no other means than the truth and valid reasoning themselves' and adds:

> thus, as the truth needs no sign – it being to possess the subjective essence of things, or, in other words, the ideas of them, in order that all doubts may be removed – it follows that the true method does not consist in seeking for the signs of truth after the acquisition of the idea, but that the true method teaches us the order in which we should seek for truth itself, or the subjective essences of things, or ideas, for all these expressions are synonymous.[17]

It thus follows that when we are faced with two apparently contradictory teachings of Spinoza's, there is no alternative method other than to resolve the contradiction, so that what had appeared to be contradictory might finally appear in the form of an idea. To put that another way, there is no alternative method other than the path of situating ideas in the right order – which, when it comes to exegesis, is both deductive *and* literal.

*

Let's go back to our textbook example. In Chapter XVI, Spinoza argues that it is legitimate not to stick to one's promises, whereas in Chapter XX, he argues the opposite. Here, not only is it illegitimate, but the simple fact of professing such an opinion is seditious and thus reprehensible. As he immediately explains:

> It is subversive not so much because of the judgments and opinions in themselves as because of the actions which such views imply. By the very fact that someone thinks such a thing, they are tacitly or explicitly breaking the pact that they made with the sovereign.[18]

Spinoza distinguishes between the 'judgments' that one makes and the 'actions which such views imply'. But why distinguish between judgement and action, when it is the judgement itself that is seditious, and which must be condemned precisely because of the 'actions which such views *imply*' (my emphasis)? So it has to be possible to 'think such a thing' without this thought thus implying 'breaking the pact that they made with the sovereign'. And that is Spinoza's thinking, as he elaborates it when he addresses natural law in Chapter XVI: according to natural law, it is legitimate not to keep one's promises, in conformity with the universal law of human nature that a man will choose the lesser of two evils. Is this, too, a seditious statement which 'tacitly or explicitly break[s] the pact ... made with the sovereign'? Absolutely not, since here we are dealing with a principle that 'should play the most important role in the formation of a state'. The 'principle' is the following: an agreement of any kind only has force insofar as breaking it would entail a greater evil for whoever violated it and not a greater good. In Chapter XVI Spinoza grounds 'the pact ... made with the sovereign' in a principle that accords with the universal law of human nature. By consequence, his thinking is not seditious, but foundational. Conversely, in Chapter XX Spinoza is speaking not of natural law, but of positive law. On this subject, his doctrine holds that the sovereign and legislator must accord to each man the freedom to disagree with positive law, but not the freedom to act in discordance with this law – in other words, to transgress it. That is why he argues that the only opinions that should be forbidden are those that 'break the pact ... with the sovereign', 'because of the actions which such views imply' – and that includes the opinion holding that 'no one has to keep his promises'. To maintain that it is *legitimate* to transgress positive law is a seditious view, which breaks the pact with the sovereign. By consequence, the sovereign not only can but must condemn whoever publicly expresses such an opinion. But isn't this what Spinoza himself does in his reasoning in Chapter XVI? No. Here, Spinoza publicly argues that it is legitimate by virtue of natural law not to keep one's promises, *but that it is illegitimate by virtue of positive law*. So his thinking is not seditious, precisely because it neither tacitly nor expressly breaks the pact made with the sovereign. Rather, it warns that no authority can claim to abolish the universal law of human nature that the greater good legitimizes the breaking of the agreement.

Is the *TTP*'s philosophy seditious? Spinoza defends himself from this charge twice, firstly in the conclusion to his Preface and then in the conclusion to the book itself:

> I must give notice here, as I do again at the end of the treatise, that I maintain nothing that I would not very willingly submit to the examination and judgment of the sovereign authorities of my country. If they judge anything I say to be in conflict with the laws of my country or prejudicial to the common good, I wish it unsaid. I know that I am

human and may have erred. I have however taken great pains not to err, and to ensure above all that everything I write entirely accords with the laws of my country, with piety, and with morality.[19]

The repetition of these words invites us to reflect on the *TTP*'s anonymous author's warning: that there is no law other than that of a life led by reason. Isn't this Milner's own explanation, distinguishing between breaking an agreement legitimately – because it is broken on account of a 'rational judgement' – and breaking it illegitimately – because it is broken on account of an 'enslaving passion'? Yes. But whereas we have taken a detour via contradiction that allows us to shed light on Spinoza's idea, Milner's detour via prejudice denatures it, all the better to suppress it. Spinoza's idea is the following:

> To understand this better, imagine that a highwayman forces me to promise to give him all I have, at his demand. Since my natural right is determined by my power alone, as I have already shown, it is certain that if I can free myself from him by deceit, by promising whatever he wants, I may by the law of nature do so, i.e., I may fraudulently agree to whatever he demands.[20]

A 'worker'-theorist wants the human to recover his good [*bien*][21]. He knows how to achieve this, if necessary by fraud. A 'bourgeois' theorist imagines that he possesses some good, which he fears he will be dispossessed of, if necessary by force. Whereas the 'worker' theorist works toward knowledge of what is good, the 'bourgeois' theorist develops a police arsenal. Is the contradiction between them impossible to mediate? At the very least, it is of principal importance.

*

Milner's exegesis is in the service of the ruling class and is thus a violent one. Taking the explicit meaning of Spinoza's manifesto for a tissue of untruths, contradictions and false appearances, he terms it 'deceptive'. In order to know its true meaning we have to force the philosopher to speak, even if that means resorting to robust interrogation techniques. Finally, the text offers up its confession: Spinoza was setting out a programme for the disappearance of the word 'Jew'.

There is another method for exegesis – a literal one, conditioned by the explicit meaning. It is literally *under its law*, because it is not at liberty to free itself of this law. However, this is not *obedience to the Law*, because in the last instance it is not the Letter that sets the Law, but the *understanding* of this Letter: the internalization of its explicit meaning.

The master violates the Letter, the slave is enchained by it and vice-versa: they are the two sides of one same nudity. But there is a third man, who lives guided by knowledge. Scripture says 'an eye for an eye, a tooth for a tooth'. The Talmud explains: for an eye, the value of an eye, for a tooth, the value of a tooth. If Levi slashes out Simeon's eye, and the Letter sets the Law, then Levi must lose an eye as reparation for Simeon losing an eye: justice consists of slashing out his eye. This is the law of an eye for an eye. This is the violence of the Letter. But if it is the *understanding* of the Letter that sets the Law here, and 'an eye for an eye' means Simeon's loss must be *repaired* by Levi losing an eye, we must ask: what is reparation (*tikkun*)? Of course, Levi must lose his eye. But reparation would demand not the slashing out of Levi's eye, but him giving his eye to Simeon. How could Levi give an eye to Simeon? By giving him the value of an eye.

What is the Law? If we set up Scripture as a Law, it follows that poking out Levi's eye is a good thing and justice for Simeon. Conversely, this is not the case if we set up knowledge as a Law. In this case, the good thing – justice for Simeon – would be for Levi to give him the gift of vision. This is a utopian justice, which provides the basis for understanding the Letter in the here and now.

PART TWO

SPINOZA'S BIBLE

The time is out of joint. O cursed spite,
That ever I was born to set it right!
Nay, come, let's go together.

WILLIAM SHAKESPEARE, *HAMLET* I, 5

INTRODUCTION

Spinoza betrayed the Jews' cause, they say, firstly in breaking with the Synagogue – or, more precisely, in forcing the Synagogue to excommunicate him; then in becoming a Christian – at least in spirit, if not through baptism and the sacraments; and finally, in providing a tortuous, disfigured, execrable presentation of Judaism. Did the *TTP* open the way to what Poliakov calls 'the rationalist or secular anti-Semitism of modern times' or did it instead keep alive the ancient, reasoned elaboration of an emancipatory, universal and egalitarian idea? Was Spinoza a traitor to Judaism or a *worker* theorist of the name 'Jew'?

The *TTP*'s argument is that whereas the Bible calls for the practise of justice and charity, and its teaching takes the form of laws, parables and stories, philosophy instead proceeds according to the order of reason. Spinoza constantly goes back to this point: 'the teachings of Scripture are very simple', aiming at 'inculcating obedience not knowledge' among common men.[1] He had first expounded this principle in 1665, before he began writing the *TTP*. In his first reply to Blyenbergh, who had written to him about Descartes's *Principles of Philosophy*, he explained:

> Scripture, being particularly adapted to the needs of the common people, continually speaks in merely human fashion, for the common people are incapable of understanding higher things. That is why I think that all that God has revealed to the Prophets as necessary for salvation is set down in the form of law, and in this way the Prophets made up a whole parable depicting God as a king and lawgiver, because he had revealed the means that lead to salvation and perdition, and was the cause thereof. These means, which are simply causes, they called laws, and wrote them down in the form of laws; salvation and perdition, which are simply effects necessarily resulting from these means, they represented as reward and punishment. All their words were adjusted

to the framework of this parable rather than to truth. They constantly depicted God in human form, sometimes angry, sometimes merciful, now looking to what is to come, now jealous and suspicious, and even deceived by the Devil. So philosophers and likewise all who have risen to a level beyond law, that is, all who pursue virtue not as a law but because they love it (*non ut Legem sed ex amore*) as something very precious, should not find such words a stumbling-block.[2]

Scripture was addressed to the common man, unable to understand 'higher things' (*rebus sublimibus*), whereas the philosopher addressed himself to the man who was able to understand them.

Scripture and philosophy each call on men to practise justice and charity – what Spinoza called 'the true conception of living' in his *TTP* – but they differ in their way of teaching it to them. Scripture does not seek to teach men to *understand* the 'true conception of living', but to make them *obey* it; philosophy does not seek to make men *obey* it, but to *understand* it. That is why Scripture adapts its reasoning to suit the greatest numbers, whereas philosophy expounds 'universal [reasons] intended to convince everybody'.[3] Scripture takes recourse to the imagination, to inadequate ideas – for example, anthropomorphisms. It continually speaks 'in the manner in which two men normally communicate their thoughts':[4] that is, in the manner of men who lead lives not guided by knowledge, but dominated by the emotions. And if Scripture is to make itself understood to such men – to convince them to adopt the true conception of living – it has to employ the language of the emotions. Spinoza formulates this principle in proposition 7 of Book IV of his *Ethics*: 'An emotion cannot be checked or destroyed except by a contrary emotion which is stronger than the emotion which is to be checked.'[5] Inadequate ideas are addressed to the man enslaved by emotions; adequate ones are addressed to the free man. There is, however, a convergence, since in each case what is at issue is inculcating 'the true conception of living' in men. Spinoza concludes that the philosophers 'must not be encumbered' by the fact that Scripture resorts to inadequate ideas to convince men to obey. After all, Scripture's goal is not for men to *understand*, but precisely for them to *obey*.

What is the main approach that Scripture takes? What is the one approach on which all the others are, in some sense, dependent? Spinoza answers: 'The means, which are nothing but causes, they called "laws" and wrote in the manner of laws'; 'The prophets ordered their words in terms of this parable rather than according to the truth.' Scripture is rendered in a juridical form – a parable addressed to the man who is unable to perceive the sublime; the man so dominated by his emotions that he will obey – it being understood that 'An emotion cannot be checked or destroyed except by a contrary emotion which is stronger than the emotion which is to be checked.' Yet the strongest of emotions is the Law. Is this the most liberating of emotions, or the most enslaving one?

*

In his *Metaphysics*, Book B, 4 (1000a), Aristotle examines the difficult question of the principles of corruptible and incorruptible beings. It is in this vein that he invokes 'Hesiod, and all the cosmologists, [who] considered only what was convincing to themselves, and gave no consideration to us'. Indeed, they 'say that whatever did not taste of the nectar and ambrosia became mortal'. Aristotle concludes: 'it is not worthwhile to consider seriously the subtleties of mythologists'. He then moves on to 'cross-examining those who offer demonstration of their statements'. So on the one hand there are 'mythologists' hiding behind 'subtleties' and on the other 'those who offer demonstration of their statements'. And the philosopher moves to disqualify the explanations of those whose wisdom is limited to 'subtleties', namely the theologian-poets, whose reasoning is based on myths.

The same opposition guides the *TTP*'s reasoning, but with a difference. Whereas for Aristotle this opposition concerns the speculative understanding of the principles of nature, in the *TTP* it concerns the 'true conception of living' – the practice of justice and charity. Spinoza does not distinguish between the principles of nature and the principles of ethics and in this sense takes his place in continuity with Plato, according to whom the idea is – in the last analysis – an idea of good. There is also a second difference: the mythological otherness that Spinoza examines in the *TTP* is not the discourse of 'Hesiod, and all the cosmologists', or that of all the other Greek theologians, but of Scripture. And Scripture, Spinoza maintains, inculcates 'the true conception of living' in men. It follows that there must be a happy compatibility between the mythological arguments in Scripture and the philosopher's reasoned proofs, both of which profess the one same conception of living: the 'true' one. However, Scripture teaches the true conception of living in the form of a Law, whereas philosophy teaches it in the form of an idea – that is to say, knowledge. So in the last analysis, are we dealing with one and the same teaching, or an essential otherness?

Is the adominated by his affect ublime:-hics "e image of the 'o recognise what is best about it. uing that the explicit meaning is decIs the argumenIsIs rgument that philosophy is in principle compatible with Scripture a sleight of hand devised out of caution, or is it a rationally founded argument? Let's pose the question more precisely: Spinoza's argument is explicit, and here we are not arguing that the explicit meaning is deceptive, but seeking to internalize this meaning. The *TTP*'s explicit argument should lead us to question whether there is a difference *of nature* between knowledge and obedience. Will this take us back to the philosopher's original act – which consists of converting man to knowledge, such that he might be free of the reasoning of 'the subtleties of mythologists'? In his response to Blyenbergh, Spinoza concludes that philosophers are 'above the law' (*supra Legem*) because they 'follow virtue not as a law but from love' (*non ut Legem sed ex amore*).[6] This is the decisive formula; the one which we must necessarily *know*, because we cannot *obey* it.

There are people who are virtuous through their obedience toward the Law – men dominated by emotions – and there are others – philosophers – who are virtuous not because that is the Law, but because they love virtue and are able to recognize what is best about it. Does this mean that the common man is in the image of the 'Jew', submissive before the Law, while the 'Christian' is in the image of the philosopher, driven by *love*? What does Spinoza mean by an ethics '*non ut Legem, sed ex amore*'? The final proposition of his *Ethics* (VP42) teaches:

> Blessedness is not the reward of virtue, but virtue itself. We do not enjoy blessedness because we keep our lusts in check. On the contrary, it is because we enjoy blessedness that we are able to keep our lusts in check.[7]

Such is the *Ethics*' last word on the matter. A man experiences good *ex amore* – through love, joy and knowledge. Love and joy are emotions that increase the capacity to act and to know. The more a man knows, the more he is animated by love and joy, and the more he is animated by love and joy, the more he knows. In contrast, whoever acts *ut Legem*, through obedience to the Law, does not experience good, any more than he experiences love, joy and knowledge. He controls his own lusts in the name of the Law, and in so doing he sets up the Law as his master. In a man's life, the intersection of the Law with man's lusts represents the serpent's arrival on the stage. This is the animal name of an impotence of thought, a wisdom of death.

Conversely, 'A free man thinks of death least of all things, and his wisdom is a meditation of life, not of death.'[8] How can we conceive Scripture and the *Ethics* as having taught one same conception of living – the true one – if while Scripture subjected the human to the Law in order to counter his lusts, the *Ethics* converted the human to knowledge so that he might experience joy and the love of good?

Spinoza's *Ethics* would advance the following proposition: the philosopher – that is to say the free man living under the guidance of reason alone – is 'above the Law'. And revolutionary practice would work to democratize the political consequences of this. But if Spinoza is an essential cog in the wheel of rationalist and revolutionary modernity, and 'remains up to the present day the accuser *par excellence* of Judaism' (Cohen), then what is modern about the 'Jewish question'? As we have seen, Benny Lévy does not step back, when faced with the abyss:

> Come on then, moderns, one more push, we must finish with Moses once and for all; we need the murder of the shepherd, in the right and proper form. This is the extremely modern programme of the final solution.

Since Moses was the legislator-prophet and the revolutionary and rationalist programme has the goal of living 'above the Law', the 'final solution' is the formula suitable for characterizing not the murder of a man or his subjects, but the abolition of the Law's transcendence. Even so, the letter of the formula – 'the final solution' – comes to be explicated in a murderous frenzy: this is where revolutionary and rationalist modernity will ultimately lead its militant sheep. For one does not innocently aspire to live 'above the law'. Jean-Claude Milner also subscribes to Benny Lévy's formula. Like Lévy he is a theorist of the 'return':[9] a secular theorist, but a consistent one. In his article 'Retour et équivoque chez Leo Strauss',[10] he shows the most lively interest in the thesis that the Bible is in-principle incompatible with philosophy. An attentive reader, he observes:

> If there are two sources [Athens and Jerusalem] and they contradict one another, then one of two things must be the case: either the contradiction can be resolved, in which case there is no research more important than finding some mediation. Or, instead, the contradiction is not resolvable, in which case there is no graver error than trying to pass something off as a mediation.[11]

Any possible mediation between the two would be of the very highest importance, since any return to Athens that is not articulated to the return to Jerusalem is nothing other than Heidegger's complicity with Nazism. 'Through his journey, Heidegger proved that the return to the Greeks – if it is unbound to the return to Jerusalem – leads to the attribution of greatness to Nazism.'[12] If, conversely, all mediation is illusory, then 'there is no graver error than trying to pass something off as a mediation'. Jean-Claude Milner does not commit this error:

The renaissance of classical political rationalism is one of the names that philosophy's return toward Athens takes in Strauss, insofar as this return responds to two distinct demands: (a) it is accompanied by a return to Jerusalem, (b) the return to Jerusalem and the return to Athens are radically separate, because their contradiction is irreducible. There is no mediation between philosophy and Revolution. There could not be, there has never been. Insofar as the West has relentlessly sought such mediation, it has been a long and vain illusion[13]

In Strauss's terms the 'return to Athens' accompanied by a 'return to Jerusalem' is the return to medieval Jewish and Muslim philosophy. In other words, it is the return to a Greek philosophy placed under the authority of the Law. Strauss's political rationalism is 'classical' only on condition that Spinoza's is 'modern' – meaning, Christian, which is to say, 'above the Law'. What remains to be cast off, other than Christianity, is Islam, the other religion of the Law. This is the object of a note of Milner's at the end of his article.

> Strauss speaks of Mohammedanism only with reference to medieval philosophy. If my interpretation is accurate, for him there was a radical difference opposing Maimonides to the Muslim philosophers, no matter how close they were. The distinction expressed itself as follows: Muslim philosophers attempted a mediation between Islam and philosophy; Maimonides approached philosophy only in order to prove the absence of mediation.[14]

Thus, the Muslim philosophers came to be integrated into the 'West', in the sense that having thrown themselves into the search for some 'mediation' between Law and philosophy, they too, pursued 'a long and vain illusion'. For Milner, only Maimonides, the most important authority of medieval Judaism, did not succumb to this illusion, having experienced and been able 'to prove the absence of mediation'. He can thus conclude:

> If we take the Revelation seriously, then there is no Revelation in the West but the Jewish one; everything that comes on top of the God of Abraham, Isaac and Jacob, everything that comes on top of the Law he gave, is foreign to the Revelation[15]

The 'Revelation' is 'Jewish' and has the form of a 'Law': the 'return to Jerusalem' is a return to the transcendence of the 'Law', as revealed by Judaism. A return to Greek philosophy is nonetheless desirable, so long as it is placed under the authority of the 'Law' – failing which it would attribute greatness to Nazism. For there is no mediation. But what is this 'Law', if not the transcendence that rationalist and revolutionary modernity claims to overcome, or even destroy?[16] The terms of the problem have now been demarcated: Spinoza's extremely modern programme is an ethics 'above the Law' (*supra Legem*). Indeed, in the eyes of the *bourgeois* theorists of the name 'Jew', that is where his essential immorality – or, as Hermann Cohen prettily puts it, his 'diabolical irony' – resides.

Did Spinoza reiterate what Benny Lévy terms 'Paul's attack',[17] the vindictive destruction of the knot between the Letter and the Law, to the benefit of a universal spirit, the allegory of the New Man? Leo Strauss's formulations on this score are equivocal. In his article 'Progress or Return?' he states that there is an insurmountable contradiction between 'Athens and Jerusalem', explaining that 'the one thing needful proclaimed by the Bible is incompatible, as it is understood by the Bible, with the one thing needful proclaimed by Greek philosophy, as it is understood by Greek philosophy'. In other words:

> To put it very simply and therefore somewhat crudely, the one thing needful according to Greek philosophy is the life of autonomous understanding. The one thing needful as spoken by the Bible is a life of obedient love.[18]

He formulated this in his lecture entitled 'How to Begin to Study Medieval Philosophy', evoking a contradiction 'between the way of life based on faith and obedience and a way of life based on free insight, *on human wisdom, alone*'.[19] Moreover, in his lecture on Thucydides he counterposed the 'obedient love' taught by the Bible to the 'free insight taught by philosophy'. He again returned to this theme in his *Natural Right and History*:

> No alternative is more fundamental than this: human guidance or divine guidance. The first possibility is characteristic of philosophy or science in the original sense of this term, the second is presented in the Bible. The dilemma cannot be evaded by any harmonization or synthesis. For both philosophy and the Bible proclaim something as the one thing needful, as the only thing that ultimately counts, and the one thing needful proclaimed by the Bible is the opposite of that proclaimed by philosophy: a life of obedient love versus a life of free insight.[20]

What is a 'life of obedient love', or indeed 'a life of love and obedience' or 'way of life founded on faith and obedience'? We immediately think of

Paul's famous formula at the beginning of the *Letter to the Romans* (1.5): 'By [Jesus Christ] we have received grace and apostleship, for obedience to the faith among all nations, for his name'.[21] In his last lectures on *The Political Theology of Paul*, Jacob Taubes commented

> The formula 'obedience of faith' is much discussed in theology. I believe that it's a polemical variant of 'obedience of laws'. It is laws that you obey, and Paul says, 'No, you obey faith'. What that means will require a long exegesis.[22]

It would indeed take a long exegesis, because the secret of the new covenant resides in this enigmatic formula. Be that as it may, Taubes is not mistaken: Paul's formula is polemical, seeking to tear down the kingship of Mosaic Law. Henceforth, Paul teaches, man must obey the Gospel of Christ.[23] Leo Strauss is thus being deliberately equivocal when he speaks of a 'life of obedient love' or a 'way of life founded on faith and obedience'. In order to get out of this equivocation, it seems that we should distinguish among three forms of life, and not two: obedience to the Law (Judaism and Islam), the 'obedience of faith' (Christianity) and autonomous understanding (philosophy). The problem is that, according to Strauss, there are only 'two roots': 'Athens and Jerusalem'. If we have established that the search for mediation is an illusion and Paul's Christianity abolished the regime of the Law, then he was thus taking Athens as his root. Yet, however much we look, we cannot find any Gospel in Athens. Indeed, Marx and Engels observe as much in *The German Ideology*:

> Sancho on page 154 makes the "Judaic reviewers" in ancient Jerusalem exclaim in opposition to the Christian definition "God is love": "Thus you see that it is heathen God that is proclaimed by the Christians; for if God is love, then he is the God Amor, the God of love!" — "Against expectation" however, the New Testament was written in Greek, and the "Christian definition" reads ὁ θεός ἀγάπη ἐστιν (1 John, 4.16 whereas "the God Amor, the God of love" is called Ερως. Sancho has, therefore, still to explain how it is that the "Judaic reviewers" were able to achieve the transformation of ἀγάπη into ἔρως.[24]

If, as Milner explains, 'everything that comes on top of the Law' is 'foreign to the revelation'; if, as Marx and Engels explain, the watchword 'God is love' is foreign to Athens; and lastly, if, as Strauss explains, there is no possible mediation between Athens and Jerusalem, then we have to conclude that the 'love' in question, ἀγάπη, is an hallucinatory psychosis, an illusion destined to a long future. There are, seemingly, only two 'roots': 'Athens and Jerusalem', respectively signifying philosophy and the Jewish revelation of the Law. And they are *antinomic*.

Leo Strauss got to the bottom of this story in a lecture that he gave at the University of Chicago on 25 January 1957, entitled 'On the interpretation of Genesis'. He proposed an exegesis of the first three chapters of Genesis. He concluded from his analysis of the story of the six-day Creation that 'heaven is depreciated in favour of the Earth, life on Earth, man',[25] and that this marks a depreciation of philosophy, which he identifies with cosmology: 'There is then a deep opposition between the Bible and cosmology proper, and since all philosophy is cosmology ultimately, between the Bible and philosophy.'[26] Leo Strauss first justifies the terms of this antinomy by opposing, on the one hand, the Biblical claim that the world was created, and on the other hand, the philosophical effort to understand the world: 'all knowledge of the createdness of the world has an entirely different character than our knowledge of the structure or articulation of the world.'[27] And at the end of his analysis of the creation story (the first chapter of Genesis) he concludes:

> There is no argument in favor of Creation except God speaking to Israel. He who has not heard that speech either directly or by tradition, will worship the heavenly bodies, will remain, in other words, within the horizon of cosmology.[28]

Strauss's alternative between, on the one hand, the word of the Biblical God addressed to Israel, and, on the other hand, the adoration of celestial bodies, is a means of translating and explicating the two fundamental categories of the Talmud; on the one hand, the man who is named an 'Israelite' and on the other hand, he who is named a 'servant of the stars' (*oved kochavim*), an expression that designates whoever worships a cult foreign to the god who 'brought the Jews out of Egypt'. Who is a 'servant of the stars'? Interpreting the first verses of the Bible, Leo Strauss responds: a philosopher. Thus, follows another question, which he immediately poses: 'What is wrong in man's effort to find his bearing in light of what is evident to man, as man? What is the true character of human life? What is the right life of man? This question is the point of departure for the second creation story, in the second chapter.'[29] Does an exegesis of the second chapter of Genesis (concerning the prohibition against the tree of the knowledge of good and evil), and then that of the third chapter (relating to the Fall) afford an answer to the question posed – the question of why the Biblical (or 'Jewish') revelation identifies philosophy with the adoration of celestial beings, that is to say, with idolatry? According to Strauss, the interest in the 'heavens', their valorization, is the expression of a desire for understanding that takes man away from obedience to the Law.[30] Autonomous understanding, knowledge, such as philosophy conceives it, becomes the very expression of disobedience; the very expression of the Fall:

> Man certainly chose to disobey. He chose therewith the principle of disobedience. This principle is called knowledge of good and evil. We may say that disobedience means autonomous knowledge of good and evil, a knowledge which man possesses by himself, the implication being that the true knowledge is not autonomous; and, in the light of later theological developments, one could say that the true knowledge of good and evil is supplied only by revelation ... Chapters two and three of Genesis are animated by the same spirit as the first chapter; what the Bible presents is the alternative to the temptation and this temptation we can call, in light of certain things we happen to know, 'philosophy'. The Bible therefore confronts us more clearly than any other book with this fundamental alternative: life in obedience to the revelation, life in obedience, or life in human freedom, the latter being represented by the Greek philosophers. This alternative has never been disposed of, although there are many people who believe there can be a happy synthesis which is superior to the isolated parts: Bible on the one hand and philosophy on the other. This is impossible.[31]

Analysing the first three chapters of Genesis, Leo Strauss reduces the alternative between Scripture and philosophy to this choice: either 'life in obedience' or 'a life in human freedom'. So there is no longer any question of 'love' or 'faith'. It is a question of either obeying the Law or living as a free man (guided by knowledge alone). As for finding a mediation, 'This is impossible'.

The 'bourgeois' theorists profess a Law whose function is to prohibit rationalist and revolutionary modernity, which is held at fault for an original sin – the sin of a knowledge raising man 'above the Law'. And for the more Judaising of these 'bourgeois' theorists our modernity is inscribed in the extension of the Christian abolition of the Law, except that in the last analysis Christianity was itself the Trojan Horse for philosophy. Let's examine this argument: Is Spinoza's modernity inscribed in the extension of the Christian abolition of the Law? Let's accept that's the case. And is the Christianity in the *TTP* the Trojan Horse for the *Ethics*? Let's accept that's the case, too. But we still have to ask what is this Law invoked by the choir of *bourgeois* theorists of the name 'Jew'. Let's examine this question from the viewpoint of a *worker* theorist of names. Let's take mastery over a memory, such that it will light up in a moment of danger.

5 THE *AT JUDAEI* MANIFESTO

At the end of the *TTP*'s third chapter Spinoza refutes the opinions expressed by 'certain people', specifying that by this he 'especially' means the Pharisees. They concluded from a passage of Jeremiah's prophecy that 'the seed of Israel will remain the people of God for ever'. Spinoza counters this with other verses and a different exegesis of Jeremiah's prophetic writings, as well as those of Ezekiel and Zephaniah. He thus concludes: 'Since this election is made solely on the basis of true virtue, it is unthinkable that it has been promised only to pious Jews, to the exclusion of other pious people.'[1] The problem is that while Spinoza was claiming to refute the 'Pharisees' – that is, as Lagrée and Moreau explain, 'the representatives of the rabbinical tradition'[2] – he was not unaware that 'Since this election is made solely on the basis of true virtue, it is unthinkable that it has been promised only to pious Jews, to the exclusion of other pious people.' This is an explicit teaching of Maimonides's Codification:[3] 'the pious of the nations' are 'heir[s] of the world to come'. And Spinoza could not have been unaware of this, because he cites precisely this text of Maimonides's at the end of *TTP* Chapter V. Moreover, the intersection of these two formulas is literal: in Chapter III, Spinoza writes that since 'election', 'concerns true virtue', it cannot be ascribed 'only to pious Jews' (*piis Judaeorum tantum*) and in Chapter V, citing and translating Maimonides, he writes that 'the pious of the nations' (*piis nationum*), are among the 'heir[s] of the world to come'.

Was Spinoza's ethical argument – namely, that election is not based on the seed, but on virtue and rational understanding (*ratione intellectus*) – a refutation of the Pharisees 'especially'? After all, Maimonides was the most renowned Pharisee in the educated Europe of the seventeenth century; Spinoza cites him on this basis; and the cited text affirms as explicitly as could be that 'election' is promised not only to pious Jews, but to all pious men whatever the seed of their provenance.

At the end of Chapter III, Spinoza claims to be refuting the Pharisees 'especially' because they relate 'election' to the 'seed of Israel'. Then, concluding Chapter V, he summarizes his doctrine, adding 'However, the Jews hold completely to the opposite view'[4] – in Latin, *At Judaei contra plane sentiunt*. There follows a citation from Maimonides's Code, which is meant to evidence what 'the Jews think'. It is the only occurrence of the Mosaic Law in Spinoza's *oeuvre*, and he presents it as antithetical – or more precisely, antinomic – to his own thinking. This, then, is the site of his break with 'the Jews'. Is this the site of a betrayal? Studying this text in depth should allow us to answer this question. We will borrow the term that Jean-Claude Milner uses in his *Le Sage trompeur* when he speaks of a 'manifesto'. I will thus speak of the *At Judaei* manifesto.

Spinoza refers to 'the Jews', then cites Maimonides's Codification. The most authoritative expression of rabbinical Judaism after the Talmud, this work was the primary indicator of what 'the Jews' thought. Spinoza cites Chapter 8, Law 11 of Maimonides's Codification, from the section 'Kings' in the book of Judgments. He first cites the text in the original Hebrew then translates it into Latin. We will translate it directly from Hebrew:

> Everyone who accepts the seven precepts [of Noah] and undertakes to observe them rigorously is among the pious of the nations and an heir of the world to come; but only if he accepts them and practises them because the Holy One prescribed them in the Torah, revealing to us through Moses that the sons of Noah had always previously [*mikodem*] been enjoined by them. But if he practises them because knowledge [*daʾat*] commands him, he is not a resident-foreigner [*ger toshav*], nor does he belong to the pious of the nations, nor[5] the learned.[6]

The 'seven precepts' are seven commandments, termed 'Noahic' (*sheva mitsvot benei noah*) and incumbent on all men. 'Sons of Noah' (*benei noah*) is the name for men who are exclusively subject to 'Noah's' seven commandments, as distinct from the 'sons of Israel' (*benei israel*) who are instead subject to the (613) Mosaic commandments. According to the Talmud (Sanhedrin 59a) at Sinai Moses repeated 'Noah's' seven commandments, which had already been given before Sinai. Maimonides immediately goes on to expound these seven commandments or precepts (*mitzvoth*) in Chapter 9, Law 1: they forbid idolatry, profaning God's name, murder, having certain sexual relations and stealing; they oblige the setting up of tribunals to render justice; and finally they forbid the consumption of a live animal's flesh. Spinoza, for his part, does not specify what they are, contenting himself with the following clarification in a footnote:

> the Jews think that God gave seven commandments to Noah, and the nations are bound only by these; to the Hebrew people alone he gave many other commandments, in order to render them happier than the rest.[7]

Spinoza explains that the Jews believe in a form of 'beatitude' to which they have the exclusive privilege (*ut eam beatiorem*). Does his explanation not contradict Maimonides's rule – which he himself cites – ascribing the world to come, supreme beatitude, to whoever observes the seven 'Noahic' commandments? The contradiction is resolved if we hypothesize that in this note Spinoza was referring to a doctrine which was not Maimonides's own but had attestation elsewhere in rabbinical literature. Indeed, it does have such attestation. That is how Menasseh ben Israel, one of the main figures of rabbinical Judaism in seventeenth-century Holland[8] addressed this question in his book *Nishmat Haim* ('The Soul of Life'). In Chapter VII, section 2, he tries to respond to an objection that Isaac Arema had formulated in his own fourteenth-century *Akedat YizHak* ('Binding of Isaac'), one of the last masterpieces of Spanish Judaism. This work had discussed the argument made by certain figures in rabbinical Judaism and particularly in kabbalistic milieus, holding that there is a difference of nature between the souls of Israel and the souls of other men. Taking a rationalist approach, Isaac Arema objected that this contradicts the Talmudic teaching, according to which all 'just' men have a share in the world to come (*Tosefta*, Sanhedrin 13.2), just like the souls of Israel do and moreover that it contradicts divine justice, which distinguishes between men according to their actions and not according to their seed. For his part, Menasseh ben Israel wanted to reconcile these two poles. He considered the distinction of nature between the souls of Israel and those of other men, to be a point of doctrine with attestation among numerous kabbalistic currents and he claimed to agree with this distinction; yet, he also understood the objections of the rationalist current as represented by Isaac Arema. This latter objection is doubly-founded, both by an ethical argument and by an explicit Talmudic teaching. He thus had to resolve this contradiction and his resolution was the following: there is indeed a distinction of nature between the souls of Israel and those of other men, but there is no injustice in that, for each man disposes of the means allowing him to correct or perfect himself and each man will be judged in function of the use that he has made of these means. This distinction of nature does not contradict the fairness of the last judgement. Menasseh ben Israel preserves the dogma of a distinction of nature between the seed of Israel and the seeds of the nations, but tries to make this compatible with the idea of a universal justice. In so doing, he reduces the division between two opposed currents: an increasingly isolated rationalist current, whose last great representative was Isaac Arema and an ever-more dominant irrationalist current, whose doctrinal foundations have attestation in many masterpieces of medieval Judaism. Indeed, in the Spain of the twelfth century, Juda Halevi had expounded what he considered to be Judaism's principal article of faith in his famous dialogue *Kuzari*, or *Book of refutation and proof on behalf of the most despised religion*:

> Al Khazari: If this be so, then your belief is confined to yourselves?
>
> The Rabbi: Yes; but any Gentile who joins us unconditionally shares our good fortune, without, however, being quite equal to us. If the Law were binding on us only because God created us, the white and the black man would be equal, since He created them all. But the Law was given to us because He led us out of Egypt, and remained attached to us, because we are the pick of mankind.[9]

This attests a belief in medieval Judaism that the seed of Israel was 'elect', just as Spinoza observed at the end of Chapter III when he endeavoured to refute the Pharisees 'especially'. And according to Juda Halevi, the foundation of this belief is the fact that the gift of the Law is not a 'direct consequence' of the creation of man (Adam), but a 'direct consequence' of the exodus from Egypt, an event that concerns the seed of Israel alone. That is also the reason why although a proselyte can join Israel, he cannot however become an 'equal' and still less if he is not a proselyte, but a non-'Israelite'.

The dogma of an 'election' of the seed of Israel was further developed in various different currents of kabbalistic literature, up to Hayyim Luzzato (in Italy), the most renowned kabbalistic rabbi of the eighteenth century. He devoted a chapter of his book *Derekh ha-Chem* ('God's Path') to the question of the relations between Israel and the nations, explaining that this question – 'one of the deepest concepts of God's providence' posed the human intellect the following problem: 'with regard to their basic characteristics [Israel and the other nations] appear exactly alike. From the Torah's viewpoint, however, the two are completely different, and are treated as if they belonged to completely different species.'[10] Luzzato then expounds his doctrine: after the Fall of Adam, human nature was degraded.

But God accorded a lapse of time at the origins of humanity, during which time man's own free will allowed him to return on his own merit to what humanity's status had been prior to the Fall. And after man succeeded in doing so, not only he but also his descendants were endowed with a non-degraded human form. Nonetheless, this 'time of effort' was limited by Providence: 'before the Generation of Separation [which followed the biblical episode of the Tower of Babel] man existed in the age of roots', after which followed the 'age of branches',[11] which continues still today. And that is why men and Israel do not make up one same species. The nature of each branch is determined by its roots, which are absolutely different from one tree to the next, according to whether they are rooted in a degraded humanity or a restored one.

Yet, only the tree named 'Israel' is rooted in a restored humanity – that is, in the humanity of before the Fall – whereas the seventy nations are irrevocably the bearers of a degraded humanity. Nonetheless, the determinism of the human condition is irrevocable only at a collective level; conversely, individual men can 'tear themselves loose from their own roots, and through their own actions include themselves among the branches of Avraham's family'[12] by converting to the religion of Israel. But it follows from this, that 'In the World-to-Come ... there will be no nation other than Israel'. Luzzato then adds: 'the souls of righteous gentiles will be allowed to exist in the Future World, but only as an addition and attachment to Israel. They will therefore be secondary to the Jew, just as a garment is secondary to the one who wears it. All that they attain of the ultimate good will have to be attained in this manner, since by virtue of their nature they can receive no more.'[13]

Haim Luzzato does not specify who the 'righteous gentiles' are. However, the question is all the more sharply posed given that this expression does not feature in the Talmud. When the Talmud refers to the universality of 'the world to come', it evokes the presence therein not of all 'righteous'[14] men, but of all 'just' men. If, conversely, we refer to Maimonides's Codification, it is indeed a matter of 'piety'. Was Haim Luzzato's kabbalistic mythology based on Maimonides's Codification? Nowhere in his Codification, or anywhere else in his *oeuvre*, does Maimonides introduce any distinction of nature between the seeds of men, any more than he distinguishes between the world to come to be inherited by the pious souls of Israel and the one inherited by the pious souls of the nations. Spinoza's footnote referring to the Jews' belief in a form of 'beatitude', that only they would inherit, and indeed what he says at the end of Chapter III on the subject of the Pharisees 'especially' – according to which it is the 'seed of Israel' that is 'elect' – thus, contradicts the rule that he cites from Maimonides at the end of Chapter V, as the illustration of what 'the Jews' think. Nonetheless, it does not contradict a strong current of rabbinical Judaism's doctrines, from Juda Halevi to Haim Luzzato.

Let's now turn to the doctrine of the codifier of Mosaic Law, Maimonides. Introducing him, Spinoza writes

> However, the Jews hold completely to the opposite view. They think that true opinions and a true conception of life make no contribution to happiness whenever people receive them by the natural light of reason alone and not as teachings prophetically revealed to Moses. Maimonides dares openly to assert this[15]

Maimonides ascribes to the 'pious men among the nations', the same retribution as the 'pious men' among the Jews – namely, the world to come, the universally shared supreme beatitude. Spinoza's disagreement with the 'Pharisee' Maimonides is thus of a totally different nature than his earlier dispute with the 'Pharisees ... especially', mentioned at the end of Chapter III. This time, the dispute concerns not the universality of the principle of election – for Maimonides explicitly recognizes this universality, in the rule in question – but the definition of what true piety is. Maimonides maintains that the 'pious man' is he who embraces the true conception of living, as a set of teachings revealed to Moses by prophecy. It is in this sense that 'the Jews hold completely to the opposite view' than Spinoza's. Whereas they – in the person of Maimonides, codifier of the Mosaic Law – maintain that the 'pious man' among the nations is he who observes the seven Noahic commandments *out of obedience to the prophecy of Moses*, he who observes them *guided by reason* is not a pious man; and not being a 'pious man', he thus has no share in the world to come.[16]

Translating from the Hebrew into Latin, Spinoza writes: *a ratione ductus* ('guided by reason'), where we have translated more literally 'because knowledge (*da'at*) commands him'. This is the formula – *a ratione ductus* – with which he designates the free man in his *Ethics*: *Homo liber, hoc est, qui ex solo rationis dictamine vivit*; 'A free man, that is, he who lives solely according to the dictates of reason' (proof of IVP 67). *Illum liberum esse dixit, qui solâ ducitur ratione*; 'I have said that a free man is he who is guided solely by reason' (proof of IVP 68).[17] This is also the formula that he employs in the *TTP*: *solus ille liber, qui integro animo ex solo ductu rationis vivit*; 'The only [genuinely] free person is one who lives with his entire mind guided solely by reason'.[18] In using the translation *a ratione ductus*, 'guided by reason', Spinoza poses the antinomy very precisely: according to Maimonides, the man who practises the commandments of the universal ethics not out of obedience to Moses's Law, but guided by reason, is impious. But for Spinoza, this latter is the definition of a free man.

I spoke of the commandments of the universal ethics, rather than of the 'Noahic' commandments. Indeed, Spinoza does not even deign to mention them. For him, the important question is not the content of the seven 'Noahic' commandments, but the distinction that Maimonides introduces between the man who observes them out of obedience to the Law of Moses and the man who observes them 'guided by reason'. That is the essential thing. Spinoza emphasizes this as he introduces Malmonides's text and again immediately afterwards:

> These are the words of Maimonides. Rabbi Joseph ben Shem Tov, in his book entitled *Kevod Elohim*, or *Glory of God*, adds that Aristotle (who he supposes has written the supreme *Ethics*, and whom he esteems above all others) missed nothing that was relevant to true morality and expounded it all in his *Ethics* and would have put it all conscientiously into practice. Nevertheless, he adds, this would not have helped him towards salvation, since he did not receive these teachings as divine doctrine prophetically revealed, but derived them from the dictate of reason alone (*ex solo dictamine rationis*).[19]

Therefore, I will sometimes take the liberty of speaking of the commandments or laws of universal ethics, rather than of 'Noahic' commandments or laws, precisely in order to pose the problem as Spinoza does. For it little mattered to him whether one was evoking the 'Noahic' laws or Aristotle's ethics, or anything else. The important thing is to determine whether true piety consists of obeying the Law rather than living guided by reason – or more exactly, guided by knowledge. For Maimonides uses the Hebrew word *da'at* (דעת), which is usually translated as 'knowledge', for example, in the case of 'the tree of the knowledge of good and evil'. Leo Strauss reformulates this choice in the following manner: 'The Bible therefore confronts us more clearly than any other book with this fundamental alternative: life in obedience to the revelation, life in obedience, or life in human freedom.' For his part, Spinoza passes the following conclusion on Maimonides's Law:

> I think it is evident to anyone who reads this attentively that all this is mere fabrication and does not rest upon the authority of the Bible, and hence one need only expound it in order to refute it.[20]

Let's continue our analysis of the rule that Spinoza cites from Maimonides's Code. This rule further stipulates that only the 'pious' men from among the nations have the status of a 'resident-foreigner' (*ger toshav*). 'Resident-foreigner' is a Biblical formula. There are three distinct categories of 'foreigner' in the Bible and the Talmud: 1) the foreigner converted to Mosaism, or 'proselyte' (*ger*), the foreigner who has fully become an 'Israelite' by converting; 2) the 'resident-foreigner' (*ger toshav*) who has not become an 'Israelite', but is nonetheless not a 'servant of the stars'; 3) the 'foreigner' to Mosaism, that is to say, the 'servant of the stars' (*oved cochavim*) who worships a *cult foreign* (*avoda zarah*) to the God who 'brought the Jews out of Egypt'. The 'resident-foreigner' is, therefore, an intermediate category between the 'Israelite' and the 'servant of the stars'. He shares with the 'Israelites' Mosaism's foundational prohibition against serving the stars, but he does not share their positive or affirmative obligation of serving the God who 'brought the Jews out of Egypt'.

Maimonides wrote that the man who observes the commandments of the universal ethics guided only by knowledge (*daät*) 'is not a foreigner-resident' (*aïn zeh ger toshav*). It thus follows that he is a 'servant of the stars', worshipping a cult foreign to Mosaism. And that is the thesis that Leo Strauss deduces from his interpretation of the Genesis: in purporting to live guided by reason alone, the philosopher avows that he has eaten from the tree of knowledge and thus, that he has disobeyed the biblical god's revelation. That is why the man who acts out of knowledge (*daät*) and not out of obedience to the Law is not a 'resident-foreigner', but a 'servant of the stars'. He worships a cult that is not only foreign to Mosaism, but in contradiction with it, and in the last analysis, *antinomic* to it. Such a man has no share in the world to come: he is destined to nothingness. Moreover, it follows that 'he does not live among us'. That is how Lagrée and Moreau translate the Latin '*hic non est incola*',[21] Spinoza's rendering of the Hebrew *aïn zeh ger toshav*, 'he is not a resident-foreigner'. Appuhn and Misrahi translate this as, 'has no right to a place among us'. That is, indeed, what Maimonides teaches in his Codification: whoever is not a 'resident-foreigner' has no place among the Israelites, just as he has no right to a place in the world to come. This double penalty is the punishment for his impiety. Only the man who observes the commandments of the universal ethics out of obedience to the Mosaic Law, acquires the right to a place in the world to come, just as he has a right to a place among the Israelites, because he alone is a 'pious' man. In linking the right to a place among the Israelites to the promise of a place in the world to come, Maimonides's Law echoes a text of Paul's:

> Wherefore remember, that ye being in time past Gentiles in the flesh, who are called Uncircumcision by that which is called the

Circumcision in the flesh made by hands; That at that time ye were without Christ, being aliens from the commonwealth of Israel, and strangers from the covenants of promise, having no hope, and without God in the world: But now in Christ Jesus ye who sometimes were far off are made nigh by the blood of Christ. For he is our peace, who hath made both one, and hath broken down the middle wall of partition between us; having abolished in his flesh the enmity, even the law of commandments contained in ordinances; for to make in himself of twain one new man, so making peace; and that he might reconcile both unto God in one body by the cross, having slain the enmity thereby[22]

Paul writes that the uncircumcised were 'without Christ, being aliens from the commonwealth of Israel, and strangers from the covenants of promise'. Is he saying that according to the 'law of commandments contained in ordinances', the uncircumcised have no right to a place among the Israelites, just as they have no right to a place in the world to come? The Greek text reads ἀπηλλοτριωμένοι τῆς πολιτείας τοῦ Ἰσραήλ, which the TOB renders as 'excluded from the city of Israel'.[23] Yet, Pharisee Judaism explicitly distinguishes between two categories of uncircumcised men, firstly the 'resident-foreigner' (*ger toshav*) and secondly the 'servant of the stars' (*oved kochavim*). Was Paul ignorant of this? We have to interpret the *caesura* 'aliens from the commonwealth of Israel'/'strangers from the covenants of promise'. Paul sets the earthly city and the celestial city in parallel: insofar as the uncircumcised are 'without Christ' – that is to say, insofar as it is the Mosaic Law that reigns – they are excluded from the earthly city, just as they are excluded from the celestial city and vice versa. In citing Maimonides's rule, Spinoza corrects this picture: the 'barrier' of the Law does not separate the circumcised from the uncircumcised, as Paul states; rather, it separates the faithful who lead a life of obedience to the Law, from the unfaithful, who live as free men.

The rule that Spinoza cites from Maimonides, wrong-foots Paul's argument 'now in Christ Jesus ye who sometimes were far off are made nigh by the blood of Christ'. Bringing together the circumcised and the uncircumcised in the community of the covenant did not require the 'blood of Christ', because there had long already existed a community of covenant between the circumcised and the uncircumcised. After all, the Mosaic Law was perfectly universal, in its 'Noahic' aspect.[24] The *At Judaei* manifesto is thus of doubly decisive importance: on the one hand, it combats the 'blood of Christ'[25] argument and on the other hand, it combats the argument of the Law.

In his book on St Paul, comrade Badiou draws out numerous theorems that serve his goal of defining what he calls a 'materialism of grace', including theorem 3: 'The law is what constitutes the subject as the impotence of thought'.[26] The sole mention of the (codified) Jewish Law appearing in the *TTP* or elsewhere in Spinoza's work, is far from anodyne. It brings to light the point of rupture: the Law whose 'barrier' has to be taken down is not the Law of the Jews, in the sense of a law particular to the Jews alone which thus divides the human race. Indeed, the transcendence of the Law, whether it is addressed to the Jews or to all men (through its 'Noahic' variant) itself, *prevents* humanity in precisely the same manner as it 'constitutes the subject as the impotence of thought'.

Jean-Claude Milner and the *bourgeois* theorists accuse the philosopher of having set out a programme for the disappearance of the name 'Jew'. Their proof is that he had the intimate conviction, deep down, that 'Jew' is a name that poses an obstacle to the universality of the human race. But what *prevents* humanity, in the philosopher's eyes, is not the name 'Jew' or a law particular to the Jews, but the universal reign of the Law. Spinoza's citation of Maimonides's rule allows us to verify the *bourgeois* theorists' use of the name 'Jew': it symbolizes the transcendence of the Law. Spinoza's 'unpardonable crime', is that he asserts the power of thought, outside the Law. Moreover, in his writing that is the meaning of the name 'Christ': it is the name of an outlaw ethics.

6 A 'CHRIST' WITHOUT THE PASSION

Having invoked 'the Jews', Spinoza immediately identifies this term with Maimonides – medieval Judaism's greatest rabbinical authority, in the eyes not only of Jewish scholars but even Christian ones, who held him in much higher esteem than they did the Talmud. Through its concision and clarity, his Codification responds to the University's aesthetic and rhetorical criteria. By comparison, the Talmud is wild and untamed. For European Bible scholars, Maimonides's Codification was a bit like 'a villa in the jungle'. But Spinoza got a wicked pleasure out of pulling the master apart, and he does so at many points in the *TTP*. Was this because when he addressed Maimonides and 'the Jews', he was also speaking about others? Was the *TTP* using the name 'Maimonides' as a mask? Not in the sense that Spinoza wasn't referring to Maimonides, but in the sense that he was also talking about someone else, apart from Maimonides?

In an article appearing in the *Harvard Theological Review*[1] under the title 'A hidden Opponent in Spinoza's Tractatus' J. Samuel Preus shows that when the *TTP* invoked the name of 'Maimonides', it was also referring to another 'hidden opponent'. Preus's proof revolves around a passage of Chapter VII concerning the proper method for Bible exegesis. Spinoza is opposed to Maimonides, whose *Guide for the Perplexed* argues that when the literal meaning of a verse contradicts Aristotelian science, we must interpret it in an allegorical manner, so that the verse's meaning concords with science. Spinoza characterizes this as a 'dogmatic' principle. In the first chapter of the *TTP*, he speaks of 'Maimonides and others', who are 'only concerned to derive Aristotelian trifles and some figments of their own from Scripture'.[2] This is his first line of attack, denouncing Maimonides's subjection of the letter of Scripture to a heterogeneous exegetic principle that thus, does violence against it. Spinoza opposes this 'dogmatic' exegetic principle with a literal principle founded on Scripture alone (*sola scriptura*): in matters of exegesis the only rule, or law, is the explicit meaning.

Preus shows that Maimonides's exegetic principle, denounced by Spinoza, is the same one that Lodewijk Meyer used in a work appearing in the Netherlands in 1666, entitled *Philosophia S. Scripturae interpres*.[3] In his presentation of Meyer's book, Moreau summarizes its guiding idea as follows: 'Reason, that is to say philosophy, is the only interpreter of the Holy Scripture.' He specifies, 'On condition, it should be understood, that "philosophy" is understood as "the true [philosophy]", that is, the "natural light" identified in Descartes's philosophy.'[4] Meyer's approach was the same as Maimonides's, except insofar as he substituted Cartesianism, or the new philosophy, for Aristotelian philosophy. The principle was nonetheless the same in Spinoza's eyes: each is 'dogmatic' in that it imposes an extraneous reason on Scripture. So according to Preus, when Spinoza advanced his own exegetic method, he was opposing Meyer, but rather than cite him by name he disguised him under the traits of Maimonides. That was his way of evidencing the 'dogmatic' tradition to which Meyer belonged, regardless of his replacement of Aristotelianism with Cartesianism. Preus's article observes that some of the criticisms that Spinoza levels against Maimonides in fact better apply to Meyer, or at least that 'Meyer is as good a candidate as Maimonides for being cast as Spinoza's archetypal dogmatist'. Spinoza's 'hidden opponent' was, therefore, Lodewijk Meyer. Indeed, this did not escape Spinoza's contemporaries' attention.[5]

When Spinoza attacked Maimonides by name, for having been 'only concerned to derive Aristotelian trifles' from Scripture, he was also surreptitiously, targeting Descartes's learned opponents – the scholars who condemned modern science. Thus, implicitly targeting Meyer, he also let it be understood that to substitute Cartesianism for Aristotelianism was to pass from one dogmatism to another. The conclusion: we know that Spinoza proceeded with caution and that manoeuvres made out of prudence contain indecent hidden propositions. And we also know, that the name 'Maimonides' may have masked another name, or other names and that just as 'Maimonides' sometimes stands in for 'the Jews' in the *TTP*, the same also goes for the term 'Jew' – for it too, may have masked other terms. Finally, we know that in order to reveal the disguise we have to proceed in a deductive *and* literal manner. Otherwise, reason loses its thread, becomes impassioned and goes astray.

Concluding Chapter V, Spinoza seeks to return to the essential point, namely that 'whatever the nature of these histories, belief in them is not relevant to the divine Law, nor do they make men happy in themselves, nor do they serve any purpose other than for their doctrine, and this is the only reason why some of them may be more important than others'.[6] That is, he says, 'the conclusion we set out to prove'.[7] Spinoza's conclusion is not that the Biblical histories are without truth, but that belief in these histories does not 'serve any purpose other than for [men's] doctrine'.[8] At this stage, the philosopher's argument is consonant with that of the theologian intent on establishing the dogma of the faith. The rupture comes immediately afterward:

> Hence if anyone reads the stories of holy Scripture and believes all of them without paying attention to the doctrine that the Bible uses them to teach, and without amending his life, he might just as well read the Koran[9] or the dramatic plays of the poets, or at any rate the common chronicles, with the same attention that the common people usually give to their reading. On the other hand, as we have said, he who is completely ignorant of them, and nevertheless has salutary opinions and a true conception of living, is truly happy [*absolute beatus*] and truly has within him the spirit of Christ.[10]

If it is possible to be totally ignorant of the Holy Scripture and yet experience *absolute beatus*, then the revelation is deposed in favour of thought – that is, the 'divine law' as defined by Spinoza in Chapter V:

> We showed in the previous chapter that the divine law which makes men truly happy (*vere beatos*) and teaches the true life, is universal to all men. We also deduced that law from human nature in such a way that it must itself be deemed innate to the human mind and, so to speak, inscribed (*inscripta*) upon it.[11]

Spinoza's break with the theological-political authorities is consummate and his lack of caution manifested: for nothing could have further contradicted the common morality of Europe of the seventeenth century. If belief in the histories of the Scripture is not necessary for salvation, it follows that it is unnecessary to believe that Jesus is the son of God, that he suffered the passion, that he was crucified and resurrected. The whole doctrinal apparatus of the Christian religion, whether Catholic or Protestant, is trashed. So Spinoza needs a decoy, devised out of caution: he 'truly has within him the spirit of Christ'. But he also says that having 'the spirit of Christ' in oneself, does not depend either on blessing or belief in the history of Christ's incarnation, crucifixion and resurrection, but on the 'true life' whose absolute universality is founded on the single axiom 'Man thinks'.[12] The philosopher's decoy thus counts for little in light of his explicit audacity.

The Christian friends with whom Spinoza corresponded were themselves worried by this. This was the case when Oldenburg wrote to him in 1675, as he worked on a re-edition of the *TTP* expanded with new annotations. Oldenburg told Spinoza that he could only 'approve your programme for the book, in which you indicate that you want to clarify and soften things that readers found troubling'. He gathers these passages under three headings: the relations between God and Nature; miracles; and finally, Jesus Christ. On this latter subject, he warns Spinoza

> Furthermore, they say that you are concealing your opinion with regard to Jesus Christ, Redeemer of the World, sole Mediator for mankind, and of his Incarnation and Atonement, and they request you to disclose your attitude clearly on these three heads.

Oldenburg concludes: 'If you do so, and in this matter satisfy reasonable and intelligent Christians, I think your position will be secure.'[13] His arguments are instructive. Let's note three things in particular: firstly, that he advises the philosopher to write in a way that 'satisf[ies]... Christians' in order for his 'position [to] be secure'. Secondly, if Oldenburg makes himself the spokesman for 'reasonable and intelligent Christians' – including himself – we can conclude that nothing can be done for the rest: the *TTP* together with its author is condemned. Thirdly, though Oldenburg is one of the philosopher's correspondents, a citizen of the Republic of letters, he thinks that Spinoza has concealed his 'opinion' regarding Jesus Christ, hidden from him as well as the Christian readers whom he purports to echo. Here, we have a context which justifies Spinoza's need to show caution and which provides confirmation of the rule that he used in his writing: to expound his thought at the same time as concealing it; saying enough to be heard by the wise but nothing beyond that, for fear of being heard by others; advancing in disguise, such that potential persecutors would only understand the things that they could tolerate. The danger, here, principally came from the Christian authorities, including 'reasonable and intelligent Christians'. Spinoza did not, however, give satisfaction to Oldenburg's requests. He replied that 'Christians are distinguished from other people not by faith, nor charity, nor the other fruits of the Holy Spirit, but solely by an opinion they hold, namely, because, as they all do, they rest their case simply on miracles, that is, on ignorance, which is the source of all wickedness, and thus they turn their faith, true as it may be, into superstition'. He then comes to Christ:

> for salvation it is not altogether necessary to know Christ according to the flesh; but with regard to the eternal son of God, that is, God's eternal

> wisdom, which has manifested itself in all things and chiefly in the human mind, and most of all in Christ Jesus, a very different view must be taken. For without this no one can attain to a state of blessedness, since this alone teaches what is true and false, good and evil. And since, as I have said, this wisdom has been manifested most of all through Jesus Christ, his disciples have preached it as far as he revealed it to them, and have shown themselves able to glory above all others in that spirit of Christ. As to the additional teaching of certain Churches, that God took upon himself human nature, I have expressly indicated that I do not understand what they say. Indeed, to tell the truth, they seem to me to speak no less absurdly than one who might tell me that a circle has taken on the nature of a square.[14]

This is without doubt Spinoza's most explicit – or least cautious – text relating to Christian dogma. He begins by specifying that the Christians 'are distinguished from other people' – that is, the Jews, the Turks, heretics, pagans, the Chinese etc. – but they are distinguished from them 'solely by opinion', once it is established that the true life comes from understanding and virtue and not belief in 'miracles'. 'Opinion' designates the particularism of a religious belief, for example, Oldenburg's belief in 'Jesus Christ, Redeemer of the world' and in his 'Incarnation' and 'Atonement'. When this 'opinion' governs people's minds, belief in the histories, miracles and dogmas is decisive: and this is 'ignorance', the source of all wickedness. As against this 'ignorance', the *Ethics*' purpose is to re-establish understanding of the divine Law, which flows exclusively from the axiom 'Man thinks'. That is why the elements of Christian dogma are only apparently universal, for they are only a particular 'opinion' and in the last analysis, 'ignorance'. So *exeunt* the 'Incarnation', the 'Atonement' and the 'Redemption'. Conversely, the 'spirit of Christ' (*Christi spiritum*) is an eminently Christian formula that Spinoza willingly uses. Indeed, he even concedes in the first chapter of the *TTP* that whereas a man cannot 'know things which are not contained in the first foundations of our knowledge and cannot be deduced from them', Christ seemingly benefited from a perfection, unknown among ordinary mortals:

> I do not believe that anyone has reached such a degree of perfection above others except Christ, to whom the decrees of God which guide men to salvation were revealed not by words or visions but directly; and that is why God revealed himself to the Apostles through the mind of Christ, as he did, formerly, to Moses by means of a heavenly voice. Therefore the voice of Christ may be called the voice of God, like

the voice which Moses heard. In this sense we may also say that the wisdom of God, that is, the wisdom which is above human wisdom, took on human nature in Christ, and that Christ was the way of salvation.[15]

Here, the philosopher seems to approve of the Christian 'opinion'. The question posed is what relation the 'wisdom of God', which is 'above' human wisdom (*quae supra humanum est*), has with Jesus's humanity. Spinoza formulates the answer as follows: *naturam humanam in Christo assumpsisse*. Pierre-François Moreau translates this as saying that God's wisdom 'assumed human nature in Christ'; Charles Appuhn translates that 'in Christ, it took on human nature'; and Madeleine Francès that it 'was incarnated in Christ'.[16] How should we interpret Spinoza's formula? Evidently, this is the passage in the *TTP* where he pushes his rule of caution furthest: 'To speak in a manner intelligible to the multitude, and to comply with every general custom that does not hinder the attainment of our purpose.' The difficulty lies in appreciating the 'goal' that caution conceals, but does not disavow.

Spinoza accepts that Christ was unique, but not that God was incarnated. From his reply to Oldenburg, we learn that while incarnation is an absurdity, Christ can, conversely, be called 'the eternal son of God' if that is taken to mean 'God's eternal wisdom, which has manifested itself in all things but most in the human mind and most of all in Christ Jesus'. Christ is thus attributed his singularity not out of a distinction of nature, or of substance, but a superlative one: the wisdom of God manifested itself 'most of all' in Jesus Christ. In other words, he is more a 'son' than any of the other 'sons of God', for one is a 'son of God', in proportion to one's 'wisdom'. Spinoza could make no greater concession to the 'reasonable and intelligent Christians' pressing him to make his meaning explicit. In writing the *TTP* he had to concede the utmost, in order to try to shelter himself from the foolish.

Spinoza's reference to Christ in the *Ethics* comes in Book IV, in the *scholium* to proposition 68. This reference is of very particular interest, because it is not necessitated by the context in which it appears, since the *Ethics* is not an exegesis of scripture. Nonetheless, in this *scholium* Spinoza does mention the Biblical story of Adam and Eve and the manner in which they lost freedom: a freedom, he continues, 'which the Patriarchs later regained under the guidance of the spirit of Christ, that is, the idea of God, on which alone it depends that a man should be free and should desire for mankind the good that he desires for himself, as I have demonstrated above'.[17] In writing that the Patriarchs recovered freedom 'under the guidance of the spirit of Christ', Spinoza would seem to be subjecting his *Ethics* to Christian 'opinion', if it were not for the fact that he immediately adds 'that is, the idea of God, on which alone it depends that a man should be free'. Is this a profession of allegiance to Christianity, or a determined yet cautious attempt at subversion? What we do know for sure is that Spinoza subjected Christian 'opinion' to the demands of his philosophy, such that whether he was professing his allegiance to Christianity or subverting it, he certainly was rationalizing it.

In Spinoza's writing, the 'spirit of Christ' becomes the 'idea of God', which is nothing other than reason. After all, proposition IV, 68 teaches that the *free* man is he who lives guided only by reason and the *scholium* goes on to explain, that the Patriarchs recovered *freedom* guided by the Spirit of Christ, 'that is, the idea of God' (*hoc est, Dei idea*). The spirit of Christ – that is, the idea of God – takes the same place in the *scholium* that reason does in the body of the proposition: he who lives guided by it is a free man. If Spinoza places the Patriarchs under the guidance of 'the spirit of Christ', he thus does so not only out of caution, but also so that his reader will discover an indecent proposition. That is, having the 'spirit of Christ' in oneself, does not depend on the 'opinion' that one has developed on 'Jesus Christ, Redeemer of the World, sole Mediator for mankind, and of his Incarnation and Atonement' – as 'reasonable and intelligent Christians' imagine – but rather on a succession of adequate ideas. We could also conclude, it is true, that the 'spirit of Christ' resides in the *blessing* of a succession of adequate ideas.

*

Doesn't the manner in which Spinoza subjects the name 'Christ' to the theoretical demands of his *Ethics* reiterate – with reference to the Christian texts – the same exegetic principle that Maimonides used and which Spinoza himself denounces in the first chapter of the *TTP* – a denunciation to which he returns in Chapters VII and XV? In Chapter VII, after expounding his method 'admit[ting] no other criteria or data for interpreting Scripture and discussing its contents than what is drawn from Scripture itself',[18] Spinoza addresses the methods that diverge from his own. On the one hand is the so-called 'sceptical' method, which is 'the opinion of those who hold that the natural light of reason does not have the power to interpret Scripture and that for this a supernatural light is absolutely essential',[19] and on the other hand there is the so-called 'dogmatic' method, Maimonides's method, which Spinoza portrays in the following terms:

He thought that every passage of Scripture yields various, even contradictory, senses and that we cannot be certain of the truth of any of them unless we know that that passage which we are interpreting, contains nothing that is contrary to or that does not accord with reason. If its literal sense is found to conflict with reason, no matter how evident that may seem to be in itself, he insists it should then be construed differently.[20]

Spinoza's response to the 'sceptic' who invokes the supernatural, is that man can only know through his own understanding and that the supernatural is a name for ignorance. Meanwhile, his response to the 'dogmatist' who subjects the verses' meaning to heterogeneous philosophical doctrines, is that the principle of an exegesis is knowledge of the explicit, or literal meaning – whether that contradicts or confirms what reason would *otherwise* hold to be true. As such, faced with the inadequate ideas of God that the prophets conveyed, Spinoza rejects any explanation in terms of allegory: 'even though their literal sense conflicts with the natural light of reason, unless it is also clearly in conflict with the principles and fundamentals derived from investigating the history of Scripture we must still stick to this, the literal sense'.[21] In establishing a verse's meaning, the decisive things are biblical intertextuality and knowledge of the Hebrew language and culture, and not what reason holds to be true on the subject of God or Nature. The Scripture's purpose is not for man to know; in this sense, the revelation is ignorant:

> God adapted his revelations to the understanding and opinions of the prophets, and that the prophets could be ignorant of matters of purely philosophical reasoning that are not concerned with charity and how to live; and indeed they really were ignorant in this respect and held contradictory views.[22]

Spinoza proposes to read Scripture as it is, rather than interpret it as it ought to be: that is, to read it as a revelation addressed to the common, ignorant man, such that he will practise justice and charity out of obedience to the prophecy. Its arguments are not a matter of educating this man, but of making him submit. However, in his final letter to Oldenburg Spinoza writes, 'The passion, death and burial of Christ I accept literally, but his resurrection I understand in an allegorical sense'[23] and then explains, that while it is beyond doubt that the authors of the Gospels believed this in a literal sense, it remains the case that 'they could have been deceived' about this.[24] He ultimately concludes, 'But Paul, to whom Christ also appeared later, rejoices that he knows Christ not after the flesh, but after the spirit'.[25] Oldenburg replies:

> In the gospels, Christ's resurrection seems to be narrated as literally as the rest. And on this article of the resurrection stands the whole Christian religion and its truth, and with its removal the mission of Christ Jesus and his heavenly teaching collapse.[26]

Does Spinoza interpret Christ's resurrection allegorically because he is being a 'dogmatist'? He does recognize that the Gospels have a determinate literal meaning and that they do indeed convey belief in the resurrection, just as the belief in anthropomorphic representations of the divine is conveyed elsewhere in the Scripture. But if the literal meaning is determinate, it is not, however, determining and Spinoza does not take it at face value. He maintains that the resurrection is an allegory, providing a metaphor for the eternal beatitude to which Christ elevated himself, because he had a singularly clear and distinct idea of God. But if that is the case, how can Spinoza reproach Maimonides's allegorical interpretations, which he characterizes as 'dogmatic'?

Spinoza cites a passage from the *Guide* in order to illustrate his opponent's method. He first provides it in Ibn Tibbon's Hebrew translation, and then translates it into Latin.[27] In the extract in question (*Guide*, II, 25), Maimonides explains that if, counter to Aristotle, he defends the thesis that the world was created, this is not because the literal meaning of Biblical verses compels him to do so. This is a puzzling claim. Then Maimonides develops his thinking. The literal meaning of the verses is not determinate and never is: for while the literal meaning abounds with all sorts of anthropomorphisms, God cannot be a body, for corporeity is a mark of finitude, contradicting the very idea of God. Therefore, all these verses should be understood as having an allegorical meaning. As such, it is possible to interpret the verses concerning the creation of the world allegorically, and thus to reject their literal meaning and instead make them confirm the thesis of the world's eternity. However, Maimonides concludes, there is a difference of two orders between the story of the creation of the world and the anthropomorphic representations of the divine. Firstly, in that while we have an idea, a proof of the non-corporeity of God we have no such idea or proof of the eternity of the world, so there is no basis for rejecting the literal meaning of the verses concerning the creation *ex nihilo*. Second, in that the creation of the world is the 'foundation' of the religion:

> If we were to accept the Eternity of the Universe as taught by Aristotle, that everything in the Universe is the result of fixed laws, that Nature

A 'CHRIST' WITHOUT THE PASSION   89

does not change, and that there is nothing supernatural, we should necessarily be in opposition to the foundation of our religion, we should disbelieve all miracles and signs, and certainly reject all hopes and fears derived from Scripture, unless the miracles are also explained figuratively. The Allegorists amongst the Mohammedans have done this, and have thereby arrived at absurd conclusions.[28]

Spinoza concludes that 'if it was clear to [Maimonides] on the basis of reason that the world was eternal' he would explain the meaning of these verses allegorically so that they appeared to teach that the world existed eternally. This is not quite true. Maimonides concludes Chapter II, 25 explaining that 'If, on the other hand, Aristotle had a proof for his theory, the whole teaching of Scripture would be rejected, and we should be forced to other opinions.'[29] Maimonides is consistent: if the religion's very foundation were refuted by reason, its whole edifice would collapse 'and we should be forced to other opinions' in order to avoid 'arriv[ing] at absurd conclusions'. So here there is no question of Maimonides providing a different interpretation of the Bible verses concerning creation, as Spinoza has him doing. Rather, it is a question of whether to abandon the Bible in favour of Aristotle. This is not because it is impossible to interpret the verses in conformity with the thesis that the world is eternal, but because monotheist religion would no longer make any sense if it *were proven* 'that Nature does not change, and that there is nothing supernatural'.

However, for Spinoza the question is not so much whether in the last instance Maimonides submits faith to reason or the other way round.[30] Rather, he is concerned with establishing a method for exegesis. In maintaining that the literal meaning is not binding since we also have the possibility of resorting to allegory – which can demonstrate something or its opposite – Maimonides is undermining the very basis of Biblical exegesis. Indeed, it follows that the verses no longer have any *literal* meaning, because their meaning depends exclusively on what reason establishes *elsewhere*. Maimonides's 'dogmatism' consists of the fact that he makes short shrift of the verses' explicit, or literal meaning. In other words, he strips them of their immanent meaning in favour of something else – in this case, Aristotle's metaphysics – which thus imposes its own law on the Hebrew letter.

What does this have to do with Spinoza's allegorical interpretation of the resurrection of Christ? His approach apparently corresponds to the one that Maimonides attributes to the Allegorists among the Muslims, namely those who interpret allegorically all the stories that contradict the order of nature. Maimonides forcefully rejects this view. He considers miracles the foundation of religion, in that they credit God's oneness as an omnipotent being, the corollary of which is the absolute contingency of the laws of nature – for without this, the whole edifice would collapse. This is also Oldenburg's response to Spinoza: without belief in resurrection, 'the mission of Christ Jesus collapses, as does his heavenly teaching'. Nonetheless, Spinoza's recourse to allegory is based on different foundations than Maimonides'. In fact, contrary to Maimonides, Spinoza recognizes that there is a determinate, literal meaning, for he does not deny that the Gospels' authors believed in the literal truth of the resurrection and related it accordingly, just as the Hebrews believed that Joshua had made the sun stand still. Spinoza does not deny that the literal meaning is determinate, but he does not believe in the stories of miracles. For him, precisely insofar as a miracle lies beyond rational comprehension it is a name for ignorance – and it is senseless to place one's faith in ignorance. Even so, Spinoza does not settle for interpreting the story of the resurrection of Christ in conformity with our knowledge of nature, but moreover interprets it 'in the allegorical sense'. This is rather singular. Writing on the subject of the sign of the 'Noahic' covenant he explains 'At Genesis 9.13 God informs Noah that he will put a rainbow in the clouds. This action of God's is assuredly no other than the refraction and reflection affecting sun rays seen through drops of water.'[31]

So here there is no question of an allegorical meaning. Spinoza does not, however, simply take the dead letter as proof that the resurrection cannot be understood allegorically. He concludes his reply to Oldenburg by evoking Paul, who 'gloried that he knew Christ not according to the flesh, but according to the spirit'. The 'flesh' designates the fabled literal story and the 'spirit' the understanding of the allegory. So here we are as close as could be to Maimonides, who says no different except insofar as he sees the story of the world's creation as just as allegorical as the story of Christ's resurrection.

Ultimately, then, is Spinoza any more or less 'dogmatic' than Maimonides? Spinoza rationalizes Christianity while Maimonides is held to have rationalized Judaism. But beyond the fact that Maimonides's rationalism demands a deeper examination of its own, the Christian covering borrowed by Spinoza's philosophy, is but a manoeuvre devised out of caution. In his writing, the 'spirit of Christ' is a deliberately rhetorical formula, for it is used strategically: 'To speak in a manner intelligible to the multitude, and to comply with every general custom that does not hinder the attainment of our purpose. For we can gain from the multitude no small advantages, provided that we strive to accommodate ourselves to its understanding as far as possible: moreover, we shall in this way gain a friendly audience for the reception of the truth'. And as it happens, the truth is almost explicit: the 'spirit of Christ' resides in successions of adequate ideas. We might say that Spinoza contradicted himself when he reproached Maimonides for arrogating the sovereignty to decide the meaning of Scripture through his free recourse to allegory. However, this would mean arguing that Maimonides, too, was taking this approach out of caution, in order 'to speak in a manner intelligible to the multitude, and to comply with every general custom that does not hinder the attainment of our purpose', despite himself also being ready to dismiss the revelation, judging it inessential for teaching the 'true conception of living'. Yet, Maimonides concludes that 'If, on the other hand, Aristotle had a proof for his theory, the whole teaching of Scripture would be rejected, and we should be forced to other opinions.' In Spinoza's eyes, this is the proof that he does not *know* the true conception of living, but that he *obeys* a revelation. His Codification – Rule 11, Chapter 8, 'Kings', book of Judgments – confirms as much.

It is immediately after Spinoza dismisses 'belief in the stories' and provides his conclusion on the 'spirit of Christ', that he invokes 'the Jews', designated as those who 'hold completely to the opposite view'. The argument once again seems to owe to an old Christian tradition, from the Fathers of the Church to Luther's diatribes, a sort of literary genre in itself: that is, the genre of polemics directed *Against the Jews* because of their persistence in denying 'the spirit of Christ'. Indeed, it is clear that the Jews instructed by Juda Halevi or Maimonides thought the opposite to what Spinoza did with regard to the 'divine law'. However, in the *TTP* the name 'Jew' is also a mask. Oldenburg warns that 'reasonable and intelligent Christians' are worried: for the author of the *TTP* seems to have concealed his thinking on the subject of 'Jesus Christ, Redeemer of the world', etc. from them. However, Spinoza had not concealed his thought, but only tried to 'accommodate [himself] to [the multitude's] understanding as far as possible'. Moreover, in Chapter V he twice literally says it all: firstly, when he explains that since 'all of Scripture was revealed for the benefit of a whole people in the first place and, ultimately, for the entire human race', 'its contents had necessarily to be entirely adjusted to the capacity of the common people and substantiated by experience alone'. He thus concludes:

> From this I think it is clear for whom and for what reason belief in the biblical narratives is necessary. From what we have just shown it very plainly follows that knowing them and believing them is supremely necessary to ordinary people whose minds are not competent to perceive things clearly and distinctly. It also follows that anyone who

rejects these histories because he does not believe there is a God or that He provides for men and things, is impious. But in the case of someone who is ignorant of them but who does know, by the natural light of reason, that there is a God and so forth, as we have expressed it above, and who also possesses a true code for living, he is entirely happy, and happier than the common people, because, besides true opinions, he possesses a clear and distinct understanding of them.[32]

He returns to this a second time at the end of Chapter V, when he concludes that the 'spirit of Christ' resides in anyone – be they Christian, Jewish, Turkish or Chinese – who possesses a 'true conception of living'. In fact, Spinoza totally ignores the historical stories, starting with that of the Incarnation, Passion and Redemption. He exclusively concerns himself with what can be put across in the form of a 'clear and distinct understanding'. It is now incumbent on the attentive reader to decide whether or not to take literally the adverb 'truly' when Spinoza writes, 'he who is completely ignorant of [the stories], and nevertheless has salutary opinions and a true conception of living, is truly happy [*absolute beatus*] and truly has within him the spirit of Christ'. If the reader decides that it should be taken literally, he will conclude that those who stick to the letter of these stories, for want of a clear and distinct understanding, do perhaps have a share in salvation, but without 'truly' having within themselves the spirit of Christ. He will then note that the signifier 'Cross' does not appear in the *TTP* even once. Spinoza was evidently wary of it. Spinoza's Christianity is not only rationalized, but has literally had the passion taken out of it. For we have to be consistent: if circumcision is nothing, then neither is the crucifixion.

7 THE ORIGIN OF THE LAW

In his critical analysis of the *TTP* (from 1915) Hermann Cohen noted that the clause introduced by Maimonides does not appear in the Talmud. He adds that Spinoza could not have been unaware of this, since the commentary in apposition to each page of the Code's text – appearing in all traditional editions available in the seventeenth century – explained that Maimonides's way of seeing things was *private* to him and not attested to by the sources themselves. Hermann Cohen relentlessly accused Spinoza of bad faith and of manipulating the texts rather than explaining them. In his foreword to *Spinoza's Critique of Religion*, Leo Strauss replies on this point

> [Cohen] notes that according to the most authoritative commentator on the Code, Joseph Caro, the qualification stated by Maimonides (viz. that piety requires recognition of the Mosaic revelation) is his private opinion, but Cohen fails to add that Caro adds that the opinion is correct. Caro would not have said this if Maimonides' opinion contradicts the consensus of Judaism.[1]

Joseph Caro (in the sixteenth century) was the author of the *Shulchan Aruch*, the Codification that orthodox Judaism considers authoritative. In writing this he principally based himself on two sources: on the one hand, Maimonides's Codification (from the twelfth century) and on the other hand Jacob ben Asher's (from the fourteenth century). He wrote a running commentary on each of them, which served as the basis for his own Codification, a sort of synthesis of the Sephardic (Maimonides) and Ashkenazi (Jacob ben Asher) sources. His commentary on Maimonides's *Mishneh Torah* was entitled the *Kessef Mishneh*. This commentary accompanied all the traditional editions of Maimonides's

Code and appeared in the outer column of the text. For each rule he tried to specify its source in the Talmud and to account for Maimonides's juridical conclusion. No one studies a rule of Maimonides's Codification without taking note of Joseph Caro's commentary. Spinoza certainly could not have been unaware of it. But as Leo Strauss notes, Cohen 'fails to add' that Joseph Caro agreed with Maimonides's opinion. Spinoza thus, knew that it was authoritative. That is why he could legitimately cite Maimonides's Law as the illustration of what 'the Jews' think, it being understood that he wanted to name a doctrinal position that was dominant in rabbinical – otherwise called Pharisaic – Judaism.

In his commentary on Maimonides's Law, Joseph Caro refers to a famous discussion between two masters of the Talmud, rabbi Joshua and rabbi Eliezer, which appears in Sanhedrin 105a. In according the world to come to 'the pious men among the nations', Maimonides was sticking to the teaching of one of the two masters (rabbi Joshua). He thus had a foundation, more than just a source.[2] Conversely, as for the clause his Codification introduces concerning the impious man who observes the commandments of the universal ethics guided by reason alone, Joseph Caro writes: 'It seems to me that our master concludes this by himself, and his conclusion is correct.' So according to Caro, there is no Talmudic source to justify Maimonides's clause that excludes the man living under the guidance of reason alone from the world to come: it is a conclusion that he makes of his own accord, and *rightly so*.

Indeed, no explicit teaching in the Talmud provides a foundation for the clause in question. Joseph Caro thinks that its source lies not in the Talmud, but in Maimonides's own thinking. That cannot but pose a serious problem: if the clause is not based on a teaching in the Talmud, how can we explain Maimonides introducing it into his Codification ... of the Talmud? Joseph Caro writes that this is a *svara de-nafsheh*. The Hebrew word *svara* denotes a logically articulated thought, and *de-nafsheh* signifies, in this context, that this thought is not deduced from a Talmudic teaching. The problem is that a Codification of the Talmud is not meant to expound what Maimonides thinks, but what the Talmud teaches. And by any logic, if no teaching in the Talmud compels Maimonides to introduce this clause, this means that it is extraneous to the Talmud; hence the proofs from other commentators who try to ground it in implicit Talmud teachings, in order to justify Maimonides's clause *juridically*.

Joseph Caro's commentary is itself intrinsically paradoxical. According to Caro, Maimonides has concluded on his own account that the man who thinks and acts by himself is therefore impious, whether or not he thinks and acts in conformity with the Law, for the very reason that he thought and acted by himself and not out of obedience. The more that Joseph Caro's explanation is explicated, the more it contradicts itself. Is not the impious man, as defined by Maimonides, precisely the man who observes the commandments of the universal ethics *mi-svara de nafsheh*, by reasoning of his own initiative? This is, however, only an apparent contradiction. Joseph Caro like Maimonides maintains that rational knowledge is legitimate, but on the express condition that it is placed under the authority of the Law. That is the argument of Maimonides's clause. And that is why Joseph Caro concludes that the clause 'is correct' – that is, it is well-founded, even if it is not a teaching from the Talmud. But is that not contradictory, in a Codification of the Talmud? The answer is that Maimonides's clause is founded on the notion of the Law – on the Law's transcendence. The very principle of a Codification – its ethical and political consequence – is that the man who does not act out of obedience to the law is impious.

Up until the twentieth century, there were two opposing answers to the question of what was the source of Maimonides's clause. Some maintained that it necessarily must have had a foundation in the Talmud's teachings and they tried to produce the proof of this; the others rallied behind Joseph Caro's commentary, concluding that the clause was founded not in a teaching from the Talmud but in the very principle of a codification of the Law. Yet, there also existed the trace of a third option, as was apparent from a book by Shlomo Zalman of Vilnius (in the nineteenth century). In his *Toldot Adam*, he spoke of a *midrash* which he held to be Maimonides's source.[3] Since this *midrash* was unknown and impossible to find, it was thought to have been made up, until 1933, when H. G. Enelow discovered an old manuscript in New York and published it as *The Mishnah of Rabbi Eliézer. The Midrash of thirty-two Hermeneutic Rules*. According to him, this was a collection dating from the era of the *Tannahim*, the masters of the *Mishnah* in the first and second centuries AD. Here, in Chapter 6, *Mishnah* 28, was Maimonides's source. The Hebrew reads[4]

> What distinguishes the pious men of Israel from the pious men among the nations is that the men of Israel are called 'pious men' only when they fulfil the whole *Torah*, while the men among the nations are called 'pious men' if they fulfil the seven precepts that were commanded to the sons of Noah, and their general and particular dispositions. Of which case do we speak? The case in which they fulfil them in the express recognition that this is out of obedience to what 'our father Noah' commanded in Strictness of speech; in this case, they have a share in the world to come in the same way as Israel, even though they do not observe the Sabbath and the feast days, because they are not enjoined to observe them. But

if they practice the seven precepts saying 'such-and-such commanded me' or if they practice them by themselves, because knowledge (*daʾat*) commanded them to do so, or indeed with reference to some idol, then even when they fulfil all the commandments of the *Torah*, they will have no retribution except in this world [and not in the world to come].

It is in this teaching from *The Mishnah of Rabbi Eliézer* that we see the first appearance of the distinction between, on the one hand, the 'pious' man who observes the 'Noahic' laws out of obedience to prophecy and for that reason has a place in the world to come, and on the other hand the impious man who observes them guided by knowledge (*daʾat*) alone. And there is proof elsewhere that Maimonides did know of a book named *Mishnat Rabbi Eliézer*, since we can find two explicit references to this text in his writing. The first appears in the *Sefer Hamitzvot* (*mitzvot aseh*, no. 5) and the second in his *Responsa* (*teshuvah*, no. 148).[5] Moreover, in this second case he is explicitly relating a ritual act to Moses's prophecy, specifying that this is 'as R. Eliezer's *beraita* teaches, and as we explained at the end of our great book'. The 'great book' in question is his Codification of the Talmud – indeed, the famous clause appears in its final pages. Finally, and most importantly, in the clause in question Maimonides cites from the text of the *Mishnat Rabbi Eliezer*: firstly, with regard to the qualification of 'pious men' (*hassidei*), where he takes the relevant formulation from the *Mishnat Rabbi Eliezer* because the *Tosefta* of the Sanhedrin refers not to 'pious' men (*hassidei*) but to 'just' men (*zadikei*). Second, with regard to the man guided by reason – or more literally, the man who observes Noahic laws, because knowledge (*daʾat*) inclines or commands him to do so. Again on this point, Maimonides's formula is a citation from the *Mishnat Rabbi Eliezer*. Maimonides's source was thus identified: a teaching that had appeared in a collection of *midrashim* whose existence was known, but which was considered lost, until Enelow discovered it among some old Hebrew manuscripts and published it in the USA in 1933.

An article welcoming this fortunate discovery appeared in the *Revue des Études juives* in 1935, 'Maïmonide. Sur l'universalité de la morale religieuse', signed by Michael Gutmann. Following Enelow's conclusions, Gutmann dated the redaction of the *Mishnat Rabbi Eliezer* to the second century AD, which helped legitimize the use Maimonides had made of it in his Codification, given that it was contemporary to the *Mishnah* and, in a sense, came from the same hand. He concludes:

> Up till now we believed that it was thanks to Maimonides's own theological reflection that he came to deduce the universally human

validity of morality not from a sort of theory of natural law, but from a primordial revelation addressed to all humanity, which also led him to deny its equivalence with atheist and irreligious morality. Eight hundred years later, the study of [Maimonides'] sources allows us to state that the universal morality founded on unalterable divine will and the primordial revelation is, in reality, one of Judaism's most ancient articles of faith. In times of intense religiosity, people barely felt the need to insist on this argument. In our own time, however, when we see certain schools attempting to build systems of morality unbound from God and religion, it is interesting to recall this ancient Jewish doctrine.[6]

Twenty years earlier (in 1915), Cohen could still write that Maimonides's way of seeing things was *private* to him and not attested to by the sources themselves. Enelow's discovery was thus not only valuable, but necessary, since it was of the greatest importance to combat 'certain schools seeking to build systems of morality unbound from God and religion'. This was 1935 and communism was on the rise in Europe. From the censors of the *TTP* in the Holland of the seventeenth century, to the pious men of the twenty-first, one same argument is professed: the essence of wickedness, or impiety, is an ethics unbound from obedience to the Law. And thanks to Enelow's discovery, this argument had become 'one of Judaism's most ancient articles of faith'.

Dazzled by the excitement aroused by an unexpected discovery, Enelow and Guttmann hurried to date the *Mishnat Rabbi Eliezer* as far back as possible – and thus to confer on it the very greatest authority. Indeed, in situating it in the era of the redaction of the *Mishnah* – the text of the principles of the oral Torah – they in a sense integrated it into the same corpus. Indeed, given that the book was peppered with Talmudic teachings and sections of text near-identical to an exegetic literature contemporary to the Talmud, it must either have emerged downstream of the Talmud and Midrashic literature, or else been further upstream. It necessarily must either have preceded the redaction of the Talmud (and date from the second century), in which case it was the source-text that the redactors of the Talmud and the Midrash borrowed from (in the sixth century), or else have been subsequent to it (and thus date from the seventh century, at the earliest), in which case it was the author of the *Mishnat Rabbi Eliezer* who compiled ancient sources in order to compose his book. As spirits calmed, reason again took its rightful place: a rapid examination suffices to establish that the *Mishnat Rabbi Eliezer* is very clearly a later work than the different sources from which it borrows, and today there is a consensus on dating it to around the eighth century, the so-called era of the *Geonim*. The title,

Mishnat Rabbi Eliezer, claims a relation between this book and a second-century master of the *Mishnah*, but this should not deceive us. It is, in any case, a well-established convention to relate a collection of texts written centuries later to an ancient master of the Talmud. Thus the *Zohar*, whose redaction probably dates to the thirteenth century, was attributed to Rabbi Shimon bar Yohai, a second-century master of the *Mishnah*.

Did Maimonides believe that the *Mishnat Rabbi Eliezer* really dated to the era of the *Mishnah*, and that it had the authority that went with this? That seems difficult to believe. As such, while he still conferred such authority upon this text, he nonetheless allowed himself to change it on one capitally important point. Whereas the author of the *Mishnat Rabbi Eliezer* demanded that 'the pious man' follow the Law of 'our father Noah', for his part Maimonides demanded that he follow the Law of 'our master Moses'. And this is a far from anodyne correction. In his commentary on the *Mishnah*[7], Maimonides explains that the fulfilment of the commandments of the Torah must refer exclusively to what the biblical god revealed to 'our master Moses', even though – for example in the cases of circumcision or the prohibition on eating the sciatic nerve – the biblical precept was first revealed to Abraham (circumcision) or to Jacob (sciatic nerve). Moreover, a teaching of the Talmudic tractate Sanhedrin (59a) specifies that 'Noahic' laws are the laws that were decreed before Sinai and then repeated there by Moses. So it was Moses who enjoined men of all nations to observe the seven 'Noahic' commandments. In Maimonides's eyes, therefore, to argue that the pious man from among the nations must observe the seven 'Noahic' commandments out of obedience to Noah and not out of obedience to Moses, is not merely inaccurate, but a grave doctrinal error.[8]

Worse: upon closer inspection, to make such an error is to fall into heresy. As the author of the *Mishnat Rabbi Eliezer* – or at least the teaching in question[9] explains – the 'pious man' from among the nations must follow not 'such-and-such' man, but exclusively 'our father Noah'. But that means that Moses is included in the category 'such-and-such'. How could Maimonides, who was sure to correct the *Mishnat Rabbi Eliezer* on this capitally important point, simultaneously accord it such authority?

That question demands the following answer: Maimonides introduced this teaching – which is absent from post-Talmudic rabbinical literature and is at best unfortunately formulated – into his Codification, not because it made up part of the Law but because it confirmed 'his own theological reflection'. This teaching from the *Mishnat Rabbi Eliezer* did not reappear until Enelow's discovery in the twentieth century. Without doubt, then, it was never 'one of Judaism's most ancient articles of faith'. Only Maimonides's own authority made it one. And he wrote it in his Codification because this teaching – leaving aside its doctrinal blunders – was the very principle on which his own project for codifying the Talmud was based.[10]

*

The Talmud was finished around the sixth century. What was previously transmitted in an essentially oral fashion had now been systematically committed to text – the reason probably being that since the masters could no longer find disciples at the same level as themselves, there was a considerable risk of running out of oil and the flame going out. A new era began after the writing of the Talmud: the era of a *post*-Talmudic Judaism. The rabbis would henceforth legislate, while the masters of the Talmud developed their dialectics. The Codification process began with the literature of the *Responsa*[11] and, correlated to this, the elaboration of religious dogma. The task at hand was no longer a matter of thinking fidelity to Mosaism dialectically, but of governing its observance by the faithful. The rabbinical authorities now tried to define or redefine the relations between Jews and non-Jews, including Christians, as well as to the followers of a new and rapidly-developing monotheism: Islam. The Talmud accorded the world to come to 'just' men of whatever nation (*Tosefta*, Sanhedrin 13.2). Is this not to risk legitimizing the Christian and the Muslim, even though their own New Testament and Qu'ran claim to depose the Book of the Jews' authority? The author of the *Mishnat Rabbi Eliezer* reviews the Talmud teaching and reformulates it in such a way as to avoid the destitution of the Jewish revelation. For certain, people other than those named 'Israelites' do have a share of the world to come – but who are these 'just' men? He replies: they are those who observe the seven 'Noahic' laws (which are discussed elsewhere in the Talmud);[12] and we should take 'just' men to mean 'pious' men. But he does not conceive piety in terms of knowledge of the biblical god's word, but in the form of a pious obedience – that is, being subjected to the Law. All that remains is for him to conclude that there is no prophecy that establishes the Law, except what is written in the Book of the Jews. The non-Jews must imperatively obey it, if they want some share in salvation. They must place themselves under the authority of the biblical figure who is the father of post-diluvian humanity: Noah. If, conversely, they place themselves under the authority of some other – be it Aristotle, Jesus or Mohammed – then they are not pious men, and by consequence they will not be 'elect' on the Day of Judgement. Let's now again read the clause that introduces the *Mishnat Rabbi Eliezer*.

But if they practice the seven precepts saying 'such-and-such commanded me' or if they practice them by themselves, because knowledge (*da'at*) commanded them to do so, or indeed with reference to some idol, then even when they fulfil all the commandments of the *Torah*, they will have no retribution except in this world [and not in the world to come].

The first exclusion concerns the subjects of a law commanded by 'such-and-such man', who could well be Mohammed, the prophet of Islam; the second exclusion concerns the philosopher, who lives guided by knowledge alone; the third exclusion concerns the worshippers of an 'idol', which could well be the Cross. None of them have a share in the world to come, because they purport to do without the Book of the Jews, which is the height of impiety. In his Codification, Maimonides introduces the teaching from the *Mishnat Rabbi Eliezer*. The principle of a Codification demands it. However, out of the three exclusions he only retains the one concerning the philosopher, apart from the correction he makes by substituting 'our master Moses' for 'our father Noah'. Leo Strauss concludes from this that according to Maimonides, 'non-Jews cannot be saved unless they believe in the Mosaic revelation, i.e. unless, as one is tempted to say, they are Christians or Muslims'.[13] For him, Maimonides is sealing the alliance of the three monotheist religions against philosophy. Leo Strauss is cautious – or inclined to be. But we should evidently interpret it another way: since observance of the seven 'Noahic' laws must refer exclusively to the prophecy of 'our master Moses', this rules out Jesus and Mohammed in advance. The question left hanging is whether knowledge, conceived as a succession of adequate ideas, is *prophetical*. That is what Spinoza argues from the start of the *TTP*, in the first words of the first chapter, 'On Prophecy':

> Prophecy or revelation is certain knowledge about something revealed to men by God ... From the definition of prophecy just given, it follows that the word 'prophecy' could be applied to natural knowledge. For what we know by the natural light of reason depends on knowledge of God and his eternal decrees alone. But the common people do not place a high value on natural knowledge, because it is available to everyone, resting as it does on foundations that are available to all. For they are always eager to discover uncommon things, things that are strange and alien to their own nature, and they despise their natural gifts. Hence when they speak of prophetic knowledge, they mean to exclude natural knowledge.[14]

This is the subject on which Maimonides wants to dot the '*i*'s: his clause's only purpose is that of excluding the philosopher from the world to come. This is another way – an allegorical one – of making him drink hemlock.

Following their overlapping paths, the three monotheistic religions encountered one same form of adversity, or otherness: philosophy. Should this rationalist other be recognized legitimate in view of the revelation (whether Jewish, Christian or Muslim)? Or should it be identified with the enemy – with impiety and idolatry? In one dream Jerome told himself, 'Thou liest, you are a follower of Cicero and not of Christ. For where your treasure is, there will your heart be also'; he then repented and vowed, '*Lord, if ever again I possess worldly books, or if ever again I read such, I have denied You*'.[15] Cicero was also Augustine's first love – a profane one. It was he who taught philosophy and the art of writing. But being a Christian demanded ultimately breaking from him, to the point of damning him. At the other extreme, in his *De consolatione philosophiae*, written in prison, Boethius (sixth century) did not even mention the name 'Christ', to the point that doubts were raised over the sincerity of his faith. Boethius's *Consolation* is comparable to Al-Farabi's *Philosophy of Plato and Aristotle* in this regard: in both cases, the search for salvation, or perfection, seems to take the path of philosophy more than religion. In his commentary on Al-Farabi's text, Leo Strauss writes:

> Through the mouth of Plato, Farabi declares that religious speculation and religious investigation of the beings, and the religious syllogistic art do not supply the science of the beings, of which man's highest perfection consists, whereas philosophy does supply it. He goes so far as to present religious knowledge in general and "religious speculation" in particular as the lowest step of the ladder of cognitive pursuits, as inferior even to grammar and to poetry. With grammar, or rather with language, religion has this in common that it is essentially the property of a particular community.[16]

Nonetheless, these texts by Boethius and Al-Farabi are the exception that proves the rule: in the three monotheistic religions, piety demands that philosophy be placed under the authority of the revelation. Thus, in Islam the question is whether the study of philosophy, as well as its use in the interpretation of the Qu'ran, is forbidden, permitted or commanded. Notably, Averroes's *Decisive Treatise* (twelfth century) sought to determine the answer to this question in juridical terms. And it was in continuity with the controversies that exercised Islam scholars, that Maimonides elaborated his own doctrine in the *Guide for the Perplexed*. A few centuries previously, probably in the eighth century in the surroundings of Baghdad, the author of the *Mishnat Rabbi Eliezer* had provided evidence of the doctrinal position that was then emerging in post-Talmudic Judaism. In this twelfth century, this would result in one of the great classics of apologetic literature: the *Kuzari*, or *Book of refutation and proof on behalf of the most despised religion*. In his introduction to this work, Charles Touati writes: 'Having lived in Christian Spain and Muslim Spain, on the receiving end of humiliations by the Cross and the Crescent, a witness to the spread of Greco-Arab philosophy among the Jews who deplored its seductive power and the ravages it provoked', Juda Halevi composed the *Kuzari* in order to defend 'his faith against philosophy, Christianity and Islam'.

Leo Strauss devoted a chapter to this work in his *Persecution and the Art of Writing*.[17] The *Kuzari* is a king of the Khazars who has successive dialogues with a philosopher, a Christian, a Muslim and a rabbi. He wants to know where the truth lies and hence he interrogates the representatives of each of the four wisdoms in dispute. Convinced by the rabbi's reasoning, the king converts to Judaism and the rabbi initiates him in the religion of Israel. That is its argument. What most particularly interests Leo Strauss is the status that the rabbi confers on rationality. His principal opponent in the dialogues is not the Christian or the Muslim, but the philosopher: 'one is entitled to consider the *Kuzari* primarily as a defence of Judaism against philosophy and to raise the question as to whether the setting of the disputations is fit for such a defence'.[18] Yet, the fact is that the rabbi and the philosopher do not have a dialogue between themselves, for the question of whether the search for truth commands a conversion to philosophy is only discussed between the philosopher and the king, and then between the king and the rabbi. Strauss draws out the implications of this method:

> Halevi knew too well that a genuine philosopher can never become a genuine convert to Judaism or to any other revealed religion. For, according to him, a genuine philosopher is a man such as Socrates who possesses "human wisdom" and is invincibly ignorant of "Divine wisdom". It is the impossibility of converting a philosopher to Judaism which he demonstrates ad oculos by omitting a disputation between the scholar and the philosopher. Such a disputation, we may say to begin with, is impossible: contra negantem principia non est disputandum. The philosopher denies as such the premises on which any demonstration of the truth of any revealed religion is based. That denial may be said to proceed from the fact that he, being a philosopher, is untouched by, or has never tasted, that "Divine thing" or "Divine command" (amr ilâhî) which is known from actual experience both to the actual believer, the Jewish scholar, and the potential believer, the king. For in contrast with the philosopher, the king was from the outset, by nature, a pious

man: he had been observing the pagan religion of his country with great eagerness and all his heart; he had been a priest as well as a king.[19]

Later on Strauss returns to this, insisting 'To conclude: Halevi's defence of Judaism against its adversaries in general, and the philosophers in particular is addressed to naturally pious people only.'[20] In order to recognize the truth and to convert to it, it is necessary to be a 'naturally pious man', to be susceptible to divine command, and have 'tasted' it. The man who lives guided by reason alone is the opposite of such a man, his *antinomic* other: that is, an impious man. It remains the case that the 'naturally pious' man might have doubts, and that is why it is necessary to convince him with arguments that adopt a rational form. But rationality is conditioned by the revelation, failing which it is impious. This is the argument of Maimonides's clause: only a man who has 'tasted' divine command has a share in the world to come. And the philosopher is irreducibly foreign to this, because he lives guided by reason alone, thus proving that he is an exceptionally immoral man – an *outlaw*.

If 'a genuine philosopher is a man such as Socrates who possesses "human wisdom" and is invincibly ignorant of "Divine wisdom"', as Leo Strauss explains in his comments on the *Kuzari*, it follows that the condemnation of Socrates by the city of Athens strikes a hard blow at his own doctrine of the 'two roots of the Western world', or at least on the famous metaphor that seals his argument: 'Athens and Jerusalem'. The impossible mediation between the two 'roots' has, in fact, been found: the (historical or allegorical) putting-to-death of the philosopher. Yet, Strauss continually asserts that there is no possible mediation. The contradiction could not have escaped him. This leads him to a surprising exegesis of Plato's *Euthyphron*, a dialogue on piety:

> Justice in the narrower sense is primarily law-abidingness, or obedience to the law. Piety therefore must be a part of justice in this sense, that it must be a part of obedience to law. But law is primarily ancestral custom. Therefore piety stands or falls by obedience to ancestral custom. It is here that Socrates agrees with orthodoxy over against the heretic, Euthyphron. Euthyphron disobeys ancestral custom by accusing his own father of impiety. Socrates shows Euthyphron *ad hominem* that he has no right to disobey ancestral custom … We may say that both the orthodox and Socrates have common sense, whereas Euthyphron lacks common sense. By this I mean that a society is possible on both orthodox and Socratic principles, whereas a society is not possible on Euthyphron's principles.[21]

Leo Strauss's commentary brings three figures onto the stage: Socrates, Euthyphron and 'the orthodox'. For him, Socrates and 'the orthodox' share one same conception of justice, understood as 'obedience to law'. The Law is primarily 'ancestral custom'. Euthyphron 'disobeys' it 'by accusing his own father of impiety'. 'Athens', Strauss explains, is a metaphor for philosophy. And in his exegesis of the *Kuzari*, he explains 'a genuine philosopher is a man such as Socrates who possesses "human wisdom" and is invincibly ignorant of "Divine wisdom"'. So how can 'the orthodox' – the pious man – and Socrates – the philosopher – be so much in agreement, as if by enchantment, as to express 'a common sense' that Euthyphron lacks? Evidently, Leo Strauss is conferring two antinomic meanings on the name 'Socrates', thus naming the philosopher 'invincibly ignorant' of the command of the divine Law, and also the opponent of Euthyphron: and this is an utterly different 'Socrates', strangely recalling the King Kuzari, in that he is a 'naturally pious' man, and as such, susceptible to conversion to the transcendence of the Law. So, in Leo Strauss's writing there are two 'Socrates', or two antinomic meanings for this name: if the 'return to Athens' is conditioned by a return to Jerusalem, then Socrates is in accordance with the pious man, but if it is not conditioned by a return to 'Jerusalem', then no such accordance is possible. To put that another way, if a return to Plato is possible and desirable, it has to be conditioned by Maimonides's clause. Since Leo Strauss is a pious man, he produces a pious exegesis of Plato's *Euthyphron*.

*

Taking a closer view, however, it may be that Leo Strauss's exegesis of the *Euthyphron* is taking its lead from Aristotle, even before it passes by way of Maimonides or 'Jerusalem'. His Aristotelian exegesis of Plato's dialogue proceeds in two phases. In the first phase, he is concerned to conceive justice on the model of money, which alone allows 'a sort of equality among things to be established'. He then observes together with Aristotle, that 'money has become by convention a sort of representative of demand; and this is why it has the name "money" (νόμισμα) because it exists not by nature but by law (νόμος) and it is in our power to change it and make it useless'.[22] Dissociating the essence of knowing the principles of justice from that of knowing the principles of nature, we have broken with Plato. Aristotle's disqualification of the poets and theologians who vaunt 'the semblance of wisdom without the reality' does not concern the subject of justice, or at least not in the same manner as it does the subject of nature. This disassociation allows Strauss to salvage 'ancestral custom'. All that remains, in the second phase, is to establish that justice consists of obeying the Law, because it is the Law. And once again he invokes Aristotle:

> As we say that some people who do just acts are not necessarily just, i.e. those who do the acts ordained by the laws either unwillingly or owing to ignorance or for some other reason and *not for the sake of the [ordained] acts themselves* (though, to be sure, they do what they should and all the things that the good man ought), so is it, it seems, that in order to be good one must be in a certain state when one does the several acts, i.e. one must do them as a result of choice and for the sake of the acts themselves. Now virtue makes the choice right, but the question of the things which should naturally be done to carry out our choice belongs not to virtue but to another faculty.[23]

One can observe the Law in spite of oneself, unwillingly; and since this act is a matter of constraint and not a voluntary one, it is not a worthy one. But what is observing the Law without knowing that it is the Law, if not a matter of one's judgement according with the legislator's judgement, with each of them conceiving it as a just action? According to Aristotle, if one is to deserve the qualifier 'just man', one has to act with a view to obeying positive law, as ordained by the legislator and not guided by rational judgement, which only comes into play insofar as it is used to appreciate what means will allow the accomplishment of the just act as ordained by the Law.[24] Strauss's exegesis of Plato's *Euthyphron* is simultaneously both Aristotelian and Maimonidean. It is perhaps first of all Aristotelian – for certain, it is not Platonic.

*

In Leo Strauss's work, the theme of the 'Return' is governed by the theme of the 'father's house'. In his lecture 'Progress or Return?' he explains:

> Return is the translation for the Hebrew word *t'shuvah*. *T'shuvah* has an ordinary and an emphatic meaning. Its emphatic meaning is rendered in English by "repentance". Repentance is return, meaning the return from the wrong way to the right one. This implies that we were once on the right way; deviation or sin or imperfection is not original. Man is originally at home in his father's house. He becomes a stranger through estrangement, through sinful estrangement. Repentance, return, is homecoming.[25]

In both his exegesis of the *Kuzari* and of the *Euthyphron*, for Leo Strauss the 'return' is the invocation of a pious observance of ancestral custom. He considers the Talmudic notion of *t'shuvah* – 'return' in the sense of 'repentance' – in the form of a 'homecoming', returning to the 'roots' after having got lost in the illusion of a 'progress' that is all the more illusory, and culpable, because it is rationally articulated, outside of the Law. For us, the Talmudic notion of *t'shuvah* has an entirely different meaning: it is the injunction to re-subjectivate the idea, to re-appropriate its intelligibility, such that it can indicate *anew* a path through existence. Comrade Alain Badiou has excellently formulated this principle, at two points in his pamphlet on the 'Meanings of the word "Jew"'. Firstly, when he writes 'The external enemy – as were the Nazi anti-semites – can attack and kill your physical being. That is the law of terror and war. But the loss of the name and of its meaning always comes from within'. And then when he writes: 'A "goy" says it with passion: saving the name of the Jews is essential to him, because this is a matter of his own conceptual and operative determination.'[26] The *t'shuvah* is, indeed, the internal, subjective re-conquest of the name and of its meaning – in other words, the re-conquest of its innermost conceptual and operative determination, which had previously been lost.

In his study on the *Kuzari*, Leo Strauss notes that 'in contrast with the philosopher, the king was from the outset, by nature, a pious man: he had been observing the pagan religion of his country with great eagerness and all his heart; he had been a priest as well as a king'. He concludes from this that it is his piety that allows him to recognize the truth – that is, to convert to the Law. Around three thousand years ago, a handful of scribes opposed the common piety with the rectitude of an active thought. According to their doctrine, set into a narrative story, a certain Abraham proved that he was a pious man – a *hassid* – by walking straight through the river. In order to do so, he had to free himself from the 'house of his father' – a father who very sincerely and wholeheartedly respected the pagan religion of his country, Ur of the Chaldees – the idolatrous name for the Origin.

8 TRUE OTHERNESS

Upon a first approach, it seems that in his *At Judaei* manifesto Spinoza is polemicizing against 'the Jews' because the doctrine of the most eminent of the 'Pharisees', Maimonides, condemns the free man. However, Spinoza was not unaware that the Christians also maintained that 'true opinions and a true conception of life make no contribution to happiness whenever people receive them by the natural light of reason alone and not as teachings prophetically revealed'. That was a dogma of the Church, if not the Christian dogma *par excellence*: as 'reasonable and intelligent Christians' reminded him through the voice of Oldenburg, only faith in Christ brought salvation, for he was 'the sole Mediator for mankind'. So when Spinoza named 'the Jews', this was partly because he was in fact opposed to Maimonides, their representative in learned Europe, and partly because it would have been at least imprudent to write 'the Christians'. But his reader knows perfectly well that the question has been posed as to whether men ignorant of Christ and his church have a share in its salvation – and that it is still posed. Indeed, the formula is a famous one: 'Outside the Church there is no salvation'. Bernard Sesboüé, a Jesuit theologian, has devoted a book to this.[1] This formula appeared for the first time in the mid-third century, in the writings of Cyprian of Carthage, who addressed it to the schismatics – those who detached themselves from the church and founded a dissident Christian sect. At that time, this formula had the violent polemical force so characteristic of fratricidal splits. But in the writings of Origen, also in the third century, it was addressed to the Jews – privileged yet recalcitrant witnesses to the coming of the Christ:

> Even if anyone from that people wants to be saved, let him come in order to be able to attain salvation. Let him come to this house in which the blood of Christ is the sign of redemption ... Let no one persuade himself, let no one deceive himself. Outside this house, that is, outside the Church, no one is saved.[2]

The formula originally concerned all those who were aware of the coming of Christ and the institution of his church and yet, refused to believe and rally to it (the Jews), or else broke away from it (the schismatics). But with the conversion of the Roman Empire, the question of the salvation of non-believers acquired another dimension, out of all proportion:

> ... a decisive event took place after Lactantius and before Jerome. The persecutor Empire officially converted to Christianity. From being threatened and necessarily minoritarian, Christianity passed to the status of the official religion of the Empire. It was publicly known and recognised: no one in the Empire could be unaware of its presence. However, it had not converted the entire society. A certain number of pagans remained faithful to their ancestral religion; the Jews maintained a position of refusal. The problem of the salvation of the pagans, living side-by-side with a Church that was very much visible, was thus posed in a new manner. Their numbers even became an objection against the faith.[3]

From then onward, the doctrine of the Fathers of the Church became ever more radicalized, from Jerome and Augustine to Fulgentius of Ruspe, who struck the decisive blow at the beginning of the sixth century: 'Most firmly hold and by no means doubt, that not only all pagans, but also all Jews, and all heretics and schismatics who die outside the Catholic Church, will go to the everlasting fire that was prepared for the devil and his angels'. Sesboüé comments:

> The formula now escaped its original context. It was generalised in the name of an abstract logic, becoming a principle for reasoning. It condemned all those who are materially foreign to the Catholic Church, without any other consideration. This text became a standard reference in the Middle Ages, and all the more so because it was long attributed to St. Augustine. All the more importantly for its subsequent history, it was the matrix for the council of Florence's definition.[4]

The council of Florence in 1442 affirmed that 'no one outside the Church – not only pagans, but also Jews and heretics or schismatics – can become participants in the eternal life, but they will go "into the everlasting fire prepared for the devil and his angels" (Mt. 25.41), unless they join [the Church] before the end of their lives'.[5] This is the acme of Christian exclusivism. Subsequently, with the discovery of the New World, the church was driven again to question the fate of those who had necessarily been ignorant of the coming of Christ. Indeed, among the Jesuits there was an attempt to relativize the condemnation of unbelievers, and then to save them. Nonetheless, in the seventeenth century a severe stance was still taken toward all who knew and yet did not rally to the church. Spinoza was not unaware of this, and nor were his readers.

*

Ever since the Fathers of the Church, throughout history Christian theologians have battled against heresies, the Jews and pagans. The question that was particularly at stake was 'election'; one of the most redoubtable questions, namely the matter of who is 'elect' for the Kingdom of the heavens. The condemnation of Pelagius and Pelagianism at the beginning of the fifth century is particularly instructive in this regard. Augustine determinedly and almost obsessively combatted the doctrine of the monk Pelagius. He relentlessly pursued Pelagius and his disciples, until they were condemned as heretics by the pope Zosimus in 418. It is difficult to establish Pelagius's doctrine with any precision, since he wrote little, often under the cover of anonymity and disowned books and theses that were ascribed to him; it is thus impossible to determine with any certainty, whether he truly disavowed these works, or only did so out of caution. We are guided less by his own thinking, than by the indictment against him. In the French-language collected works of Augustine, four volumes are devoted to the *Pelagian Crisis* and what followed from it.[6] Here we see that Augustine accused Pelagius of having destroyed two foundations of Christian dogma, thus leaving the whole edifice in ruins: the doctrine of original sin and the doctrine of grace.

Pelagius was a theorist of free will. He maintained that the possibility of doing good is inherent to human nature, such as it was created by God, and that in order to actualize this possibility man must will it – and this depends on him. Pelagius did also refer to 'God's aid' and sometimes to 'grace', a supernatural aid that helps man in his determination to do good. Nonetheless, the principle remains that whereas one element of this concerns God – in that he made the capacity to discern between good and evil part of human nature – another element concerns man's own merit – namely, his putting this capacity to good use. The example of sight illustrates this: it is in man's nature that he is seeing, for God created him like this; but the way he uses it depends on him and it may be that the way he uses it makes him more blind than seeing. If, conversely, he uses it well, he will see, consistent with his nature. In Augustine's eyes, adopting such a doctrine amounted to denying the dogma of original sin. Indeed, it follows from Pelagius's doctrine that man is culpable through his own fault alone, and not by nature. In denying original sin, Pelagius is necessarily led to deny election by the 'Cross'. Augustine administers the proof of this:

> He, however, who said, I will destroy the wisdom of the wise (Corinthians 1:19) since that cross cannot be made of none effect, in very deed overthrows that wisdom by the foolishness of preaching whereby believers are healed. For if natural capacity, by help of free will, is in itself sufficient both for discovering how one ought to live, and also for leading a holy life, then Christ died in vain, (Galatians 2:21) and therefore also the offense of the cross is ceased (Galatians 5:11). Why also may I not myself exclaim? — nay, I will exclaim, and chide them with a Christian's sorrow — Christ has become of no effect unto you, whosoever of you are justified by nature; you are fallen from grace.[7]

Only the existence of an original sin, Augustine continues, elevates Christ as a 'saviour of a corrupt human nature'. So if Pelagius denies that human nature has been corrupted, then he necessarily renounces the 'blood of Christ'. However, the difficulty that Augustine encounters in condemning Pelagius is that the heretic equivocates, trying to reconcile salvation by free will and salvation by grace. In order to draw up his indictment against Pelagius and condemn him, Augustine has to be able to catch him out. And that is what the case of infants who die before baptism helps him to do. If Pelagius is consistent, then he must hold that they do indeed enter the Kingdom of Heaven, as innocents who have not had the time or means to do evil. This would thus prove his heresy, for no one can enter the Kingdom of Heaven unless he has been baptised, as the Gospel of Mark (16.15-16) teaches:

> And he said unto them, Go ye into all the world, and preach the gospel to every creature. He that believeth and is baptized shall be saved; but he that believeth not shall be damned.

If there is no alternative other than being either saved or condemned, it follows that there is no salvation without baptism and/or faith in Christ. Confronted with the case of infants who die before baptism, Pelagius must either concede that they are destined to the flames of hell, which would prove their culpability and reduce his own doctrine to ruins; or else challenge the dogma of original sin, which would prove his own culpability – in other words, his heresy. He finds a way out: 'I do not know where they go, but I know where they do not go'. It is an elegant evasive measure, and a subtly polemical one. He admits that if they have not been baptised they do not enter the Kingdom of heaven, and thus conforms to dogma; but he refuses to believe that they will burn in hell. Their fate remains in suspense, in limbo. Augustine's tactic thus next consists of denying the possibility of a third term: there is either the Kingdom of Heaven or the flames of hell. Hieronymus Bosch delighted in this tragi-comic alternative and Augustine made it his own hobbyhorse. He unflinchingly maintained that all human beings who have not been baptized are destined to the flames, even if they are still infants and without fault. And it is brandishing this argument that he embarks on his condemnation of Pelagius and then that of his disciples:

> The new-fangled Pelagian heretics have been most justly condemned by the authority of catholic councils and of the Apostolic See, on the ground of their having dared to give to unbaptized infants a place of rest and salvation, even apart from the kingdom of heaven. This they would not have dared to do, if they did not deny their having original sin, and the need of its remission by the sacrament of baptism.[8]

The infants' fate has to come after the church's. Augustine suspects Pelagius of wanting to leave open the breach that would ultimately cause the ruin of the whole edifice. For if infants are not culpable, the doctrine of original sin is reduced to nothing and consequently, so too salvation by the 'blood of Christ'. To assert the possibility of man being impeccable by nature is to deny that Christ is the only mediator: 'Christ has become of no effect unto you, whosoever of you are justified by nature; you are fallen from grace'. In legitimizing the idea of existence guided by reason alone, the monk Pelagius's doctrine does without due obedience to the Cross; hence the accusation of 'Judaising' levelled against Pelagius and his disciples. The history of ideas is an endlessly ironic discipline.

In the *TTP* Spinoza revives Pelagius's Christianity, but his Pelagianism is consistent: he simultaneously gets rid of both the 'barrier' and the 'mystery' that is meant to remove it. For he conceives original sin as nothing more than the following: since man is part of nature, he is not born free; he conquers his own freedom. Another difference with Pelagius is that Spinoza is not a theorist of free will. According to him, the principle of action is not a decision coming from some mysterious power called 'will'; action is determined by an idea, for ideas, be they adequate or inadequate, are determinant. To imagine a will *free* to choose between good and evil is to imagine a transcendent power whose decision is free because it is not based on reason – in other words, a power (Will) whose freedom is in the last analysis *arbitrary*.[9] This power is nothing other than the Law. That is why Spinoza denies that freedom can be conceived in terms of free will.

We experience freedom in passing from an inadequate idea to an adequate one; or indeed in passing from an inadequate action to an adequate one; or, more radically still, in passing from an inadequate life to an adequate one. Did Descartes, the philosopher of free will, teach any different? In a letter to Father Mersenne of April–May 1637, he replied to his correspondent's objections regarding his *Discourse on Method*:

> You reject my statement that in order to do well it is sufficient to judge well; yet it seems to me that the common scholastic doctrine is that 'the will does not tend towards evil except in so far as it is presented to it by the intellect as some kind of good'—that is why they say that 'whoever sins does so in ignorance'—so that if the intellect never represented anything to the will as good without its actually being so, the will could never go wrong in its choice. But the intellect often represents different things to the will at the same time, and that is why they say 'I see and praise the better, but I follow the worse', which applies only to weak minds, as I said on page 26. The well-doing of which I speak can not be understood in a theological sense—for there grace comes into the question—but simply in the sense of moral and natural philosophy, where no account is taken of grace. So I cannot be accused, on these grounds, of the error of the Pelagians. It is as if I said that good sense was the only thing necessary to make a man of honour, it would be altogether irrelevant to object that it was necessary also to have the right sex and not to be a woman … As to those who asked you what religion I was, they should have looked at what I said on page 29, namely that I would not have thought myself obliged to rest content with the opinions of others for a single moment if I had not intended in due course to examine them using my own judgment. Then they would see that it cannot be inferred from my *Discourse* that infidels should remain in the religion of their parents.[10]

Error, according to Descartes, comes from the will giving its assent even when it is in the dark. When this principle is applied to the ethics of good (and no longer to the science of truth), it follows that the fault principally comes from the thing that the intellect represents to the will as good, but which is not *truly* good: 'so that if the intellect never represented anything to the will as good without its actually being so, the will could never go wrong in its choice'. Is this not, then, precisely the same as Pelagius's doctrine, in that it would thus be possible to be an impeccable man, so long as one did not hurry into assenting before having a clear and distinct idea of what one was assenting to? Descartes defends himself from this accusation, arguing that he is reasoning as a philosopher and not as a theologian. 'Grace' is a matter for theology alone; and whereas theology teaches the supernatural routes to salvation, he 'simply' deals in 'moral and natural philosophy'. But it is precisely when 'election' is accessible to man through natural routes that the edifice of religion crumbles, because then no 'grace' is necessary – and *therefore Christ died for nothing*. Concluding, Descartes assures Father Mersenne that he does not think that 'infidels should remain in the religion of their parents' and this would suggest *in fine,* that salvation depends exclusively on faith in Jesus Christ, the sole Mediator for mankind, etc.

As we know, the philosopher was masking his approach. The accusation of being a Pelagian amounted to condemnation. So he had to distinguish between, on the one hand, the philosophical order of nature and on the other hand, the theological order of grace: 'if I said that good sense was the only thing necessary to make a man of honour, it would be altogether irrelevant to object that it was necessary also to have the right sex and not to be a woman'. The natural no more intersects with the theological than rationality intersects with sexual difference: if someone has 'good sense' – 'of all things among men, the most equally distributed' – that suffices to make them a 'man of honour', and to object that they would also have to have a member that is extraneous to the female body – to be a *man* – 'would be altogether irrelevant'. So be it. But does *honesty* alone suffice for 'election'? Descartes's conclusion seems to be that honesty is not sufficient, because even the 'man of honour' must also convert to the true religion. If we continue with the analogy, ultimately he is missing the 'member' that grace comes from.

Nonetheless, Descartes's concluding argumentation justifying the theological dogma is singularly philosophical: 'I would not have thought myself obliged to rest content with the opinions of others for a single moment if I had not intended in due course to examine them using my own judgment'. So the infidel's error – remaining with the religion of their parents – is that of having contented themselves with others' opinions without having used their 'own judgment' to examine them. But is 'grace' a matter of judgement? According to Descartes, judgement is the articulation of a will and an understanding: good judgements consist of assenting to a clear and distinct idea, whereas bad judgements consist of hurrying to assent while the idea remains confused. Theology's place is left vacant. Continuing with the same analogy, it follows that the member that grace comes from is not missing; if it is evidently supernatural, that is because it is redundant. Ultimately, the theological argument falls all by itself, as it was precarious even to begin with. God is dead.

Mersenne returned to these charges in 1641. Collecting his *Second Set of Objections to the Mediations*, he wrote to Descartes 'if the will never goes astray or falls into sin so long as it is guided by the mind's clear and distinct knowledge, and if it exposes itself to danger by following a conception of the intellect which is wholly lacking in clarity and distinctness, then note what follows from this. A Turk, or any other unbeliever, not only does not sin in refusing to embrace the Christian religion, but what is more, he sins if he does embrace it, since he does not possess clear and distinct knowledge of the truth'.[11] Descartes then ducks this charge, hurrying to concede to the Jesuit priest that 'the clarity or transparency which can induce our will to give its assent is of two kinds: the first comes from the natural light, while the second come from divine grace'.[12] And when it comes to unclear things like 'the Christian religion', only divine grace can legitimately compel the will to assent to it. What remains to be done is to explain why the Turks and other infidels do not enjoy the support of divine grace:

> The sin that Turks and other infidels commit by refusing to embrace the Christian religion does not arise from their unwillingness to assent to obscure matters (for obscure they indeed are), but from their resistance to the impulses of divine grace within them, or from the fact that they make themselves unworthy of grace by their other sins.[13]

Descartes resurrects the member that we'd thought was dead: the philosopher without the theologian's help, is thus worth nothing more than a Turk or the other infidels. But Descartes is crafty: as if hammering the nail in deeper, he immediately adds,

> Let us take the case of an infidel who is destitute of all supernatural grace and has no knowledge of the doctrines which we Christians believe to have been revealed by God. If, despite the fact that these doctrines are obscure to him, he is induced to embrace them by fallacious arguments, I make bold to assert that he will not on that account be a true believer, but *will instead be committing a sin* by not using his reason correctly.[14]

The word is out: it is a *sin* to assent to what you do not have a clear and distinct idea of. In order to appreciate Descartes's guile and the way in which he is playing with the good priest Mersenne here, we have to look a little beyond this, to the objections raised by the ardent young Jansenist Arnauld (the *Fourth Set of Objections*). Arnauld recommends to the author of the *Meditations*, that he specify that his teachings regarding error, will and understanding are exclusively a matter of discerning true and false, and not good and evil. And he adds a 'second point' repeating the first

The second point I should like our author to stress is that, where he asserts that we should assent only to what we clearly and distinctly know, he is dealing solely with matters concerned with sciences and intellectual contemplation, and not with matters belonging to faith and the conduct of life[15]

What does this have to do with 'the conduct of life'? Citing a treatise of Augustine's (Chapter 15 of *On the Profit of Believing*), Arnauld explains that there are three instances, or ways, of assenting: understanding, belief and opinion. Understanding applies to discerning true and false and belief to discerning good and evil, whereas opinion has no proper application, 'If we understand something, then we owe it to reason; if we believe something, we owe it to authority; and if we are opinionated about something, this is based on error.'[16] So it is important that Descartes be advised not to lead the readers of his *Meditations* into error; for if they came to the opinion that understanding equally applies to discerning good and evil, the result would not be an error, but a *sin*: 'M. Descartes, prudent man that he is, will readily judge how important it is to make the distinctions thus outlined. For otherwise those many people who in our age are prone to impiety may distort his words in order to subvert the faith.'[17] But what was Descartes's reply to Father Mersenne's objection? That a Turk who converted to Christianity without the supernatural aid of grace would be '*committing a sin* by not using his reason correctly'. Let's now see how wily old Descartes responds to his young inquisitor:

> The next point concerns the fact that in the Fourth Meditation I dealt only 'with the mistakes we commit in distinguishing between the true and the false and not those that occur in our pursuit of good and evil', and that when I asserted that 'we should assent only to what we clearly know' this was always subject to the exception of 'matters which belong to faith and the conduct of life'. Now this is something that the entire context of my book makes clear; moreover I have explained this point quite explicitly in your reply to the Second Objections ... and I have also given advance warning of it in the Synopsis. I say this in order to show how much I respect M. Arnauld's judgement and how much I welcome his advice.[18]

In his replies to the *Second Set of Objections*, part 5, Descartes's response to Mersenne is that when a man assents to something that he does not at all understand, that is itself a *sin*, unless he is compelled by supernatural grace. He points Arnauld to this. However, to disguise the fact that it was indeed he who struck the blow, he hastens to edit the text of the *Synopsis of the Meditations*, so that it conforms to his inquisitor's demands. He thus adds the following clarification, 'in order to show how much [he] respect[s] Arnauld's judgement':

> But here it should be noted in passing that I do not deal at all with sin, i.e. the error which is committed in pursuing good and evil, but only with the error that occurs in distinguishing truth from falsehood. And there is no discussion of matters pertaining to faith or the conduct of life, but simply of speculative truths which are known solely by means of the natural light[19]

Has Descartes capitulated? It seems that he has; or more exactly, this is the function of the *Synopsis* of his *Meditations*, even though it appears in the guise of an apparatus. Descartes sets out his replies to Arnauld in an 18 March 1641 letter to Mersenne, with the Jesuit priest serving as a mediator; and it is also to Mersenne that he writes, requesting that this addition be made to the *Synopsis* of the *Meditations*. He furthermore asks him to, 'Put the words between brackets so that it can be seen that they have been added'.[20] Does Descartes do this so that Arnauld will see how diligently he has submitted to his 'authority'? Or is it that his reader, alerted to the change, will be able to recognize it as a manoeuvre devised out of prudence? The editors of the *Œuvres philosophiques de Descartes* comment, in a note:

> While here he declares, upon Arnauld's demand, that this only concerns errors of speculation, in his *Fourth Meditation* Descartes would maintain: *atque ita et fallor et pecco, and thus I err and sin.*[21]

So sin is not original; it comes from a misuse of the will, when we assent to things that are obscure to us – whether this is a matter of discerning true from false or good from evil. Descartes reiterates Pelagius's heresy; he is not ignorant of it, but feigns that he is. In a letter to Mersenne dated March 1642, he writes that he looked into Augustine in order to seek out 'the errors of Pelagius, to discover why people say that I share his opinions, with which I have never hitherto been acquainted'.[22] In his March–April 1637 letter to Mersenne, however, he was not unaware of his 'opinion'; indeed, he denied that he shared it. In March 1642, he continued:

> Pelagius said that it was possible without grace to do good works and merit eternal life, and this was condemned by the Church; I say that it is possible to know by natural reason that God exists, but I do not say that

this natural knowledge by itself, without grace, merits the supernatural glory which we hope for in heaven. On the contrary, it is evident that since this glory is supernatural, more than natural powers are needed to merit it.[23]

The supernatural has reasons of its own, unknown to reason itself. The God of Augustine, Calvin, Luther, Mersenne and Arnauld may judge men as he sees fit, whereas we have to determine our conduct in virtue of clear and distinct ideas. For Descartes, the 'authority' claimed by Augustin and Arnauld is not the principle that must guide our life. Yet he does feign agreement with this claim – indeed, prudence demanded it. In 1643, Voetius wrote that 'René [Descartes] might rightly be compared to the most subtle defender of atheism, Cesare Vanini; for he works by the same means to elevate the throne of atheism in the soul of the ignorant'. Descartes's editors specify: 'Vanini, condemned for atheism, was burned alive in Toulouse on 9 February 1619'.[24]

*

In his reply to Oldenburg, who had asked him to explain his thinking on Christ, Spinoza distinguished between knowledge 'according to the flesh' and 'according to the spirit', explaining that this latter is 'God's eternal wisdom, which has manifested itself in all things but most in the human mind and most of all in Christ Jesus'. He continues:

> No-one can attain blessedness without the wisdom that teaches — as nothing else does — what is true and false, good and evil; this wisdom was manifested most through Jesus Christ

Whether we invoke Moses, Jesus or Mohammed, ultimately this is the only question that counts: Are true and false, good and evil, two sides of the same coin? Augustine, Maimonides and Arnauld accept that *knowledge* is sovereign in matters of true and false, but not in matters of good and evil, where it is *obedience* that must reign; and it is this cleavage, this barrier, that legitimizes the condemnation of the philosopher, for he does not separate true and false from good and evil. But if the theologian condemns Spinoza, for his part, Spinoza does not condemn the theologian. In the *TTP*, at the end of fifteen chapters devoted to Scriptural exegesis, he concludes:

> I speak expressly of pious conduct and formal religious worship and not piety itself or private worship of God or the means by which the

mind is internally directed wholeheartedly to revere God. For internal veneration of God, and piety, as such are under everyone's individual jurisdiction (as we showed at the end of ch. 7), and cannot be transferred to another. Furthermore, what I mean by 'kingdom of God' here is plain enough, I suppose, from chapter 14. We showed there that a person fulfils the law of God by practising justice and charity at God's command, from which it follows that a kingdom of God is a kingdom in which justice and charity have the force of law and command. I cannot see that it makes any difference here whether God teaches and commands the true practice of justice and charity by the natural light of reason or by revelation. It makes no difference how such practice is revealed to men, provided that it possesses supreme authority and serves men as their highest law.[25]

In affirming 'the utility and necessity' of a 'revelation' Spinoza has made the theologian better-disposed to listening to him. He can thus let it be understood that 'the true practice of justice and charity by the natural light of reason' is worthy in *a different way*. And he returns to this in his Annotations (no 31) in order to make sure that there is no possibility of misunderstandings regarding the nature of the 'necessity' he attributes to 'revelation':

'that simple obedience is the path to salvation': In other words, it is not reason but rather revelation that can teach us that it suffices for salvation or happiness to accept the divine decrees as laws or commandments and that there is no need to understand them as eternal truths.[26]

A 'revelation' was necessary in order to show that a life of obedience can offer salvation – that is, 'election'. A 'revelation' was necessary in order to show that God desires that man will at least obey him, even for want of knowledge. Indeed, from the moment that man does think, he is led to conceive of a god who liberates, rather than subjects him. According to Spinoza, 'it is not reason but rather revelation that can teach us' that man's obedience is of the same value as his freedom; even to the extent that the subjected man will have a share in the world to come, just like the man living guided by reason alone. In other words, this teaching is beyond comprehension. Why? Because to conceive the 'divine decrees' as 'eternal truths' – in other words, to conceive them in the form of ideas – involves actions *of another nature*.

9 THE MASQUERADE

Hermann Cohen and others after him have reproached Spinoza for reducing Mosaic Law to a positive, state law, stripping it of its universal or divine dimension. However, in the European learned society of the seventeenth century Spinoza's doctrine on the 'election' of the Hebrews – namely, that it relates to 'the state and the other good things in this life' – was a commonplace of biblical exegesis. The tenet that there is a distinction in the Old Testament texts between what pertains to a universal or natural moral law and what pertains to a ceremonial law, particular to the Hebrews, was present even in Thomas of Aquinas. Its adoption in a political, or secular perspective dates from the Renaissance. The philological study of the 'Hebrew Republic' became the laboratory of the liberal doctrines that were then being elaborated. The reform current gave shelter to a republican orientation within its ranks, which established its doctrine under the cover of learned exegesis, as it sought to influence the course of things. Hugo Grotius was one representative of this current in the Netherlands; Thomas Hobbes in England shared this same principle of a political exegesis of the Bible, even though his orientation was monarchist and not republican. In his *On the Citizen* (1642, then 1647), almost thirty years before Spinoza published the *TTP*, Hobbes interpreted the 'election' of the Jews in the following terms:

> All law can be divided first according to its different sources into *divine* and *human law*. Then following the two modes by which God makes his will known to men, *divine law* is twofold: *natural* (or *moral*) and *positive*. *Natural law* is the law which God has revealed to all men through his *eternal word* which is innate in them, namely by *natural reason*. And this is the law which I have been attempting to expound throughout this little book. *Positive law* is that law which God has revealed to us through the *prophetic word* by which he spoke to men as

a man; such are the laws which he gave to the Jews about their constitution [*politia*] and divine worship; and they can be called *divine civil laws*, because they were particular to the commonwealth of Israel, his own particular people.[1]

So the singularity of Spinoza's biblical exegesis does not reside in the reduction of the Mosaic Law to the positive law of a particular state: rather, it is a commonplace that the *TTP*'s author adopts in order to differentiate himself on other points. He first differentiates himself on the subject of the relation between natural and positive law. His formula, from his correspondence, is well known: 'the difference which you inquire about between Hobbes and myself, consists in this, that I always preserve natural right intact, and only allot to the chief magistrates in every state a right over their subjects commensurate with the excess of their power over the power of the subjects. This is what always takes place in the state of nature.'[2] Conversely, Hobbes introduces a rupture, an interruption between 'the state of nature' and collective existence under the authority of the state. For him, justice consists of obeying the laws of established political authority; there is no good or evil, justice or injustice, beyond the positive laws that this authority carves in stone:

> Of doctrines that dispose men to sedition, the first, without question, is: *that knowledge of good and evil is a matter for* individuals. We allowed that this was true in the natural state; in fact we proved it (I,9); for in a natural state, individuals live by equal right, and have not submitted by their own agreement to other men's power [imperium]. But in the civil state it is false. For it has been shown (VI.9) that the civil laws are the rules of *good* and *evil*, of the *just* and the *unjust*, the *honourable* and the *dishonourable*, and that therefore one must accept what the legislator enjoins as *good*, and what he forbids as *evil*. The legislator is always the holder of sovereign power – in a Monarchy, the Monarch.[3]

Once a political authority is established, it determines *absolutely* what is good and evil, just and unjust; and in these matters, by consequence, reason commands nothing other than obedience to the state's laws. Hobbes incessantly returns to this, for it is the foundation on which he can clarify the whole array of political concepts. As such, distinguishing 'advice' – a precept whose own content obliges that it be obeyed – and a 'command' – a precept whose form obliges that it be obeyed – he explains:

> ADVICE is an *instruction* or *precept* [*praeceptum*] in which the reason

for following it is drawn *from the matter itself*. But a COMMAND is an instruction in which the reason for following it is drawn from *the will of the instructor*[4]

The clause that Maimonides introduces with regard to the seven 'Noahic' laws is thus entirely justified; better, it is *necessary* in order for there to be 'command'. For the man who observes the Law not because it is the Law, but because reason – knowledge (*daʾat*) – makes him see this action as just, is, indeed, not acting in virtue of the will of he who ordains it. Rather, he is observing the Law as if it were a precept 'in which the reason for following it is drawn *from the matter itself*. In so doing, the free man does away with the authority of the 'command', for he is living guided by reason alone. Maimonides, as cited and translated by Spinoza, could thus legitimately conclude, 'But if he practises them because he has been convinced by reason that he should, he is not one of us, nor does he belong to the pious or learned of the nations.'[5] And thus, is also why Hermann Cohen can justify Maimonides's clause, as against Spinoza:

> The Noahide who wants to become a foreigner-resident must, therefore, first give assurance that he is not adopting the seven commandments out of his own reason – a reason that could on any day arrive at other decisions regarding these ethical concepts, whose authority is relative – but because they are the Jewish political law. Only then will the Jewish state – which he may not, even so, consider a mere nursery for free thinkers – be safe from the perils troubling its ethical existence.[6]

Is this not the same as Spinoza's own doctrine in Chapter XX of the *TTP*, when he explains that 'seditious views' in the state are 'those that dissolve the agreement by which each person surrenders their right to act according to their own judgement'? Has not the man who lives guided by reason rather than obey the Law dissolved 'the agreement by which each person surrenders their right to act according to their own judgement'?

*

Spinoza teaches that a free man is he who lives guided by reason alone, and moreover claims that unlike Hobbes, he 'always preserves natural right intact'. Yet in Chapter XVI, when he addresses the 'agreement' fundamental to the state, he maintains that once the 'agreement' has been sealed, 'we are obliged to carry out absolutely all the commands of the sovereign power, however absurd they may be. Reason too bids us do so: it is a choice of the lesser of two evils.'⁷ And this choice, Spinoza explains, is a law 'so firmly inscribed in human nature that it may be included among the eternal truths'.⁸ There are no greater evils than the absence of a state. It follows that reason always commands obedience to the Law, because it is the Law – 'however absurd' its commands. So the same justification obtains for condemning the citizen as for condemning the soldier; for obedience rests on one and the same principle:

> it is right to condemn [him] just as everyone admits it is perfectly right to do in warfare. Any soldier who does not stay where he is posted, but attacks the enemy without his commander's knowledge, even if his tactics are good and he succeeds in driving the enemy off while yet still doing so as a personal venture of his own, is rightly condemned to death, since he has violated his oath and the right of his commander. Not everyone sees with equal clarity that all citizens, without exception, are equally always bound by this right, but the reasoning remains absolutely the same.⁹

Once it is accepted that justice and good are measured by the yardstick of obedience and not of thought, Spinoza's teaching is the same as Maimonides's. In other words, it is the same as Hobbes's. For one of two things must be the case. Either life guided by reason alone consists exclusively of obeying the Law – that is, 'command'. Otherwise, even if such a life might per chance lead to good action, this will be outside the Law, and thus a fault that is to be condemned (as the example of the soldier proves; and this is an allegory for the case of the citizen). Either way, Spinoza's teaching is thus the same as Hobbes's, which is none other than Maimonides's, although it is secularized or laicized. Hobbes laicizes 'command' such as Maimonides conceives it in his Codification; he laicizes the will of the instructor. The 'commandment' is no longer a 'commandment', because it expresses God's will through the intermediary of the prophet, but because it expresses the will of the sovereign. Moses, the man, is a legislator.

But if Spinoza himself adopts Hobbes's doctrine that reason commands obedience to the Law, because it is the Law and that there is no other definition of justice, then why does he denounce Maimonides's famous clause? As against Hobbes, Spinoza 'always preserves natural right intact'. What does that mean? The answer comes in the explanation that immediately follows: he 'only allot[s] to each magistrate in every state a right over their subjects commensurate with the excess of their power over the power of their subjects. That is what always happens in the state of nature.'¹⁰ So

Hobbes was still too idealist; Spinoza was a consistent materialist and thus a cynic; there is no foundation for law other than power, and consequently a theory of political authority is necessarily founded on 'what always happens in the state of nature'. A theory of justice is an objective description of the existing power relations between the sovereign and his subjects. So long as the sovereign has the power [*puissance*] necessary to maintaining his authority [*pouvoir*], he has the right to it; once he loses that, he loses this right. Spinoza is explicit in this regard, in another passage of Chapter XVI of the *TTP*:

> sovereigns, we showed, retain the right to command whatever they wish only so long as they truly hold supreme power. If they lose it, they at the same time also lose the right of decreeing all things, which passes to the man or men who have acquired it and can retain it.[11]

Marx and Engels's remark on Hobbes would thus, seemingly, even further apply – if not exclusively so – to Spinoza, precisely because he always 'preserves natural law intact:' 'If power is taken as the basis of right, as Hobbes, etc., do, then right, law, etc., are merely the symptom, the expression of other relations upon which state power rests'.[12] So was the divergence between Spinoza and Hobbes purely descriptive and not normative? It seems that Spinoza would legitimize the revolutionary act, in the descriptive sense, in that the overthrow of an enfeebled regime is something natural and thus legitimate; whereas Hobbes would condemn it in the name of the Law. But each of them are essentially indifferent to the nature of the old regime – and indeed the new one. Whether it is a revolutionary or counter-revolutionary act, Spinoza would seemingly analyse it as an evolution of power relations that in itself justifies sovereign right. However, such a reading would fail to understand the art of Spinoza's writing and indeed, both the spirit and letter of his example of the 'agreement' – 'To understand this better, imagine that a highwayman forces me to promise to give him all I have, at his demand.'[13] Spinoza always preserves natural law intact, and in natural law the dispossessed man could legitimately recover his good – which is his freedom – once he could put up the force necessary to recovering it. His doctrine is a materialist politics of the free man. That is the thread that he never loses from sight, on pain of falling into the nihilist alternative: either the transcendence of the Law, or else the law of the strongest. These alternatives are the (dogmatic) face and (sceptical) reverse side of one same coin.

*

Spinoza always preserves natural law intact. In so doing he desacralises the will of the sovereign, which is only a sovereign will on account of his power: 'it is foolish to call for someone else to keep faith with oneself, in perpetuity, if at the same time one does not try to ensure that violating the agreement will result in greater loss than gain for the violator'.[14] The gain in question is in his interest, in the sense of a good; if violating the agreement will not result in greater loss than gain, then the sovereign's will is nothing. Does Spinoza argue that there are no greater evils than the elimination of state sovereignty? Or does he maintain that there are no greater evils than what *prevents* men's freedom? In the *Ethics*, IV, *scholium* II of proposition 37, he reformulates the principle of the state:

> in order that men may live in harmony and help one another, it is necessary for them to give up their natural right and to create a feeling of mutual confidence that they will refrain from any action that may be harmful to another. The way to bring this about (that men who are necessarily subject to passive emotions (Cor. Pr. 4, IV) and are inconstant and variable (Pr. 33, IV) should establish a mutual confidence and should trust one another) is obvious from Pr. 7, IV and Pr. 39, III. There it was demonstrated that no emotion can be checked except by a stronger emotion contrary to the emotion which is to be checked, and that every man refrains from inflicting injury through fear of greater injury. On these terms, then, society can be established, provided that it claims for itself the right that every man has of avenging himself and deciding what is good and what is evil; and furthermore if it has the power to prescribe common rules of behavior and to pass laws to enforce them, not by reason, which is incapable of checking the emotions (Sch. Pr. 1 7, IV), but by threats.[15]

A sovereign governs men not by reason but by threats, that is, by fear, for 'an emotion can only be restrained by an emotion stronger than, and contrary to itself'. Only on this condition can a 'general rule of conduct' be established and govern men: the empire of fear. That is the Law of the place, the structure that governs a collective's empirical existence.

To adopt comrade Badiou's Mallarméan formula, if *nothing will have taken place but the place itself*, then in the last analysis human reason commands nothing other than obedience to the Law, because it is the Law. The transcendence of the Law was secularized, from Maimonides to Hobbes, but the principle remained exactly the same. And in the *Ethics*, IV, *scholium* II of proposition 37, Spinoza is apparently saying no different to this: as he goes on to explain, 'wrongdoing' and 'merit' do not exist in 'a state of nature', but exclusively in relation to the laws of the city: 'Wrongdoing is therefore nothing other than disobedience, which is therefore punishable only by the right of the State, and on the other hand obedience is held to be merit in a citizen because he is thereby deemed to deserve to enjoy the advantages of the state.'[16] He concludes 'From this it is clear that justice and injustice, wrongdoing and merit, are extrinsic notions, not attributes that explicate the nature of the mind. But I have said enough on this subject.'[17] When fear reigns and justice consists exclusively of obedience, the ruling class's own morality itself constitutes the Law: 'an emotion can only be restrained by an emotion stronger than, and contrary to itself'. The enslaving passion regulates the collective life of men. Nothing will have taken place but the place itself. But enough on this point.

*

The politics of free men begin with the affirmation of something other than the Law: the affirmation of an idea. In the *Ethics,* Spinoza affirms the idea of a politics, and more particularly in proposition 63 of Book IV, together with its proof:

> Proposition 63. He who is guided by fear, and does good so as to avoid evil, is not guided by reason. Proof. All emotions that are related to the mind insofar as it is active, that is (Pr. 3, III), emotions that are related to reason, are emotions of pleasure and desire only (Pr. 59, III). Therefore (Def. of Emotions 1 3), he who is guided by fear and does good through fear of evil is not guided by reason.

The free man lives guided by reason; and reason commands obedience to the laws of the city, which govern men by fear. Does that mean that in the last analysis man's freedom consists of internalizing – rationalizing – the empire of fear? Is this the internalization of its explicit meaning? Proposition 32 of Book IV teaches, 'Insofar as men are subject to passive emotions, to that extent they cannot be said to agree in nature.'[18] Fear is an enslaving passion and insofar as it is this that constitutes the Law, men cannot be said to be naturally in harmony. There is, then, no common good, but a common rule for living, which necessarily transcends what it regulates, for want of knowledge of a common good. The only common thing is the enslaving passion that establishes other men's Law. Conversely, proposition 35 of book IV teaches, 'Insofar as men live under the guidance of reason, to that extent only do they always necessarily agree in nature.'[19]

Does politics of the free man consist of internalizing fear, an enslaving passion, or of emancipating men from its empire? In Appendix IX of Book IV of the *Ethics*, Spinoza writes:

> Nothing can be more in harmony with the nature of anything than other individuals of the same species, and so ... there is nothing more advantageous to man for preserving his own being and enjoying a rational life than a man who is guided by reason. Again, since among particular things we know of nothing more excellent than a man who is guided by reason, nowhere can each individual display the extent of his skill and genius more than in so educating men that they come at last to live under the sway of their own reason.[20]

Reason commands obedience to the laws of the city, for this is to choose the lesser of two evils: a city's institution of a common rule for living is founded on fear – threats – since 'an emotion can only be restrained by an emotion stronger than, and contrary to itself'; fear is an enslaving passion and men under its empire, cannot be said to be naturally in harmony. What is the internalization of its explicit meaning? Is this the rationalization of fear? This is the morality of the ruling class, the morality of Saul, denounced by the prophet Samuel: it does not know its explicit meaning, but passionately submits to it, in order to perpetuate the empire of fear.[21] But let's go back to Spinoza and his materialist politics of the free man; 'in so training men that they come at last to live under the dominion of their own reason', *in hominibus ita educandis, ut tandem ex proprio rationis imperio vivant*. If the morality of the ruling class consists of rationalizing the empire of fear, Spinoza's politics consists of emancipating men from its enslaving reign, so that they might finally live under the dominion of reason itself. In Chapter XVI of the *TTP*, Spinoza writes:

> Acting on command, that is, from obedience, does take away liberty in some sense, but it is not acting on command in itself that makes someone a slave, but rather the reason for so acting. If the purpose of the action is not his own advantage but that of the ruler, then the agent is indeed a slave and useless to himself. But in a state and government where the safety of the whole people, not that of the ruler, is the supreme law, he who obeys the sovereign in all things should not be called a slave useless to himself but rather a subject. The freest state, therefore, is that whose laws are founded on sound reason; for there each man can be free whenever he wishes, that is, he can live under the guidance of reason with his whole mind.[22]

The 'slave' is the man alienated to other men's sovereignty; the purpose of his actions is not his own freedom, but someone else's benefit. In this case, it is only the sovereign's power that can legitimize his sovereignty, for in the last analysis his is the Law of the strongest. So reason commands obedience to him, just as it commands giving in to the highwayman's demands. For man to be a 'subject' and not a 'slave', there has to be a state whose 'supreme law' (*summa lex*)[23] is securing the well-being [*salut*][24] of the whole people and not of those in command. In this case, to obey the Law is to work for one's own freedom and for that of everyone else. So reason commands obedience to the laws, even when the sovereign's power is nil. The state's *true* sovereignty is thus proportional to its lack of power; it is absolute when the state ceases to exist as both a power and a Law: 'The freest state, therefore, is that whose laws are founded on sound reason; for there each man can be free whenever he wishes, that is, he can live under the guidance of reason with his whole mind.' The laws of the freest state educate men in living guided by reason, so that they can ultimately live as absolutely free men, without Law. Spinoza immediately adds: 'Similarly, though children are obliged to obey all their parents' commands, they are nonetheless not slaves, since a parent's commands are mostly directed to the good of the children.'[25] True parents educate their children to become men, that is to say, men freed of parental tutelage. Similarly, in Chapter XX of the *TTP*, Spinoza concludes

> It very clearly follows from the fundamental principles of the state which I explained above that its ultimate purpose is not to dominate or control people by fear or subject them to the authority of another. On the contrary, its aim is to free everyone from fear so that they may live in security so far as possible, that is, so that they may retain, to the highest possible degree, their natural right to live and to act without harm to themselves or to others. It is not, I contend, the purpose of the state to turn people from rational beings into beasts or automata[26]

As against Maimonides's clause, which is the foundation of Hobbes's state, Spinoza counterposes the becoming of free men. The ethics of 'command', such as Hobbes defines it, prohibits this becoming, because it conceives the Law [*Loi*] in the form of the laws [*droit*] of Other men. In his preface to the *Guide for the Perplexed*, Claude Birman writes:

> In every sense, God remains radically unknowable, in himself just as to others. So here there is no question of a dogmatic theology. What remains to be enounced is the dimensions of the relation that God

entertains with *us*. What relations? The God of Israel is defined as he who 'brought the Jews out of Egypt' (Ex. 20.1-2), meaning he who liberates from oppression and delivers from servitude.

The biblical god enjoins man to free himself from the laws of Other men. In Chapter V of the *TTP*, where Spinoza analyses the laws particular to the Hebrews and relates these laws to the foundation of their state, the philosopher explains:

> Thus, now that their state is dissolved, there is no doubt that the Jews are no more bound by the Law of Moses than they were before the commencement of their community and state. For while they dwelt among other peoples before the exodus from Egypt, they had no special laws, and were bound only by the natural law and, indubitably, the law of the state in which they were living, *so far as it did not conflict with the natural divine law*.[27]

Why specify that 'before the exodus from Egypt' the Hebrews were bound by obedience to the law of the state in which they lived, '*so far as it did not conflict with the natural divine law*'? For even when it did conflict with it, would this not be the same as the case of the commands – 'however absurd' – which reason nonetheless commands obedience to, because this is to choose the lesser of two evils? In his *Political Treatise*, Spinoza is explicit on this subject:

> So the more a man is guided by reason – that is, the more he is free – the more steadfast he will be in preserving the laws of the state and in carrying out the commands of the sovereign whose subject he is … If a man who is guided by reason has sometimes to do, by order of the commonwealth, what he knows to be contrary to reason, this penalty is far outweighed by the good he derives from the civil order itself; for it is also a law of reason that of two evils the lesser should be chosen. Therefore, we may conclude that nobody acts in a way contrary to what his own reason prescribes insofar as he does that which the law of the commonwealth requires to be done.[28]

Spinoza writes that the subjects of the 'law of the state' that governed the Hebrews 'before the exodus from Egypt', were bound to observe it '*so far as it did not conflict with the natural divine law*'. But if 'nobody acts in a way contrary to what his own reason prescribes insofar as he does that which the law of the commonwealth requires to be done', then how can 'the law of the state' 'conflict with the divine natural law'? His idea is wrapped up in this contradiction. If divine Law ordered submission to the sovereign's Law, just because he is the sovereign, and if justice thus consisted of obeying laws regardless of their content, then Moses would not have defied the Pharaoh. Rather, the divine Law enjoins men to free themselves from other men's laws. The rules governing the state are only legitimate on condition that they do not conflict with 'the natural divine law', a law that works to emancipate the human from the Law, such that he is absolutely free – that is, *elect*.

10 THE TREE OF KNOWLEDGE

In theorizing the 'command' – which is obligatory in virtue of the will of the instructor – Hobbes inscribes Maimonides's clause at the foundation of politics. This clause is itself the outcome of the dogmatic and sceptical (be it Jewish, Christian or Muslim) reaction against the danger that knowledge represents. And whereas Maimonides demands that obedience to the Law refers to 'our master Moses', Hobbes demands that we believe that Jesus 'is Christ':

> For Christ does not forgive sins for everyone, but only for those who repent, or obey, i.e. for the just (I do not say the innocent, but the just; for justice is the will to obey the laws and is compatible with a sinner; and the will to obey, in Christ's eyes, is obedience. The just man (not everyone) shall live by faith. Obedience therefore justifies because it makes just, in the way in which Temperance makes temperate, Prudence prudent, and Chastity makes chaste, that is to say essentially. And it puts a man in the position of being capable of pardon. Again Christ did not promise to condone the sins of all the just but only of those who believe that he is Christ.[1]

Spinoza instead works to universalize the remission of sins – hence the last of his seven foundations of universal faith, enumerated in Chapter XIV of the *TTP*:

> 7. Finally, God forgives the repentant their sins; for there is no one who does not sin, and therefore if this were not clearly established, all would despair of their salvation and would have no reason to believe that God is merciful. But anyone who firmly believes that God forgives men's sins

with the mercy and grace with which he directs all things and is more fully inspired with the love of God for this reason, truly knows Christ according to the spirit, and Christ is within him.

Once again, it is important to understand the significance of the adverb 'truly' in Spinoza's writing. This is a response to Hobbes who, for his part, rubber-stamps a Christian sectarianism founded on a dogmatic understanding of knowing Christ. Where Spinoza writes that the man who 'is more fully inspired with the love of God', 'truly knows Christ according to the spirit', Hobbes writes 'all that is necessary to *salvation* is contained in two Vertues, *Faith in Christ* and *Obedience to Laws*'.[2] *And when it comes to 'faith in Christ', the English philosopher submits to the dogma such as it was established by Augustine:*

> The *unum necessarium*, only article of faith, which the Scripture maketh simply necessary to salvation is this, that Jesus is the Christ. By the name of Christ is understood the King which God had before promised by the prophets of the Old Testament to send into the world, to reign (over the Jews and over such of other nations as should believe in him) under Himself eternally; and to give them that eternal life which was lost by the sin of Adam.[3]

If accession to the 'eternal life' is conditional on reparation for the 'sin of Adam', this reparation depends not on knowledge but on obedience (to laws) and faith (in Christ). That is Hobbes's interpretation of Paul's famous formula at the outset of his *Epistle to the Romans*: the 'obedience of the faith'. In *On the Citizen*, Hobbes also conceives the 'baptismal covenant' in terms of faith and obedience:

> *The men to whom St. Peter preached on the day of Pentecost*, next after the Ascension of our Saviour, asked him, and the rest of the Apostles, saying, (Act. 2.37.) "Men and Brethren what shall we doe?" to whom St. Peter answered (in the next verse) "Repent, and be Baptized every one of you, for the remission of sins, and ye shall receive the gift of the Holy Ghost. Therefore Repentance, and Baptisme, that is, believing that Jesus is the Christ, is all that is Necessary to Salvation. Again, our Saviour being asked by a certain Ruler, (Luke 18.18) "What shall I doe to inherit eternall life?" Answered (verse 20) "Thou knowest the Commandements, Doe not commit Adultery, Doe not Kill, Doe not Steal …" which when he said he had observed, our Saviour added, "Sell all thou hast, give it to the Poor, and come and follow me".[4]

Augustine, Maimonides, Hobbes and Strauss are in agreement: it is not *knowledge* that repairs 'the sin of Adam', but *obedience* (to the Law) and *faith* (in the only mediator between God and men). Spinoza keeps 'the spirit of Christ', but not without specifying: the spirit of Christ, 'that is, the idea of God'. He thus blows apart the Christian dogma to which Hobbes made his pledge of allegiance.[5] But also and above all, he introduces the *idea* – that is, knowledge – instead of obedience. This is an unpardonable crime.

Hobbes conceives just and unjust and good and evil on the model of the divine word that prohibits eating from the tree of knowledge. But does his exegesis of the Scripture determine his doctrine, or is it his doctrine that determines his exegesis of the Scripture? He writes:

> Legitimate kings therefore make what they order just by ordering it, and make what they forbid unjust by forbidding it. When private men claim for themselves the knowledge of good and evil, they are aspiring to be as Kings. When this happens the commonwealth cannot stand. The most ancient of all God's commands is, (Gen. 2.17): *Do not eat of the tree of knowledge of good and evil*; and the oldest of all the devil's temptations is (3.5): *You will be as gods knowing good and evil.*[6]

A man who takes it upon himself to choose good from evil, just from unjust, independently of 'command', is a culpable man; he impedes the exercise of divine authority, whether that of God or of the state; he gives in to 'the most ancient of the devil's temptations'. And even if this does happen to mean acting in conformity with the Sovereign's laws, he is still at fault, because in referring to his own knowledge of good and evil he shows that he has eaten the forbidden fruit. Hobbes returns to this point, specifying:

> Note *in passing* that by the precept not to eat of the *tree* of the knowledge of good and evil (whether it is judgement of Good and Evil that is forbidden here, or eating some fruit from a tree), God required utterly simple obedience to his precepts, without argument as to whether the precept was Good or Bad; for without the command, the fruit of the tree has nothing in its nature by which its eating could be morally bad, i.e. a sin.[7]

The reason for the prohibition is not 'drawn from the matter itself' – here meaning the fruit of this tree – but from 'the will of the instructor', be that the God or the Sovereign. This 'instructor' has 'required utterly simple obedience to his precepts', 'without argument'; that is to say, without seeking to know their *raison d'être*, for in the last analysis, 'Legitimate kings therefore make what they order just by ordering it, and make what they forbid unjust by forbidding it.' And that is that. The prohibition on eating the fruit of the tree of knowledge is not something for knowledge to concern itself with: 'for without the command, the fruit of the tree has nothing in its nature by which its eating could be morally bad, i.e. a sin'. No; the prohibition on eating the fruit expresses a prohibition on knowledge (in matters of good and evil) and this prohibition is the principle of obedience to 'command'. It is not the idea of justice, but the *absence* of such an idea.

Yet, this is, seemingly, Spinoza's own doctrine, as he elaborates in *scholium* II to proposition 37 of his *Ethics*, Book IV:

> Thus in a state of nature wrongdoing cannot be conceived, but it can be in a civil state where good and bad are decided by common agreement and everyone is bound to obey the state. Wrongdoing is therefore nothing other than disobedience, which is therefore punishable only by the right of the State, and on the other hand obedience is held to be merit in a citizen because he is thereby deemed to deserve to enjoy the advantages of the state ... From this it is clear that justice and injustice, wrongdoing and merit, are extrinsic notions, not attributes that explicate the nature of the mind. But I have said enough on this subject.[8]

Thus defined, 'justice and injustice' are not 'attributes which display the nature of the mind'. Does there exist, according to Spinoza, a knowledge of justice and injustice, good and evil, that displays the nature of the mind? In his letter to Blyenbergh, he writes that philosophers practise virtue not in the manner of obedience to a Law, but out of love (*non ut Legem sed ex amore*) and it is on this basis that he interprets the prohibition against eating from the tree of knowledge:

> Therefore the command given to Adam consisted solely in this, that God revealed to Adam that eating of that tree brought about death, in the same way that he also reveals to us through our natural understanding that poison is deadly. If you ask to what end he made this revelation, I answer that his purpose was to make Adam that much more perfect in knowledge.[9]

The incompatibility of Spinoza's and Hobbes's interpretations of the prohibition to Adam seems to lack any possibility of mediation. For the former, God enjoined man not to obey, but to know; for the latter, he enjoined man not to know, but to obey.

In his interpretation of the first three chapters of Genesis, Leo Strauss counterposes 'a life of obedience' commanded by the Bible to 'a life of human freedom', commanded by philosophy. For Strauss, the deprecation of the celestial in the creation story is a condemnation of philosophy, identified with cosmology because it claims to discern good from evil on the basis of a knowledge of nature. To claim to know the distinction between good and evil, Strauss concludes, is to serve the stars, to fall into an idolatry of human nature, and make oneself culpable of the sin of Adam and Eve:

> man certainly chose to disobey. He chose therewith the principle of disobedience. This principle is called knowledge of good and evil. *We* may say that disobedience means autonomous knowledge of good and evil, a knowledge which man possesses by himself, the implication being that the true knowledge is not autonomous; and, in the light of later theological developments, one could say the true knowledge of good and evil is supplied only by revelation.[10]

Strauss identifies the rectitude of operative thought with the adoration of celestial bodies. And it is on this foundation that he establishes the principle of a fidelity to the biblical god: a 'life of obedience'. Is this a life of ignorance? In his lecture 'Progress or Return?' he again addressed the biblical story of the tree of knowledge:

> the knowledge of good and evil means, of course, not one special branch of knowledge, as is shown by the fact that in God's knowing of the created things, they always end, "And He saw that it was good." The completed thing, the complete knowledge of the completed thing, is knowledge of the good, the notion being that the desire for, striving for, knowledge is forbidden. Man is not meant to be a theoretical, a knowing, a contemplating being; man is meant to live in childlike obedience. Needless to say, this notion was modified in various ways in the later tradition, but it seems to me that the fundamental thought was preserved, if we disregard some marginal developments.[11]

Strauss can only conceive of the unity of truth and good in the Bible in the following form: 'Man is not meant to be a theoretical being'. In other words, man is not meant to be a man. The child obeys the will of whoever instructs him – his father, his mother, his teacher, or simply an adult. Obedience is 'childlike', in the meaure that there is 'command'. Leo Strauss is consistent: he does not hesitate in concluding that 'man is meant to live in childlike obedience'. Indeed, if the prohibition made to Adam does concern knowledge – in Hebrew, *daat* – it is a castrating measure, because it is written that Adam *knew* Eve (Gen. 4.1) – the knowledge in question designating the intimate relations between a man and a woman. Continuing his reflection, Strauss goes on to address the biblical episode of the institution of kingship, when the Hebrews demanded a king:

> Fundamentally, the institution of human kingship is bad—it is a kind of rebellion against God, as is the *polis* and the arts and knowledge. But then it becomes possible by divine dispensation that these things, which originate in human rebellion, become dedicated to the service of God, and thus become holy. And I think that this is the biblical solution to the problem of human knowledge: human knowledge if it is dedicated to the service of God, and only then, can be good, and perhaps, in that sense, it is even necessary. But without that dedication it is a rebellion. Man was *given* understanding in order to understand God's commands. He could not be freely obedient if he did not have understanding. But at the same time this very fact allows man to emancipate the understanding from the service, from the subservient function for which it was meant, and this emancipation is the origin of philosophy or science from the biblical point of view. And so the antagonism between them.[12]

Strauss concedes that knowledge is 'necessary' and legitimate when its purpose is for man to be 'freely obedient'; but he terms 'rebellious' the fact of man 'emancipat[ing] the understanding from the service, from the subservient function for which it was meant'. To what 'service' was the understanding meant, if not that of knowing the God who 'brought the Jews out of Egypt'? That is the *worker*-theorist's question; the question to which a *bourgeois* theorist responds that man is meant to obey and not to know, and that by consequence knowledge is legitimate if – and only if – it is a function 'subservient' to the Law.

What is Spinoza's exegesis of the story of the tree of the knowledge of good and evil? It appears in Chapter IV of the *TTP*:

> If, for example, God said to Adam that he did not wish him to eat of 'the tree of the knowledge of good and evil', it would entail a contradiction for Adam to be able to eat of it, and therefore it was impossible that Adam should eat of it; for that eternal decree must have contained an eternal necessity and truth. However since Scripture narrates that God gave this command to Adam and in spite of this Adam did eat of the tree, we must necessarily infer that God only revealed to Adam

the bad effects that would necessarily befall him if he ate of that tree, but not the necessity whereby that bad consequence would follow. This is how it was that Adam perceived that revelation not as an eternal and necessary truth but rather as a ruling (*sed ut legem*), that is, as a convention that gain or loss follows, not from the necessity and nature of the action done, but only from the pleasure and absolute command of the prince. Therefore that revelation was a law and God was a kind of legislator or prince exclusively with respect to Adam, and only because of the deficiency of his knowledge. It is for the same reason too, namely deficiency of knowledge, that the Ten Commandments were law only for the Hebrews (*Decalogus respectu Hebraeorum tantum lex fuit*)[13]

Did God make this prohibition to Adam like one forbids a child something, without teaching of the 'necessity whereby th[e] bad consequence would follow'? In other words, was Adam forbidden the fruit so that he would obey, and not so that he would know? Or, is it that Adam misunderstood God's teaching, such that instead of perceiving 'that revelation … as an eternal and necessary truth', he took it 'for a law'? We learn from Spinoza's letter to Blyenbergh that God made this prohibition to Adam only 'To make him that much more perfect in knowledge' (*ut eum tanto scientia perfectiorem redderet*). So this is a teaching, and not a law: 'advice' in the sense of a precept that reason makes us follow on account of its own content and not a 'command', in the sense of a precept that reason makes us follow on account of the will of whoever instructs it. If Adam took the teaching for a 'command', that was the failing of *his* reasoning alone (*solum defectum ejus cognitionis*).

God revealed to Adam that he would die if he ate the forbidden fruit, but he did not *demonstrate* to him that eating from the tree of knowledge would bring death. Adam concluded from this that the relation was an arbitrary one – that God's word was not a teaching, *but a Law*. The Latin text says *sed ut legem*. This is Adam's fault. In turn, this sheds light on the formula in Spinoza's letter to Blyenbergh, where he refers to those who practise virtue not out of obedience to the Law (*non ut legem*), but out of love (*sed ex amore*). The philosopher's ethics corrects Adam's fall, in the sense of what kabbalistic Hebrew calls *tikkun* (תקון) – *repairing* the original sin.

Spinoza explains that the same was the case at Sinai: 'It is for the same reason too, namely deficiency of knowledge, that the Ten Commandments were law only for the Hebrews.' The Hebrews at the foot of Mount Sinai repeated Adam's fall. If we go back to the explicit sense of the Bible, the Hebrews' fault at the foot of Mount Sinai was that of having set up a golden calf. Even in the terms of the kabbalistic tradition, this was the repetition of the fall of Adam. Setting up a golden calf was the act of setting up a Law, for want of knowing it; hence Moses's reparatory act of breaking the tablets. This was the affirmation of a reparatory *orality*; or, in Spinoza's terms, it was the affirmation of the primacy of the idea over the Law. Again with regard to the revelation at Sinai, the Talmud (tractate Shabbath 145b–146a) teaches:

> Why are idolaters lustful? Because they did not stand at Mount Sinai. For when the serpent came upon Eve he injected a lust into her: [as for] the Israelites who stood (עמדו) at Mount Sinai, their lustfulness departed; the idolaters, who did not stand at Mount Sinai, their lustfulness did not depart.

In his *Guide for the Perplexed*, II, 30, Maimonides devotes a chapter to the 'philosophical explanation' of Genesis I–IV and cites this passage from the Talmud:

> The following is also a remarkable passage, most absurd in its literal sense; but as an allegory it contains wonderful wisdom, and fully agrees with real facts, as will be found by those who understand all the chapters of this treatise. When the serpent came to Eve he infected her with poison; the Israelites, who stood at Mount Sinai, removed that poison; idolaters, who did not stand at Mount Sinai, have not got rid of it. Note this likewise.[14]

What does standing at Mount Sinai mean? In his famous clause, Maimonides answers that it means obeying the commandments ordered by God through the intermediary of Moses. By virtue of his obedience to the ('Noahic') laws, the pious man of whatever seed is delivered from the poison that has contaminated humanity to its very bones. This is the rupture that Maimonides introduced within post-Talmudic Judaism, together with Juda Halevi, whose *Kuzari* takes a literal reading of the Talmudic apologue in Shabbath 146a; only the 'Israelites' are delivered from the seed of the serpent. The fall of Adam abolished the universal Law of man's creation. After the fall, only the Law of Sinai delivers humans from the serpent's seed; and this is the Mosaic Law, addressed to 'Israelites' alone – the *nation* that God brought out of Egypt. Maimonides objects that this apologue's passage is 'most absurd in its literal sense'. Indeed, a teaching from the tractate Sanhedrin 59a teaches that at Sinai Moses repeated the 'Noahic' commandments, from which it follows that the Mosaic Law included a fully universal 'Noahic' element and that by consequence, all pious men from whatever seed have an equal share in the world to come, at least so long as they obey the Law. Viewed in comparison with Juda Halevi's doctrine, we see that Maimonides's Codification universalized the Law, and it is this universalization of the Law that guides the argument of the *At Judaei* manifesto; the 'barrier' that prevents humanity is not the particularism of the Jewish law, but the universality of the Law, because it subjects the human to the impotence of thought. So who out of Juda Halevi, Maimonides or Spinoza was able to read the Talmud?

The Talmudic allegory contents itself with revealing that it is the fact of standing at Mount Sinai that delivers humanity from the serpent's seed, but it does not reveal the necessary consequences that follow from this. The Talmud tests us, just as the word of God tested Adam. What does standing at Mount Sinai mean? Spinoza writes that 'It is for the same reason too, namely deficiency of knowledge, that the Ten Commandments were law only for the Hebrews.' The pact at Mount Sinai repeats the fall of Adam; it is on account of *their* deficiency of knowledge that the Hebrews make God's word at Sinai into a Law. But is the Talmud – which is essentially dialectical, two-sided and contradictory – a Law? The codifier Maimonides interprets the revelation at Sinai as a Law. For his part, Juda Halevi interprets the revelation at Sinai as the election of the seed of Israel.

Spinoza's move is that of a *worker* theorist of the name 'Jew'; in his exegesis of the Scripture, 'true virtue' and 'understanding' come in place and instead of the 'seed of Israel' *and* the universality of the Law. Having established that much, let's read the Talmud; let's proceed from the explicit meaning toward the implicit one, such that we can internalize its teaching and know it. The Mosaic Law is only addressed to the 'Israelites' alone because they have come out of Egypt. Let's translate that: only a collective of free men linked by a common experience of a god who has 'brought them out of Egypt' can recognize his godliness and live under his law. Indeed, since Abraham the liberating word has been addressed to men endowed with an inner freedom, because it is they who can understand it. After the sin of the golden calf came the second tablets. And this time the Hebrews were prepared to understand; in other words, they accepted that writing is subordinate to orality – that is, a god who speaks; what Spinoza calls 'the *idea* of God'.

The serpent had told Eve that if she and Adam ate the fruit from the tree of knowledge they would be as gods, knowing good from evil (Gen. 3.5). Hobbes observes that this is the first of the devil's temptations and interprets it as follows: it is forbidden to eat the fruit from the tree of knowledge because eating it provides knowledge of good and evil, and having this knowledge amounts to freeing the understanding from the subordinate function that it was meant to have. According to this interpretation, therefore, the devil invites woman to know; he invites the human to liberate her understanding, inviting her to live above the Law like gods. Again in Chapter IV of the *TTP*, Spinoza returns to the story of the tree of knowledge:

> Now let us pass to the second point, running through Scripture, to see what it teaches about the natural light of reason and this divine law. The first thing that strikes us is the history of the first man where it is narrated that God forbade Adam to eat of the fruit of 'the tree of the knowledge of good and evil', which seems to mean that God instructed Adam to do good, and to seek it under the aspect of good and not as the opposite of what is bad, that is, to seek good for the love of good rather than from the fear of harm. For as we have already shown, he who does good from a true love and knowledge of good, acts freely and with a constant purpose, but he who does good from fear of suffering injury, is simply driven to avoid what is bad, like a slave, and lives at the command of another. Hence, this one prohibition laid by God on Adam entails the whole divine law and agrees fully with the dictate of the natural light of reason. It would not be difficult to explain the whole history, or parable, of the first man on this basis, but I prefer to let it go. I cannot be absolutely sure whether my explanation agrees with the intention of the writer, and many people do not concede that this history is a parable, but insist it is a straightforward narrative.[15]

According to Spinoza, God enjoined man to know good. That is why God forbade man the fruit of the tree in question: so that he would not know good *in relation* to evil, like a man 'driven to avoid what is bad, like a slave, and [who] lives at the command of another' like a man subjected to the Law. This, conversely, is what the serpent expects of man; that is what he, as the master of pleasure and death, expects of him. From Hobbes to Spinoza, the serpent has become God and God has become the serpent.

*

In terms of literal exegesis, Hobbes's interpretation is principally founded on the verse from Gen. 3.22 where after Adam and Eve have eaten the forbidden fruit God says, 'Behold, the man is become as one of us, to know good and evil.'[16] The proliferation of translations across history all – or almost all – converge: in eating the fruit from the tree of knowledge, man became in the image of god – 'as one of us'. Consequently, the verse from Gen. 3.22 confirms the truth of the serpent's word when – in Gen. 3.4-5 – he foretold to Eve that if she and Adam ate the forbidden fruit, they would not die but would be like gods, knowing good and evil. So the prohibition was against knowing – against living as a sovereign, free man. Is this the explicit meaning of the Scripture? The letter of the Hebrew text in Gen. 3.22 reads:

כאחד היה האדם

Sticking to the letter of the Hebrew, God says that 'Adam was like [a god]' and not that he *became* like one. How should this be translated? This is an important question: whether humanity was in the image of God *before* eating the fruit from the tree, or *after* doing so. In the first case, the serpent has tricked the woman, because he has stripped humanity of its grandeur while claiming to embellish it. In the second case, the serpent speaks the truth, but finds that truth and the Law do not intersect.

If we translate 'Adam was like a God' – the implication being, he no longer is, after eating the fruit – it follows that God enjoined man to live guided by knowledge; that is to say, in the understanding of a divine word that forbids man to die. For *eating* the fruit from the tree of knowledge is a death – a way of getting to know death. *Eating* from the tree of knowledge is not a knowledge, but the symptom of an impassioned ignorance, which Spinoza names 'the deficiency of knowledge'.

If, conversely, we translate 'Adam is become like a God' after having eaten the fruit from the tree, it follows that God enjoined man not to know and that in eating the fruit – transgressing the prohibition against knowledge – Adam and Eve came to know; they freed their existence of the subordinate function that it was meant to have.

How should this be translated? From the Septuagint to the Vulgate and Protestant, Jewish, academic and poetic versions, the enormous majority of translations in all languages have adopted the interpretation that corroborates the serpent's word: after eating from the tree of knowledge, Adam 'is become like [a god]'. Yet, the Hebrew says 'was like one' (כאחד היה). In his translation of Genesis, Henri Meschonnic conforms to the ruling interpretation: 'voilà, l'homme est comme un' ('behold, man is like one'). And in a note he justifies his choice to translate in the present tense a verb (*hayah*) that is, conversely, conjugated in the past tense in the Hebrew:

'is', *hayah*, the perfect form of the verb 'to be' – the present result of a past action, which forbids saying 'was' (which would mean the opposite – that he is no longer). Hence as an exceptional case, here the finished action takes the present tense. There are two solutions to this: those who have transposed it into 'is become' (Osterwald, Segond, Fleg, the Jerusalem Bible and the TOB); with two variants: Lemaistre de Sacy's ('behold Adam become ...') and the Rabbinate's ('here, man become'). The other solution is to use the present: Cahen's (adding 'now' – 'now man is like ...') and similarly Grosjean's ('now man is ...) and Chouraqui's ('here, the husbandman is ...')[17]

Meschonnic invokes Hebrew grammar: the perfect tense of the verb 'to be', *hayah*, is the 'present result of a past action, which *forbids* saying "was"' (my emphasis). So in this view to be 'like one' – to be knowing – is the 'present result of a past action', namely the action of having eaten the forbidden fruit. Is it the Law of Hebrew Grammar that forbids understanding and thus translating it as 'was'? Or, is it that an underlying interpretation of the Bible narrative is instead laying down the Law, here? What Meschonnic puts in brackets – 'which forbids saying "was" (which would mean the opposite – that he is no longer)' – is singular, in this regard. And why not understand it as saying precisely that Adam 'is no longer [like a god]' *after* having eaten from the tree of knowledge? Meschonnic concludes, 'Hence *as an exceptional case*, here the finished action takes the present tense' (my italics). To translate the Hebrew *hayah* as 'is' or 'is become' rather than 'was' is, indeed exceptional, and a very singular one. In fact, it is an exception that makes what the serpent says true: he spoke the truth in explaining to Eve that when God forbade man the tree of knowledge, he did so because he was forbidding him from knowing. Conversely, what is the meaning of the Hebrew word *hayah* if we read the plot of the Bible story a different way – if we have a different understanding of the word of God? Translating it poses no problems: it is a finished past action. Adam 'was' *like a god*, which means that he *is no longer like one* after the fall and not that he *is become like one*. This gives an entirely different meaning to what follows: 'and now, lest he put forth his hand, and take also of the tree of life, and eat, and live for ever, Therefore the Lord God sent him forth from the garden of Eden'. It is because man is no longer 'like a God'; because he no longer lives guided by knowledge; because he has lost his *understanding* of the word of God, that the tree of life is now forbidden to him and he is sent forth from the garden of Eden.

Meschonnic maintains that Hebrew grammar *forbids* this reading, but according to very learned Bible scholars it is the conjugation of the verb 'to be' in the past tense – in Hebrew, *hayah* – that poses a problem to those who want to read it as saying that Adam 'is' or 'is become' *like a God*. The commentary by Adam Clarke (1760–1832) is testament to this, as is that of Haim ben Attar (1696–1743), both of whom were astonished to find the word 'to be' conjugated in the past tense where they had expected it to be in the present. The former is a highly reputed Protestant exegete and the latter an equally reputed Jewish exegete (author of the well-known commentary *Or ha-Haim*). Even before them, Isaac Abravanel (1437–1508) had already objected to Maimonides's interpretation, on the basis of the Hebrew *hayah*. And nor did Renaissance Bible scholars going back to the letter of the Hebrew text fail to interrogate its grammar. We might take the case of Brian Walton's 1657 Bible, a work of scholarship if there ever was one. It includes six Latin translations of six different versions of the Bible: from the Hebrew version (the so-called Masoretic Text) to the Greek (the Septuagint), the Aramaic (*Targum Onkelos*), the Samaritan, the Syriac and the Arabic versions. Since this polyglot Bible had a philological purpose, the Latin translations are strictly literal. It sought to set the variations among the oldest versions of the Scripture in the hands of a very great number of European Bible scholars. Yet, of the six Latin translations of Genesis 3.22, the only column that reads, 'Adam was like [a god]', is the literal translation from the Hebrew *hayah*: 'Ecce homo *fuit* sicus unus'.

The interpretation that lays down the Law by invoking grammar demands a short philological digression:[18] it is not the Hebrew *hayah* that 'forbids' understanding this as 'the Adam (*ha-adam*) *was* like [a god], rather than that he *is become* like one by sinning. *The Adam* – that is, the human – was 'like one' before the fall, during the encounter between man and woman in Genesis 2.22-24: 'This is now bone of my bone, and flesh of my flesh'. This is the ethics of the encounter outside of the Law: in the image of the God who 'brought the Jews out of Egypt'.

*

Why does the woman transgress the prohibition against dying? Let's read. The woman, Eve, was not present when God forbade Adam to eat from the tree of knowledge of good and evil. If we hold to the second story of man's creation (Gen. 2), she had not yet been created. So we have to ask what Adam taught her on this subject, such that she would be instructed in the word of God. So seeing things from Adam's perspective: What would we have said to Eve? Hobbes would have told her, 'That's the Law, my dear, like it or not – the Sovereign told me in person: don't eat from this tree, hands off! For that is His will'. And that is, indeed, what Adam, broadly speaking, had to tell her. Spinoza explains that this expresses the deficiency of *Adam*'s knowledge; we would add – where the serpent slithered. For the serpent is the symptom of a word that polices, under the cover of being policed. With Adam having made Eve his slave, it was the serpent who ruled the roost. The enslaving passion of fear reigned in the garden. The Law of impassioned ignorance succeeded the ethics of the encounter outside the Law.

We learn from the Bible story of Adam and Eve that after the man had made God's teaching a Law, the woman no longer spoke to a man (to Adam) but to a serpent, an animal that arises from Adam's fall: or more precisely, which makes itself a home thanks to the deficiency of *Adam*'s knowledge. She eats the fruit, then gives it to the man to eat. Humanity is ignorant of God's teaching and this ignorance thus comes in two phases; firstly, Adam makes the teaching a Law, thus making himself the woman's master; then, second, Eve transgresses it. This is the (dogmatic) face and (sceptical) reverse-side of one and the same coin. Adam and Eve have become master and slave. They are naked. Exiled.

*

Proposition 68 of Book IV of the *Ethics* teaches, 'If men were born free, they would form no conception of good and evil so long as they were free'. In the proof, Spinoza explains: 'I have said that a free man is he who is guided solely by reason. Therefore, he who is born free and remains free has only adequate ideas and thus has no conception of evil … and consequently no conception of good.'[19] There follows a *scholium*:

> It is clear from Pr. 4, IV that the hypothesis in this proposition is false and cannot be conceived except insofar as we have regard solely to the nature of man, or rather, to God not insofar as he is infinite but only insofar as he is the cause of man's existence. This and other truths that we have already demonstrated seem to be what Moses intended by his history of the first man. For in that narrative no other power of God is conceived save that whereby he created man; that is, the power whereby he had regard only for man's advantage. And this is the point of the story that God forbade the free man to eat of the tree of the knowledge of good and evil, saying that as soon as he should eat of it he would straightway fear death instead of desiring to live. Again, the story goes that when man had found woman, who agreed entirely with his own nature, he realized that there could be nothing in Nature more to his advantage than woman. But when he came to believe that the beasts were like himself, he straightway began to imitate their emotions (Pr. 27, III) and to lose his freedom, which the Patriarchs later regained under the guidance of

the spirit of Christ, that is, the idea of God, on which alone it depends that a man should be free and should desire for mankind the good that he desires for himself, as I have demonstrated above (Pr. 37, IV).[20]

The hypothesis of proposition 68 is 'false'; man, part of nature, is not born free and he does not naturally and necessarily live the experience of freedom. The fact that this proposition is false – that it is an untruth – provides an introduction to the Bible story, to the fiction of Adam and to experience guided by the idea. For this is what 'seem[s] to have been signified by Moses in the history of the first man'. Spinoza proposes an exegesis of this history: the free man lives guided by reason alone, beyond 'good and evil' – if that means a 'good' which is 'good' relative to some 'evil' – but he does not live without good, if that means a good which has the form of truth; and as Spinoza argues in his treatise *On the Improvement of the Understanding*, 'the truth needs no sign – it being to possess the subjective essence of things, or, in other words, the ideas of them, in order that all doubts may be removed'. True is not relative to false, but is true on its own account; similarly, it is not attested to by some law, or some fine rule verifying that it conforms to the Law. And the same is also true of *true good*. So God forbade man to die – that is, to conceive good only relative to evil (scepticism) or only relative to the Law (dogmatism). He forbade him to be ignorant.

Spinoza writes: 'God forbad man, *being free*, to eat of the tree of the knowledge of good and evil' (our emphasis). Let's translate that: he forbade Adam to think and act out of obedience to the Law (*ut Legem*) rather than out of the love of good (*ex amore*). He forbade him to hand himself over to death: 'as soon as man should have eaten of it, he would straightway fear death rather than desire to live'. Which we should take to mean: as soon as he ate the fruit, his existence would be subjected to the fear of death, and powerlessness to affirm his desire to live as a free man.

Where does Adam's sin come from? In the *scholium*, Spinoza answers: 'after he believed the beasts to be like himself, he straightway began to imitate their emotions, and to lose his freedom'. In the *TTP* he explains that it is, 'only because of the deficiency of his knowledge', that this 'revelation was a law'. When the Law reigns, the imitation of animal emotions is unleashed. As the Law represses animal emotions it simultaneously unleashes their imitation. This knotting of the Law and animal emotions is the starting point for the infinitely malign union that rots humanity down to its bones.

The human has to convert to knowledge – that is, to *repair* (*tikkun*) the fall – in order that the serpent's seed might cease to have its effect. And this is the last word of the *Ethics*: we do not rejoice in virtue because we control our lusts, but it is because we know this joy that we can control our lusts. The Law and the appetite for pleasure each feed one another, because they start out from one same cause: the passion of ignorance. That is the fall of the first man, Spinoza explains: it is because of his deficiency of knowledge that the serpent works his way in. This is the ill-fated tangle of a man and a woman: whereas man's desire is joy in the Law, woman's is its transgression. 'Heavens, it's my husband!' – such is the key to 'bourgeois' love.

*

At the beginning of the *Guide for the Perplexed*, Maimonides relates the 'question of great importance' that 'a learned man' posed him 'some years ago':

> It would at first sight, "said the objector," appear from Scripture that man was originally intended to be perfectly equal to the rest of the animal creation, which is not endowed with intellect, reason, or power of distinguishing between good and evil: but that Adam's disobedience to the command of God procured him that great perfection which is the Peculiarity of man, viz., the power of distinguishing between good and evil – the noblest of all the faculties of our nature, the essential characteristic of the human race.[21]

Maimonides replies to this objection by distinguishing between a first kind of knowledge, which consists of discerning true from false and a second kind of knowledge, which consists of discerning good from evil, or the fine from the ugly. This first kind is a true knowledge and the second, a probable opinion. Here we can recognize Augustine's doctrine as related by Arnauld, calling Descartes to order: we owe to *reason* what we understand in relation to true and false; we owe to *authority* what we believe in relation to good and evil. Since – Arnauld continues, citing Augustine – opinion, the third instance, is ignorance, it follows that if discerning good and evil exclusively pertains to opinion (that is, ignorance), a reasonable man will always follow authority on these matters – and here we again end up with Hobbes's doctrine. So before Adam ate from the tree of knowledge of good and evil, he only concerned himself with true knowledge, the knowledge of intelligible things and not of opinions relative to good and evil, fine and ugly. Maimonides continues:

> After man's disobedience, however, when he began to give way to desires which had their source in his imagination and to the gratification of his

bodily appetites ... he was punished by the loss of part of that intellectual faculty which he had previously possessed. He therefore transgressed a command with which he had been charged on the score of his reason; and having obtained a knowledge of the apparent truths, he was wholly absorbed in the study of what is proper and what improper.[22]

Why did Adam disobey? Why did he give in to the imagination and the pleasure of the senses – that is, giving in to apparent truths relating to good and evil, the fine and the ugly? The answer has been known for centuries: in the economy of the Bible story, women's role is that of introducing the imagination and the pleasure of the senses. Leo Strauss explicitly formulates this in his exegesis of the first three chapters of Genesis: 'Woman, that is the presupposition, is lower than man. And this low creature, I apologize, woman, lower still than man, begins the transgression.'[23] Indeed, if we repeat Adam's deficiency of knowledge, we will reach the conclusion that the sovereign appearance of the serpent is woman's deed: it is she who inaugurates transgression and who enthrones the pleasure of the senses, the seduction of nihilist pleasure. If, conversely, one does not repeat Adam's fall, one will conclude that the serpent works its way in on account of *Adam*'s deficiency of knowledge. If Adam had not subjected Eve to his Law, she would not have been a slave to pleasure. That is why Spinoza explains that the imitation of animal emotions *chez Adam* begins with the deficiency of *his* knowledge. That is why he explains that woman is the free man's good and if man loses his freedom, this is caused by the deficiency in *his* knowledge of woman:

> when man had found a wife, who was in entire harmony with his nature, he knew that there could be nothing in nature which could be more useful to him; but that after he believed the beasts to be like himself, he straightway began to imitate their emotions ... and to lose his freedom.

How do we get from woman 'in entire harmony with [man's] nature' to the imitation of animal emotions? Out of ignorance of love. Spinoza writes of love in his *Ethics* (Part IV, Appendix XX):

> As for marriage, it is certain that this is in agreement with reason if the desire for intercourse be engendered not simply by physical beauty but also by love of begetting children and rearing them wisely, and if, in addition, the love of both man and woman has for its cause not merely physical beauty but especially freedom of the spirit.[24]

The imitation of animal emotions begins from the subjection of the human to the Law.

There is a contradiction in connection to the story of the tree of knowledge, which we can see in Spinoza's letter to Blyenbergh: on the one hand, he explains that 'all that God has revealed to the Prophets as necessary for salvation is set down in the form of law',[25] while on the other hand he explains that the revelation God made to Adam had no goal other than 'To make Adam that much more perfect in knowledge'.[26]

God addressed himself to man so that man would know; but the prophets put God's word in a juridical form, either because they poorly understand it, or because they are translating it for the common man incapable of perceiving the sublime. That is what happened with Adam, just as it happened at Sinai: 'It is for the same reason too, namely deficiency of knowledge, that the Ten Commandments were law only for the Hebrews (*Decalogus respectu Hebraeorum tantum lex fuit*)'. Lagrée translates this as, 'the Ten Commandments were a law regarding the Hebrews alone', in order to render the Latin word *tantum* (only, uniquely, exclusively). But for whom were the Ten Commandments not a law? In his letter to Blyenbergh, Spinoza replies: 'philosophers and likewise all who have risen to a level beyond law'.[27] But was this a Law for the redactor [*der Redaktor*] of the Scripture? Spinoza's conclusion on Scripture in the *TTP* is seemingly the following: '[these texts are] manifestly speaking according to the [utterly deficient] understanding of the common people, whom Scripture strives to render not learned but obedient'.[28] Scripture expounds God's word in the form of a Law. It must take that approach, because of the deficient knowledge of the common man. He cannot know or grasp higher things but he can nonetheless obey. Spinoza goes further still: just like in the case of Adam or the sons of Israel at Mount Sinai, the prophets misunderstand:

> What we say about the Israelites and about Adam, must also be said of all the prophets who issued laws in the name of God: they did not perceive the decrees of God adequately as eternal truths.[29]

Moreover, Spinoza adds, this is even true of Moses, the greatest of the prophets of Israel: 'he perceived all these things not as eternal truths but as precepts and teachings, and prescribed them as decrees of God'.[30] Only Christ understands properly:

> I emphasize that these things must be said only about the prophets who gave laws in the name of God, but not about Christ. For concerning Christ, although he too appeared to issue laws in the name of God, one must see,

that he [on the contrary] understood things truly and adequately. Christ was not so much a prophet as the mouth-piece of God.[31]

So on the one hand is Moses, and together with him the prophets of the Old Testament, including Adam, who interpreted the word of God as a Law; and on the other hand, Christ, whom one must see ... understood things truly and adequately'. However, in the *scholium* to proposition 68 of Book IV of the *Ethics*, Spinoza names Moses as redactor of the story of Adam, referring to 'what seem[s] to have been signified by Moses in the history of the first man'. And in the *TTP*, speaking of this 'history', he concludes that 'Hence, this one prohibition laid by God on Adam entails the whole divine law and agrees fully with the dictate of the natural light of reason'[32] and that 'it would not be difficult to explain the whole history, or parable, of the first man on this basis'. So Moses, redactor of the story of Adam, does not suffer from the deficiency of knowledge that Adam does.

In the *scholium* from the *Ethics*, Spinoza exhibits minimal caution: he speaks of 'what *seem[s]* to have been signified by Moses in the history of the first man' (my emphasis). In the *TTP* he exhibits a maximum of caution, concluding his interpretation of the story of Adam with a double reservation: he is not certain that his explanation of the parable is right; and many deny that this is, indeed, a parable. Is there some problem with this precise point in the biblical text, which justifies his caution? Or, is there a problem with his *own* doctrine of the Scripture? Evidently, Spinoza was grappling with a contradiction: if we maintain to the last that 'Scripture strives to render not learned but obedient', then it is Augustine, Maimonides, Arnauld, Hobbes and then Leo Strauss who are interpreting the story of Adam, in conformity with the thinking of the Bible's redactor, and not Spinoza. Indeed, one cannot explain the parable of the first man like Spinoza does in the aforementioned *scholium* from the *Ethics* and in Chapter IV of the *TTP*, without it being manifest that Scripture seeks to render men learned, not obedient: hence the first part of his reservations, 'I cannot be absolutely sure'.

Then comes the second part: most deny that this is a 'parable', arguing that it is *literally* a 'straightforward narrative'. What does this mean, if not that it is a law? The 'parable' that Spinoza imputes to the prophets and by extension the Scripture itself, at each point contradicts the 'parable' of the first man, since Adam set up a law on account of the deficiency of *his* knowledge. There is one parable too many and the two are contradictory, or more exactly, antinomic: the one *forbids* the other, for if Moses at Sinai repeated Adam's lack of knowledge, then he cannot at the same time have been the *redactor* of the story of the first man, such as Spinoza understands it. The philosopher thus expresses some reservation: I am not sure, and many will not understand. He stops short, as he reaches the threshold of a revelation. Is this a historical-critical revelation? This contradiction is, indeed, resolved if we hypothesize that the redactor of the story of Adam is not Moses. Is this the 'critical' teaching that Spinoza has kept secret? In the *At Judaei* manifesto, after citing Maimonides's famous clause he concludes:

> I think it is evident to anyone who reads this attentively that all this is mere fabrication and does not rest upon the authority of the Bible, and hence one need only expound it in order to refute it.[33]

But if the 'Scripture' concerned – here meaning the Old Testament, or the Hebrew Bible – is the work of 'the prophets', whose 'words were adjusted to the framework of this parable rather than to truth',[34] then it follows that Maimonides the Codifier's clause, is backed up 'by the authority of Scripture', even if perhaps not by reason. Spinoza has stopped at the threshold of a biblical revelation, not a critical one: Scripture is a law in the eyes of the ignorant; it is the passion of ignorance that sets up obedience as a law and, with this, forbids knowledge. But for whoever knows how to read it, the ethic of the redactors of the Hebrew Bible, the ethic of 'Moses', is *different in nature*:

> The God of Israel is defined as the god who 'brought [the Jews] out of Egypt' (*Exodus* 20: 1–2); that is to say, the god who liberates from oppression and delivers from servitude. The four-letter Name (YHWH) is the name of a liberating god: and this is not just an add-on, as if it were one of his 'qualities' among others; rather, this god is *essentially* liberating. Such a god is incompatible with any other (*Exodus* 20:3-6) in the measure that the ultimate meaning of the creation is absolute freedom. And the Revelation's role is to enlighten processes of liberation, such that they might aptly discern, in the course of the world, what this freedom does and does not entail (Ex. 20:7).

In the terms of the Talmud, this would be expressed as follows: the Torah is not a Law; it is a dialectical, dual and contradictory knowledge of good. It is Maimonides's *Codification* that repeats the deficiency of Adam's knowledge and not Moses, the man who defied the Pharaoh, divided the sea and broke the tablets.

Like the *Hodie Judaei* manifesto, the *At Judaei* manifesto is testament to faith in the old Hebrew tradition. An evidently inspired Leo Strauss accurately identified the emotion driving the philosopher: 'Spinoza recognized the universalism of the prophets in some respects more clearly than some of the greatest traditional Jewish authorities'.[35]

What authorities is Leo Strauss thinking of? We don't know. But we do know that in the *TTP* Hobbes is a hidden enemy of Spinoza's. Nevertheless, Maimonides is mentioned at the end of Chapter V, instead of Hobbes – for if we unmask this Maimonides, it is indeed Hobbes. Conversely, the unmasked Hobbes is Maimonides's Codification: 'theology, which today, as we know, is wizened and has to keep out of sight'.[36]

Hobbes's ethics subject man to the Law, whereas Spinoza's frees the understanding and action that find themselves implicated by the Law. Two antinomic exegeses of the story of the first man follow from this, together with two antagonistic conceptions of politics.

So Spinoza's Bible is not Augustine, Maimonides, Hobbes or Leo Strauss's Bible: his Bible is a knowledge of the god who 'brought the Jews out of Egypt', while theirs is a Law that subjects mankind at the expense of human knowledge:

> The highest good of those who pursue virtue is common to all, and all can equally enjoy it.[37]

EPILOGUE

The consciousness of exploding the continuum of history is peculiar to the revolutionary classes in the moment of their action.
WALTER BENJAMIN, THESES ON THE PHILOSOPHY OF HISTORY

If we stick to the explicit meaning of the *Hodie Judaei* manifesto, in the first paragraph Spinoza is inviting the theological-political authorities to allow the Jews the possibility of exercising honorific functions. In the second, he is envisaging the re-establishment of their state, because the sign of circumcision could by itself assure the Jews an eternal existence (and across the changing course of things, this would probably eventually come to pass). Jean-Claude Milner claims that the hidden meaning is something else: that Spinoza is theorizing the disappearance of the name 'Jew' and working toward this end.

If we stick to the explicit meaning of the *Hodie Judaei* manifesto, Spinoza is reproaching 'the Jews' for being ignorant of 'the spirit of Christ', because Maimonides, codifier of Mosaic Law, condemns the free man. We would argue that the hidden meaning is something else: Spinoza is reproaching the theological-political authorities of being ignorant of the God who 'brought the Jews out of Egypt'. He is working so that God might be known.

Is each of these exegetes practising the same art? Are they, in the end, the two sides of one same coin? Apparently so – or more precisely, in a formal sense they are. But for competent readers, the contradiction is manifest and of principal importance. In the one case, sophistication makes a pact with violence; in the other, it is the idea that regulates sophistication.

It is interesting to retrace the institutional, editorial and media journey of Jean-Claude Milner's 'free arguments' on 'Spinoza and the Jews': a seminar at the *Institut d'études lévinassiennes*, a book published by Verdier, two TV programmes on France Culture, an article in *Le Monde*, a symposium at the Sorbonne, etc. That's how a debate on ideas can take place. 'Is Spinoza the theorist of the "perfect persecution" of the Jews? Let's discuss it at the Sorbonne'. Like Éric Marty's free ramblings on Badiou and the Jews,[1] Jean-Claude Milner's do not only have the function of impassioning honest folk, but also – and above all – a crucial function in the elaboration of their common morality.

A theorist of historical materialism knows how to identify a manoeuvre like this. It is a matter of making sure there is no choice other than the following one: hatred against the Jews or love for the ruling class. That is why today the 'bourgeois' theorists' argument *par excellence* is to hurl the accusation of anti-semitism against the 'worker' theorist of names; hence Spinoza, Badiou and I are patented anti-semites.[2] The alternative 'hatred against the Jews or love for the ruling class' was conceived in order to forbid the thinking, action and existence of the 'worker' theorist of names, while also allowing for the diversion of people's anger.

*

Dressing man's nudity is the act of subjectively reconquering his internal liberty; the act of knowledge. Spinoza's hole-marked coat symbolizes the hatred to which this act is subject. This is the Law's hatred for knowledge – a bourgeois hatred.

However, the Law is itself knowledge, for it establishes a common rule for living where there is none, where 'man is wolf to man'. Yet, it is also violence, for it forbids knowledge. The Law is ambivalent. It is the naked signifier of the sleeping father, drunk and alone.

Is Ham's violence – wanting to expose his father's nudity to his brothers – a revolutionary violence? That is the 'bourgeois' theorists' thesis; that is their exegesis of the Bible. So they repress the name 'worker', like how one represses an impulse. Do they truly believe that the theorist of the name 'worker' is setting out a programme for the liberation of impulses, or just feign to do so? Whatever the case may be, the true exegetes of the Bible know that Ham's violence is set in comparison with Shem's reparatory act – the act of dressing man's nudity, the act of knowledge. Where there was a Law – that is, where there was an ambivalence – the 'worker' theorist of names introduces the law of knowledge, the law of the emancipatory relation.

The ethics of the *worker* theorist of the name 'Jew' is thus an ethics *ex amore*, in the sense that Spinoza writes that 'the love of both, to wit, of the man and of the woman, is not caused by bodily beauty only, but also by freedom of soul'; conversely, the ethics of the *bourgeois* theorist of the name 'Jew', is an ethics *ut Legem*, in the sense that Milner writes that the return of the name 'Jew' has the corollary of the disappearance of the name 'worker'.

Meaning: the return of the name 'Jew' is legitimate if and only if it has the corollary of the disappearance of the name 'worker'.

Yet, the two names, 'Jew' and 'worker' were like one. A practitioner of historical materialism knows how to commemorate them.

APOLOGUE: THE SPECTRE'S MANIFESTO

There's something rotten in the Kingdom of Denmark.

Let's improvise, *in extremis*, a 'worker' apologue. Once there was a bad joke. The police ministers were worried about it. They banned the bad joke and its author. He then made yet more bad jokes as if to say: 'if the police ministers want to muzzle me, I will make lots of other bad jokes of the same type, even worse ones, for I have no fear of the police ministers'. The police ministers doubled down, then he did the same, and so on and so forth. The police ministers were worried by the rise of anti-semitism, for the man and his bad jokes were more and more popular the more they tried to muzzle him and he laughed in their faces. So they doubled down ever further and so did he, and so on and so forth. In repressing the comic affect they did even more to feed it. If they had not themselves laid this egg, they did incubate it and then fed the chick. In truth, the man with his bad jokes and the police ministers were the (sceptical) face and (dogmatic) reverse of one same dark disaster – indeed, they could have been swapped around. Thus, the liberalism of the Western democracies was long the comic reverse-side of the Stalinist tragedy, just as in the present the 'new anti-Semitism' is the sceptical reverse-side of a police dogmatism. Thus a new police arsenal was developed in order to combat the 'new anti-semitism'. But since it fed it, rather than combated it, how should we understand it? We know Leo Strauss's rule: 'If a master of the art of writing commits such blunders as would shame an intelligent highschool boy, it is reasonable to assume that they are intentional.' So it was a decoy, devised out of caution: in the last analysis, the police arsenal that was thus developed sought not to combat the popularity of bad jokes, but *something else*.

*

Indeed, some people were not completely duped. The French Communist Party spokesman observed: '[the minister of the police] has already saturated the political space with other subjects. Each time he does so, it's a clever way of drawing a curtain over subjects we consider rather more of a priority'.[1] It is vital, for those who have no idea of good, to build up a representation of evil. The bad jokes ended up saying that the ruling class is under the control of 'the Jews' and that evil comes from 'the Jews'. This allowed the theorists of bad jokes to reconcile the 'French', redefined to mean non-Jews. The reconciliation was thus the most conciliating possible – ultimately, the most charitable one. For their part, the ministers of the police ended up saying that they needed to have a free hand to combat the 'new anti-semitism' effectively, when this was not a matter of the means for combating 'terrorism'. Most importantly, this allowed them to unite the French around a common conception of politics: it must essentially be a policing matter, if it is to exist at all. Police institutions and anti-semitic jokes were the (dogmatic) face and (sceptical) reverse of one and the same coin, struck by an easily identifiable die: the die of nihilism. To cite Badiou – himself citing Deleuze, we have the 'disjunctive synthesis of two nihilisms'. Or else we can conclude, like Lacan, that we have 'Kant with Sade'.

It was said that the purpose of the police arsenal was to combat anti-semitism. They had nothing left to do except to characterize the 'worker' theorists of names as anti-semites: Spinoza, Badiou, others, soon also the name 'worker' and finally, the *idea* of a God who 'brought the Jews out of Egypt'. And that was that: the Law forbids knowledge; sophistication makes a pact with violence; man's nudity reigns. A deceptive animal establishes its uncircumcised kingdom.

*

Let's conclude, then, with Hamlet: *Nay, come, let's go together.*

NOTES

Prologue

1   Jean-Claude Milner, *L'Arrogance du présent*, Paris: Grasset, 2009, 212–13.
2   Ephesians 2.14-16, *King James Bible*.
3   Karl Marx and Friedrich Engels, *The German Ideology*, in *Marx/Engels Collected Works* (henceforth *MECW*), Vol. 5, London: Lawrence and Wishart, 1975, 329.
4   Or 'royalty'. See Chapter 3.

Part One: Introduction

1   Baruch Spinoza, *Theological-Political Treatise*, Cambridge: Cambridge University Press, 2007, 3.
2   Georges Friedmann, *Leibniz et Spinoza*, Paris: Gallimard, 1962, 260–1.
3   See Leo Strauss, *Spinoza's Critique of Religion*, Chicago: University of Chicago Press, 19.
4   See Strauss's 'Cohen's Analysis of Spinoza's Bible Science', in *The Early Writings (1921–32)*, New York: SUNY, 2002, 160. In the note to the French version (*Le Testament de Spinoza*, Paris: Cerf, 2004, 76–7) the translators note Freudenthal's judgement, which concludes, 'We cannot blame the community for having regarded Spinoza as an enemy within its own walls, or for casting him out; what cannot be excused is the violent manner in which the Herem was pronounced.' We would express reservations on the form, but not on the basic point: Spinoza was an 'enemy within'. This is a particularly happy formula …
5   Leo Strauss, *Spinoza's Critique of Religion*, 19.
6   Emmanuel Levinas, *Difficile liberté*, Paris: Albin Michel, 1963, Livre de Poche, 155.

7   Benny Lévy, *Le Meurtre du pasteur. Critique de la vision politique du monde*, Paris: Grasset/Verdier, 2002, 172–5.

8   Jean-Claude Milner, *Le Sage trompeur. Libres raisonnements sur Spinoza et les Juifs. Court traité de lecture I*, Paris: Verdier, 2013.

9   *Histoire de l'antisémitisme*, Vol. 1, Paris: Calmann-Lévy, 1954, 228.

10 Paris: Verdier, 2003; Paris: Grasset, 2005 and Grasset, 2009 respectively.

11 Milner, *Le Sage trompeur*, 27. We will note here that the present book was conceived during a writing residence with our comrades at the 'Envie de lire' bookshop in Ivry – a collective business created and functioning on the model of a workers' co-op – whereas Milner conceived and professed his doctrine of the name 'Jew' in an Institute founded in Jerusalem by Benny Lévy, Alain Finkielkraut and Bernard Henri Lévy. Hence there is a clash between two schools.

12 Milner, *Le Sage trompeur*, 93.

13 See translator's note.

14 Spinoza, *Theological-Political Treatise*, 55–6.

15 Milner, *Le Sage trompeur*, 90.

16 Ibid., 91.

17 Milner, *Le Sage trompeur*, 108.

18 Milner's choice and his analysis are probably not without connection to the story surrounding Spinoza's excommunication. The philosopher has been attributed the authorship of a Spanish-language *Apologia*, a sort of response to the Amsterdam Jewish community that had excommunicated him. Spinoza purportedly made use of this *Apologia* as he wrote the *TTP*, many of whose passages supposedly originate in this polemical text. In picking out an extract from the *TTP* and setting it up as a manifesto, Milner proposes to deduce the doctrine of the *Apologia*, if not the original text itself. Themselves writing on this supposed *Apologia*, Lagrée and Moreau conclude from their analysis of the historical documents that, 'all this comes from a rumour, and not from a book' (Spinoza, *Traité théologico-politique*, 7).

Chapter 1: Discourse on Method

1   Milner, *Le Sage trompeur*, 91.

2   Tacitus, *Annals*, XV, 44.

3 Ephesians, 2.14-15.

4 Milner, *Le Sage trompeur*, 20.

5 Ibid., 113.

6 Spinoza, *Ethics* in *Complete Works,* translated by Samuel Shirley, Indianapolis: Hackett, 2002, 357 (IVP 72).

7 Spinoza, *Theological-Political Treatise*, 46.

8 Ibid., 53.

9 Ibid., 55.

10 The Latin text reads '*postquam se ab omnibus nationibus ita separaverunt, ut omnium odium in se converterint*'. Appuhn as well as Lagrée and Moreau translate this as 'such as to attract hatred' (*de façon à attirer la haine*), which is a way of translating as literally as possible the Latin preposition *ut*. This preposition can express the idea of finality, thus meaning that the Jews have lived apart from the nations with the goal of attracting hatred; it could also express the idea of a result or consequence, with the Jews having lived apart for certain reasons, with the consequence that the nations resent them. Sensitive to this problem, Misrahi chooses to modify Appuhn's translation, such as to get rid of the idea of finality in favour of the idea of consequence: *les Juifs ayant vécu à l'écart de toutes les nations jusqu'à s'attirer la haine universelle* ('the Jews having lived apart from all nations, to the point of attracting universal resentment'. The Latin is equivocal: 'such as to attract hatred', may suggest that the Jews are responsible for the resentment they arouse. Spinoza is evidently not unaware of the Jews' religious fervour, for he is working to refute its arguments. It is, indeed, religious fervour that conceives 'election' in the form of the immutable attachment between God and the people that he has chosen for himself, 'election' being substantiated precisely by the laws and rites that God has prescribed to the Hebrews alone. For his part, Spinoza understands the particularity of laws and rites in reference to the Hebrews' state. But from the point of view of Jewish religiosity, these rites' *raison d'être* is election itself, and not the sovereignty of the state; and in consequence, this is also the reason for their attachment to the rites: they are testament to their 'election'. If the Latin proposition *ut* is equivocal, the reasoning within which the phrase in question is inscribed is unequivocal. Misrahi is thus right to translate this as 'to the point of attracting universal resentment'.

11 Spinoza, *Ethics*, 344 (IVP 45).

12 Ibid., 6.

13 Milner, *Le Sage trompeur*, 20–1.

14 Milner, *Le Sage trompeur*, 79.

15 Sabbatai Zevi aroused the enthusiasm of the low-ranking Jews, who saw him as a Messiah who would restore the Jews' state in the Holy Land. He ultimately converted to Islam in 1665. The affair caused a great hubbub at the time. Guershom Sholem devoted a book to it.

16 Spinoza, *Theological-Political Treatise*, 6.

17 Ibid.

Chapter 2: The Song of the Sign

1 [Segré's original French title is a delicious pun, which does not translate into English: '*Le chant du signe*' sounds very similar to '*Le chant du cygne*', 'Swansong'.]

2 Spinoza, *Theological-Political Treatise*, 55.

3 Milner, *Le Sage trompeur*, 101.

4 Ibid., 44.

5 Ibid., 102.

6 Ibid., 103.

7 Ibid., 77.

8 Spinoza, *Theological-Political Treatise*, 55.

9 Milner, *Le Sage trompeur*, 81.

10 Ibid., 77–8.

11 Ibid., 71.

12 Ibid., 77–8.

13 Ibid., 63.

14 Ibid., 9.

15 Spinoza, *Theological-Political Treatise*, 56.

16 Ibid., 63.

Chapter 3: Kingship

1 Milner, *Le Sage trompeur*, 17.

2. Ibid., 16.
3. Ibid., 21.
4. Ibid., 9.
5. Ibid., 44.
6. Ibid., 102.
7. Ibid., 79.
8. Ibid.
9. Spinoza, *Theological-Political Treatise*, 41.
10. Spinoza, *Traité théologico-politique*, 716 n66.
11. [Or indeed the English text here cited.]
12. Jeremiah, 31.35-37.
13. Ezekiel, 20.32-33.
14. Spinoza, *Theological-Political Treatise*, 53.
15. Ibid., 54.
16. Ibid.
17. Jeremiah 31.33.
18. Spinoza, *Theological-Political Treatise*, 54.
19. Strauss, *Spinoza's Critique of Religion*, 20-1.
20. *The Rebirth of Classical Political Rationalism*, Chicago: University of Chicago Press, 1989, 231.
21. In *Un État commun entre le Jourdain et la mer*, Eric Hazan and Eyal Sivan write: 'One of the most oft-heard bad-faith arguments levelled against the one-state solution is that it is an anti-Semitic proposal seeking to destroy the Jewish state. For example, listen to the famous Harvard law professor Alan Dershowitz, 'The one-state solution proposal now being made by Palestinian lawyers and some anti-Israel academics is nothing more than a ploy. It is designed to destroy the Jewish state of Israel and to substitute another Islamic Arab state' (*Jerusalem Post*, 20 October 2005) (Paris: La Fabrique, 2013, 47). Their book is accompanied by a DVD of Eyal Sivan's film *État commun*, without doubt the finest expression of contemporary Israeli cinema.
22. Milner, *Le Sage trompeur*, 84.
23. In the *Ethics*, Spinoza firstly states that 'virtue is nothing other than to act from the laws of one's own nature' (330, *scholium* of IVP 18). He then goes on to explain in the first *scholium* of IVP 37 that 'the difference

between true virtue and weakness can readily be apprehended from what has been said above; namely, true virtue is nothing other than to live by the guidance of reason, and so weakness consists solely in this, that a man suffers himself to be led by things external to himself and is determined by them to act in a way required by the general state of external circumstances, not by his own nature considered only in itself' (340).

Chapter 4: On Contradiction

1 Spinoza, *Theological-Political Treatise*, 250.
2 Ibid., 253.
3 Milner, *Le Sage trompeur*, 94.
4 Ibid., 95.
5 Ibid.
6 Ibid.
7 Ibid., 96.
8 Milner cites a version of the prayer in question: 'All vows which we may have made from the last Day of Atonement to this one, any prohibition or sentence of anathema that we may have pronounced against ourselves, any privation or renunciation that we have made by oath, promise or our word alone, we retract; may they all be declared invalid, cancelled, dissolved null and void; may they have no force nor value; may our vows not be regarded as vows, nor our oaths as oaths (Ibid., 95–6).
9 Ibid., 97–8.
10 Spinoza, *Theological-Political Treatise*, 12.
11 Ibid., 198.
12 Ibid.
13 Ibid., 198–9.
14 Ibid.
15 Strauss, *Persecution and the Art of Writing*, Chicago: Chicago University Press, 2013, 184.
16 Spinoza, *On the Improvement of the Understanding*, New York: Dover Publications, 2012, 7.
17 Ibid., 14.

18 Spinoza, *Theological-Political Treatise*, 254.

19 Ibid., 12.

20 Ibid., 198.

21 [A 'good' also in the sense of 'goods', possessions, assets.]

Part Two: Introduction

1 Ibid., 172, 179.

2 Spinoza, *Correspondence* in *Complete Works* cit., 834.

3 Spinoza says of the revelation made to Job that 'Being accommodated to Job's understanding and meant merely to convince him, these reasons are not universal ones intended to convince everybody' (*Theological-Political Treatise*, 41).

4 *TTP*, 16.

5 *Ethics*, 325, (IVP 7).

6 Maxime Rovere translates this as saying that philosophers practise virtue 'not as a law, but out of love' [*non pas comme une loi, mais par amour*]; Charles Appuhn bypasses the negation *non ut Legem*, which he judges seemingly redundant, and translates that they practise virtue 'out of love for it [virtue]' [*par amour pour elle*]; Madeleine Francès translates *Legem* as 'obedience': they practise virtue 'not out of obedience, but out of love' [*non par obéissance, mais par amour*]; Elwes, author of a nineteenth-century English translation, renders this as 'not in obedience to law, but through love'.

7 *Ethics*, 382 (IVP 42).

8 Ibid., 355 (IVP 67).

9 The notion of 'return' first appears in Leo Strauss, who borrows it from the Jewish religious tradition (the notion of *t'shuvah*); it designates the 'return' to a way of thinking and living that is placed under the authority of the revelation, after having stood apart from it. (Note in particular Leo Strauss's lecture 'Progress or Return?', *Modern Judaism*, 1981, Vol. 1, 17.) In a spoken intervention, Benny Lévy explained that with the expression 'the thought of the return' he intended to evoke 'the return to the transcendent God' (*La Confusion des temps*, Paris, Verdier, 2004, 86).

10 Appearing in the 2004 third issue of *Cahiers d'études levinassiennes*, devoted to 'Thinking on the Return', 113–45.

11 Ibid., 119.

12 Ibid., 116.

13 Ibid., 134.

14 Ibid., 143 n.18.

15 Ibid., 142.

16 Is this Emmanuel Levinas's conclusion when he writes 'And it is not by chance that the history of Western philosophy has been a destruction of transcendence' (*De Dieu qui vient à l'idée*, Paris, Vrin, 1982, Éditions de Poche, 1992, 95)? In order to answer this we would have to mount a deep investigation of Levinas's texts, such as to determine whether he considers the ethical transcendence of the face of others a Law. We will return to this question in a future work.

17 Lévy, *Le Meurtre du Pasteur*, 102.

18 Strauss, 'Progress or Return?', 33.

19 Strauss, *Leo Strauss on Maimonides*, Chicago: University of Chicago Press, 2013, 102.

20 Strauss, *Natural Right and History*, Chicago: University of Chicago Press, 1965, 74.

21 This formula also concludes the letter, in 16.26: 'But now is made manifest, and by the scriptures of the prophets, according to the commandment of the everlasting God, made known to all nations for the obedience of faith.'

22 *The Political Theology of Paul*, Stanford: Stanford University Press, 2004, 14.

23 In Romans 10.16, Paul writes: 'But they have not all *obeyed* the gospel. For Esaias saith, Lord, who hath believed our report?' (my emphasis).

24 'The German Ideology' in *Marx-Engels Collected Works*, London: Lawrence & Wishart, 1975, Vol. 5, 381–2.

25 'On the Interpretation of Genesis', *L'Homme*, 21/1, 15.

26 Ibid.

27 Ibid.

28 Ibid., 16.

29 Ibid., 16–17.

30 He writes: 'It appears from the first account that man is separated to the highest degree, that he can move or change his place, in a very metaphorical sense even, to the highest degree. But this privilege, this

liberty, this freedom, is also a great danger. Man is the most ambiguous creature; hence man is not called good, just as heaven is not called good. There is a link between the ambiguity of man, the danger to which man is essentially exposed, and heaven, with what heaven stands for; the attempt to find one's bearing in light of what is evident to man as man, the attempt to possess knowledge of good and evil, like the gods' (ibid., 17).

31 Ibid., 19.

Chapter 5: The *At Judaei* Manifesto

1 Spinoza, *Theological-Political Treatise*, 54.

2 Spinoza, *Traité théologico-politique*, 716 n.66.

3 The *Mishneh Torah* is a codification of the Talmud, redacted by Maimonides between 1130 and 1140. This was the first time that the Talmud was fully and systematically codified – that is to say, reordered, rewritten and rethought in the form of a legal code in converting to the of individuals, men can 'terminism of the human condition is only irrevocable at the collective level; co.

4 *Theological-Political Treatise*, 79.

5 According to another reading, 'but'.

6 [Here I have made the existing English translation from the Latin conform to Segré's French translation from the Hebrew. The English (*TTP*, 79) reads: 'Everyone who accepts the seven precepts and diligently practises them is among the pious of the nations and an heir of the world to come; that is, if he accepts them and practises them because God prescribed them in the Law and revealed to us through Moses that the same requirements had been prescribed to the sons of Noah before. But if he practises them because he has been convinced by reason that he should, he is not one of us, nor does he belong to the pious or learned of the nations'.]

7 *Theological-Political Treatise*, 79n.

8 'And one of the young Spinoza's masters': Étienne Balibar, *Spinoza et la politique*, Paris: PUF, 2011, 31.

9 Juda Halevi, *Kuzari*, I, 26–7.

10 Moshe Hayyim Luzzato, *The Way of God*, Jerusalem: Feldheim, 1997, 133.

11 Ibid., 135.

12 Ibid., 139.

13 Ibid., 143.

14 [The French translation of Luzzato cited by Segré renders this word as *pieux*, pious.]

15 Spinoza, *Theological-Political Treatise*, 79.

16 Much has been written on the fact that there are two different lessons in Maimonides's text, and that Spinoza picks up on one of them while discarding the other. According to the first, the man who lives guided by reason 'is not a pious man, and not (*ve-lo*) a wise man'; according to another lesson, he 'is not a pious man, but (*ela*) a wise man'. In Hebrew, the difference lies in the single letter *aleph*: according to those who read it as לא we get 'and not', whereas those who read it as אלא get 'but'. A lot of ink has been spilled discussing which is the right lesson. The one Spinoza picks up on (i.e. he is neither pious nor wise) appeared in all traditional editions up till the twentieth century.

Whatever the case may be, while this question does have some bearing on Maimonides's doctrine on wisdom (*hokhma*), it has no impact on the sole point of doctrine of interest to Spinoza – and us – namely the question of whether the man who observes the seven Noahic commandments guided by reason alone has a share in the world to come (whether or not he deserves to be characterized as a 'wise' man). After all, according to Maimonides, *only* 'pious' men have a share in the world to come and he concludes that the man guided by reason, is neither a 'resident-foreigner' nor a 'pious man'.

17 *Ethics*, 355.

18 Spinoza, *Theological-Political Treatise*, 201.

19 Ibid., 79.

20 Ibid.

21 According to the Gaffiot dictionary *incola, ae*, designates 'inhabitant', 'he who remains in a place'.

22 Paul, *Letter to the Ephesians*, 2.1116.

23 Tremellius's Latin Bible translates this as saying that the uncircumcised man does not have the status of a citizen of Israel (*abalienatos a civili status israelis*). The Vulgate translates: '*alienati a conversatione Israhel*'; the *King George Bible*, 'being aliens from the commonwealth of Israel'; Luther translated: '*ausgeschlossen vom Bürgerrecht Israels*'; Segond renders it as '*exclus du droit de cité en Israël*'.

This has a juridical consequence: the uncircumcised man does not have the same status as the circumcised man. He is not his equal, or his neighbour.

24 This is the argument of Eli Benamozegh's book *Israël et l'Humanité*, which, moreover, draws on the rule that Spinoza cites from Maimonides.

25 Since Paul's argument is founded on a false premise, it would seem to be a vain one, unless we understand it as follows: the sign of circumcision sets up a 'barrier' because it distinguishes between bodies, such as to forbid exchange between a woman of Israel and an uncircumcised man, and in so doing substitutes hatred for love. If that is the case, Paul's teaching must be the following: a man's *true* love for a woman does not depend on the circumcision of the flesh, which is the trace of man's own hand, but the circumcision of the heart, the trace of the word of God – or, to hold to the letter of the Christian fable, the work of the 'blood of Christ'. However, while this interpretation is justifiable, it is unable to give account of the dominant interpretation, or of the letter of Paul's *Epistles*: the Mosaic Law erects a 'barrier' between the circumcised and uncircumcised, not only in relation to the women of Israel, but in relation to the 'covenants of the promise'. Certainly, we should also address Giorgio Agamben's book on this subject, *The Time that Remains: A Commentary on the Letter to the Romans* (Stanford: Stanford University Press, 2005) as well as René Lévy's *Disgrâce du signe. Essai sur Paul de Tarse* (Lausanne, L'Âge d'homme, 2012). We will return to this in another book.

26 Badiou, *Saint Paul. La fondation de l'universalisme*, Paris: PUF, 1990, 87.

Chapter 6: A 'Christ' Without the Passion

1 'A hidden Opponent in Spinoza's Tractatus', *Harvard Theological Review*, 1995, volume 88, no. 3.

2 Spinoza, *Theological-Political Treatise*, 18.

3 Lodewijk Meyer, *La Philosophie interprète de l'Écriture* (translated by Lagrée and Moreau), Paris: Intertextes, 1988.

4 Moreau, *Spinoza. État et religion*, Paris: ENS Éditions, 2005, 101.

5 However, Preus reckons that the fact that Spinoza was targeting Meyer by way of Maimonides went unnoticed. He writes, 'Also unnoticed is the probability that Spinoza's cutting criticism of "Maimonides", particularly on the issue of biblical interpretation, targets Ludwig Meyer and the implication of his views'. But in the published editions of Spinoza's *Correspondence*, we find a letter from Velthuysen to Ostens providing a synthesis of the *TTP*, which shows that this connection did not escape him. Velthuysen identifies Meyer, termed the 'paradoxical theologian', with Maimonides: '[Spinoza] considers that all those who deny that reason and philosophy are the interpreters of Scripture will be on his side. For it is generally agreed that in Scripture there are predicated of God a great many things which are not applicable to God, but are adapted to human understanding in such a way that men may be moved by them and be awakened to the love of virtue. This being so, he thinks it must be accepted that the holy teacher intended by these untrue arguments to educate men to virtue, or else anyone who reads Holy Scripture is entitled to judge the intended meaning of the holy teacher according to the principles of his own the interpreter of Scripture. For he considers that Scripture must be understood literally, and that men must not be granted freedom to interpret as they please in a rationalistic way what is to be understood by the words of the prophet, so as to decide in the light of their own reasoning and acquired knowledge when it is that the prophets spoke literally and when figuratively' (Spinoza, *Correspondence*, 897). Where Velthuysen speaks of a 'paradoxical theologian', this was an epithet given to Meyer on account of the subtitle of his *Philosophia S. Scripturae interpres*, 'exercitatio paradoxica'.

6 Spinoza, *Political-Theological Treatise*, 78.

7 Ibid.

8 Ibid.

9 Is this deprecation of the Qu'ran, profane in view of the Holy Scripture, a manoeuvre made out of caution? Certain readers of Spinoza's think so. In his account of the *TTP*, Velthuysen writes that it follows from the author's position, that 'the Koran, too, is to be put on a level with the Word of God'. (Spinoza, *Correspondence*, 903); and responding to those who accused him of professing a divine law that made no distinction between the faithful (Christians) and the unfaithful, Spinoza himself answered that 'if [someone] replies that Mahomet, too, taught the divine law and gave sure signs of his mission as did the other prophets, there is certainly no reason for him to deny that Mahomet was a true prophet'. (Ibid., 906).

10 Spinoza, *Political-Theological Treatise*, 78–9.

11 Ibid., 68.

12 *Ethics*, II, Axiom II.

13 From Spinoza, *Correspondence*, 965.

14 Ibid., 967.

15 Spinoza, *Theological-Political Treatise*, 19.

16 Francès (Folio) chooses to Christianize the formula by introducing a true and proper 'incarnation'. However, this is to force the letter of the Latin text, and is not faithful to its spirit. Appuhn (GF) and Moreau (PUF) are more measured and also more faithful to the text, with Moreau holding closest to its letter.

17 *Ethics*, 355 (IVP 68).

18 *Theological-Political Treatise*, 98.

19 Ibid., 112.

20 Ibid., 112–13.

21 Ibid., 100.

22 Ibid., 40.

23 Spinoza, *Correspondence*, 977.

24 Ibid.

25 Ibid.

26 Ibid., 979.

27 The original text from the *Guide for the Perplexed* was in Judeo-Arabic, and it was then translated into Hebrew by Ibn Tibbon; then into Latin by Spinoza; and finally into English. The passage here in question has thus undergone three distinct, overlapping translations.

28 Maimonides, *Guide for the Perplexed*, II, 25.

29 Ibid.

30 We might emphasize that on this point Maimonides distinguishes himself from Blyenbergh, who writing to Spinoza expounded a method of exegesis that placed reason under the authority of the revelation. He explained that he had 'two general rules which always govern my endeavours to philosophise'. 'One is the clear and distinct conception of my intellect, the other is the revealed Word, or will, of God. In accordance with the one, I try to be a lover of truth, while in accordance with both, I try to be a Christian philosopher. And whenever it happens that after long consideration my natural knowledge seems either to be at variance with this Word or not very easily reconcilable with it, this

Word has so much authority with me that I prefer to cast doubt on the conceptions I imagine to be clear rather than to set these above and in opposition to the truth which I believe I find prescribed for me in that book' (Spinoza, *Correspondence*, 836).

31 Spinoza, *Theological-Political Treatise*, 89.

32 Ibid., 77.

Chapter 7: The Origin of the Law

1 Strauss, *Spinoza's Critique of Religion*, 23.

2 An analysis of the Talmud teaching in question would demand a considerable study. And this is, indeed, a necessary analysis, to which we will return in a future work. This is important for gauging the effect that Maimonides's Codification had on an ancient Hebrew tradition.

3 A *midrash* is an exegesis of biblical verses. This literary form continued for some time after the completion of the Talmud; this is called late midrashic literature. It then developed among the kabbalistic tendencies; the Zohar of the thirteenth century is essentially indebted to this, at least formally speaking.

4 [What follows is a rendering of Segré's own translation from Hebrew to French, translated into English]

5 We owe these textual references to Jacob I. Dienstag. See his article 'Natural Law in Maimonidean Thought and Scholarship' (*The Jewish Law Annual*, Vol. VI, 1987, 64–77). In a concluding annex, he responds to those researchers who have hypothesized that the *Mishnat Rabbi Eliezer* was redacted after Maimonides's Codification, meaning that Maimonides was *its* source, and not the other way round. To this effect, he cites the two references to the *Mishnat Rabbi Eliezer* found in Maimonides's own writing.

6 *Revue des Études juives*, 1935, 43.

7 See his *Perush ha-Mishnayot* on the *mishnah* of the tractate Hullin, 100b.

8 The formula 'our father Noah' is, moreover, an anomaly. It has no attestation in any other text of Talmudic or Midrashic literature; it is a hapax. The formula 'our father', in Hebrew *avinou*, is traditionally related either to the god-creator or else to the patriarchs Abraham, Isaac and Jacob. If the formulas 'sons of Noah' (*ben noah*) or 'sons of Adam' (*ben adam*) are commonplace in the Talmud and Midrashic literature, conversely there is no mention of 'our father Noah' or 'our father Adam', for it is the patriarchs who the 'Israelite' must follow. The author of the *Mishnat Rabbi Eliezer* nonetheless judged the formula 'our father Noah' appropriate when we are speaking of the man who observes the seven 'Noahic' commandments, for he is a 'son of Noah' and in this respect a subject of 'Noahic' law. But however logical his conclusion may seem, it is mistaken: when the prophetic injunction is addressed to the collective in a space other than that of the 'house', it refers not to the 'father' but to the 'master'. So in Moses's case, the accepted formula is 'our master Moses', in Hebrew *mosheh rabbenou*. And that is why in Maimonides's commentary on the *Mishnah*, he specifies that all the precepts of the Torah must be fulfilled in reference to 'our master Moses' and not in reference to 'our father' Abraham or Jacob. And this is all the more the case when we are speaking of the seven 'Noahic' commandments repeated by Moses at Sinai, addressed to all men.

9 Indeed, it is probable that the *Mishnat Rabbi Eliezer* is the work of several successive hands.

10 This statement will be contradicted by Talmudists who, basing themselves on commentators other than Joseph Caro, would argue that this distinction is taught in the Talmud. I cannot here elaborate a detailed analysis of the Talmud teachings in question, so for the moment, will base my position on Joseph Caro's commentary, concluding that this is not a teaching from the Talmud, but one that comes from the Codifier's own theological reflection.

11 *Responsa*, in Hebrew *She'elot ve-Teshuvot*, are texts that examine and clarify a point of religious practice. These were the first elements of putting Talmudic teaching in a juridical form.

12 Sanhedrin 56–9. The relations between justice as it is discussed in the *Tosefta* and observance of the seven 'Noahic' laws deserves a deep examination of its own. As we earlier indicated, we will have to analyse this on some future occasion.

13 Strauss, *Spinoza's Critique of Religion*, 23.

14 Spinoza, *Theological-Political Treatise*, 13.

15 Jerome, Letter 22.30.

16 Leo Strauss, 'Farabi's Plato', *Louis Ginzberg Jubilee Volume*, American Academy for Jewish Research, 1945, 373–4.

17 Strauss, *Persecution and the Art of Writing*, 'The Law of Reason in the *Kuzari*'.

18 Strauss, *Persecution and the Art of Writing*, 103.

19 Ibid.

20 Ibid., 111.

21 Strauss, *The Rebirth of Classical Political Rationalism*, 203–4.

22 Aristotle, *Nicomachean Ethics*, 5, V, in *Complete Works*, Vol. 2, Princeton: Princeton University Press, 1995, 1788.

23 Ibid., 6, XII, 1807.

24 Richard Bodéüs's French translation reads, '*Nous disons en effet de certaines personnes qu'elles exécutent ce qui est juste alors qu'elles ne sont pas encore justes elles-mêmes, par exemple, celles qui font ce que prescrivent les lois, soit à contrecœur, soit par ignorance, soit pour un autre motif, mais non parce que c'est juste*' (Paris: Garnier Flammarion, 2004, 337). ['Indeed, we say that some people accomplish what is just even though they are still not just themselves, for example those who do what the laws prescribe, either unwillingly or out of ignorance or some other reason, but not because it is just']. The context demands that we understand 'because it is just' not in the sense of what reason considers to be just, but in the sense that justice consists of obeying the law. And 'out of ignorance' thus means that the actor concerned was ignorant that the act he judged to be just – for he has, indeed, accomplished it – was precisely the act that the law ordained.

25 'Progress or Return?', *Modern Judaism*, 1981, Vol. 1, 17.

26 Alain Badiou, *Circonstances, 3. Portées du mot "juif"*, Paris: Lignes, 2005, 25, 27.

Chapter 8: True Otherness

1 Sesboüé, *Hors de l'Église pas de salut. Histoire d'une formule et problème d'interprétation*, Paris: Desclée de Brouwer, 2004.

2 Origen, *Homilies on Joshua*, Washington, DC: Catholic University of America Press, 2002, 49–50.

3 Sesboüé, *Hors de l'Église pas de salut*, 57.

4 Ibid., 69–70.

5 Cited in ibid., 8.

6 Paris, Desclée de Brouwer, *Etudes augustiniennes*, Vols 21–24, 3rd series: 'La grâce'.

7 Augustine, *Anti-Pelagian Writings*, 47.

8 Augustine, *On the Soul and its Origin*, II/17.

9 [In French *libre arbitre* means 'free will'.]

10 *Correspondence* in *The Philosophical Writings of Descartes*, translated by John Cottingham, Robert Stoothoof and Dugald Murdoch, Vol. III, Cambridge: Cambridge University Press, 1991, 56–7.

11 *Objections and Replies*, in *The Philosophical Writings of Descartes*, translated by John Cottingham, Robert Stoothoof and Dugald Murdoch, Vol. II, Cambridge: Cambridge University Press, 1984, 90.

12 Ibid., 105.

13 Ibid., 105–6.

14 Ibid., 106, our emphasis.

15 Ibid., 152.

16 Ibid.

17 Ibid.

18 Ibid., 172.

19 Descartes, Letter to Mersenne, 18 March 1641, in *Correspondence*, 175.

20 Ibid.

21 Descartes, *Œuvres philosophiques de Descartes*, Paris: Garnier, Vol. II, 319 n4.

22 Descartes, Letter to Mersenne, March 1642, in *Correspondence*, 211.

23 Ibid.

24 Descartes, *Œuvres philosophiques de Descartes*, Paris: Garnier, Vol. III, 31.

25 Spinoza, *Theological-Political Treatise*, 239.

26 Ibid., 270.

Chapter 9: The Masquerade

1 Hobbes, *On the Citizen,* Cambridge: Cambridge University Press, 1998, 156.

2 Spinoza, *On the Improvement of the Understanding*, 369.

3 Hobbes, *On the Citizen*, 131–2.

4 Ibid., 153.

5   Spinoza, *Theological-Political Treatise*, 79.

6   Excerpted in Strauss, *Le Testament de Spinoza*, 136.

7   Spinoza, *Theological-Political Treatise*, 200.

8   Ibid., 198.

9   Ibid., 204.

10 Spinoza, *On the Improvement of the Understanding*, 369.

11 Spinoza, *Theological-Political Treatise*, 200.

12 Marx and Engels, 'The German Ideology', 329.

13 *Theological-Political Treatise*, 198.

14 Ibid., 199.

15 *Ethics*, 340–1 (IVP 37).

16 Ibid., 341.

17 Ibid., 353, (IVP 63).

18 Ibid., 336, (IVP 32).

19 Ibid., 337, (IVP 35).

20 Ibid., 359.

21 Producer Camille Robert's 2013 *Logique de la peur* (2013), filmed in Israel, is a remarkable reflection on the role of fear in politics, even beyond the Israeli case.

22 *Theological-Political Treatise*, 201.

23 In a note, Lagrée and Moreau (Spinoza, *Traité théologico-politique*, 767) quote from Cicero's *De legibus*, III: *Salus populi suprema lex esto*.

24 [Literally, 'safety', as in the example of the 'Comité de salut public' (Committee of Public Safety) of 1793, but also 'salvation'.]

25 Spinoza, *Theological-Political Treatise*, 201.

26 Ibid., 252.

27 Ibid., 71, our italics.

28 Spinoza, 'Political Treatise', in *Complete Works*, Indianapolis: Hackett, 2002: 691–2.

Chapter 10: The Tree of Knowledge

1   *On the Citizen*, 244.

2 *Leviathan*, Oxford: Clarendon Press, 1952, 458.

3 Ibid., 462.

4 Ibid., 468.

5 This is not how Jean-Claude Milner understands it in *Le Sage trompeur*: here, he ascribes Hobbes's doctrine to Spinoza. Referring to the 'minimum credo' that Spinoza expounds in seven articles in Chapter XIV of the *TTP*, he explains 'It is a minimum in the sense that its articles are both necessary and sufficient to the foundation of a universal religion; it is a Christian credo, for, as Spinoza says, he who adheres to these seven articles has truly encountered Christ' (86). So according to Milner, in seventeenth-century Europe, Spinoza stuck to rules of caution when it was a matter of persecuting the Jews, to the point that he developed bewildering writing strategies, but conversely it is out of the question that we could identify any kind of rule of caution in his use of the name 'Christ'. Jean-Claude Milner's passion is an object of interminable analysis.

6 *On the Citizen*, 132.

7 Ibid., 188.

8 *Ethics*, 341, (IVP 37).

9 Spinoza, *Correspondence*, 834.

10 'On the Interpretation of Genesis', *L'Homme*, 21/1, 19.

11 'Progress or Return?', 43.

12 Ibid., 44. Italics in the original.

13 *Political-Theological Treatise*, 62–3.

14 *Guide for the Perplexed*, II/30.

15 *Theological-Political Treatise*, 65.

16 [From the King James Bible. The *TOB* version cited by Segré reads near-identically, 'Voilà que l'homme est devenu comme l'un de nous, pour connaître le bien et le mal'. He also cites the Rabbinic Bible published in 1904 under the guidance of Zadoc Kahn in 1904, which reads 'Voici l'homme devenu comme l'un de nous, en ce qu'il connaît le bien et le mal' ('Here is man become like one of us, in that he knows good and evil').]

17 Henri Meschonnic, *Au commencement. Traduction de la Genèse*, Paris: Desclée de Brouwer, 2002, 257.

18 Particularly instructive in this regard are the Spanish translations that circulated among the Jewish community of Amsterdam in the

seventeenth century. We can clearly distinguish between two schools of thought, therein: on the one hand, those who translate it as 'was' – *el ombre* fue *como uno* – and on the other hand those who translate it as 'is' – *el ombre* es *come uno*. These two variants were in competition ever since the first Spanish or Judeo-Spanish translations. Hence the fifteenth-century *Biblia de la casa de Alba*, translated from the Hebrew by rabbi Moses Arragel de Guadalajara, translated it as 'Adam *is* like one', whereas the sixteenth-century Ladino Bible of Ferrara translates it as 'man *was* like one'. The same is true of the Latin translations of the Renaissance era: while the majority followed the dominant interpretation, there are enough exceptions among Bible scholarship that we can conclude that this is not a question of grammatical law, as Meshonnic claims, but a question of interpretation. Sante Pagnini's 1528 Latin translation is strictly literal enough to translate this exactly as did Walton's polyglot Bible more than a century later: *Ecce homo* fuit *sicus unus*. Similarly, Sebastian Münster translated it as, '*Ecce ille homo* fuit *quasi unus*'. In general, the others who instead opt for the present tense follow the Vulgate, translating it as *factus est*: he 'is become' rather than 'was' (*fuit*) like a god. Certain Italian translations are also testament to the possibility – if not necessity – of translating this as 'was'. Thus, Santi Marmochini (Venice, 1546) translated it as *Ecco che Adamo estato quasi uno*, whereas Filippo Rustici (Geneva 1562), for example, translated it as *Ecco che Adam è divenuto quasi como uno*, as would the *Giovanni Diodati Bible* (1649). From Luther to Rosenzweig and Buber, passing via Mendelssohn, German Bibles have opted for *ist geworden* (in Rosenzweig and Buber, *ist worden*) – 'is become'. English Bibles also oscillate between 'is become' and 'has become', with the notable exception of Young's translation. This text sought to stick as close as possible to the letter of the Hebrew, to the extent that it was named 'The Young's Literal Translation'. It translates these words as 'the man was as one'.

19   *Ethics*, 355, (IVP 68).

20   Ibid.

21   *Guide for the Perplexed*, I, 2.

22   Ibid.

23   Strauss, 'On the interpretation of Genesis', 18.

24   *Ethics*, 360.

25   *Correspondence*, 834.

26   Ibid.

27 Ibid.

28 Spinoza, *Theological-Political Treatise*, 177.

29 Ibid., 63.

30 Ibid.

31 Ibid.

32 Ibid., 65.

33 Ibid., 79.

34 Spinoza, *Correspondence*, 834.

35 Strauss, *Spinoza's Critique of Religion*, 23.

36 Walter Benjamin, *On the Philosophy of History* in *Illuminations* (New York: Schocken Books, 1968), 253.

37 *Ethics*, 338, (IVP 36).

Epilogue

1 See *Une querelle avec Alain Badiou, philosophe*, Paris: Gallimard, 2007. His book is based on a long article that first appeared in *Les Temps modernes*.

2 Reporting on my excellent book *La Réaction philosémite* (Paris: Lignes, 2009, found in all good bookshops and notably at *Envie de Lire* (rue Gabriel-Péri, Paris – metro stop Mairie-d'Ivry), one weekly presented it as 'a new *Protocols of the Elders of Zion*'.

Apologue: The Spectre's Manifesto

1 *Le Monde*, Wednesday 1–Thursday 2 January 2014, 6. Already Lenin had written 'Everywhere the reactionary bourgeoisie has concerned itself, and is now beginning to concern itself in Russia, with the fomenting of religious strife – in order thereby to divert the attention of the masses from the really important and fundamental economic and political problems', cited by Pierre Tevanian, *La Haine de la religion*, Paris, La Découverte, 2013, 93. (Text here from English version of 'Socialism and Religion' in Lenin, *Collected Works*, Vol. 10, Moscow: Progress Publishers, 1965, 87).

INDEX

Abravanel 145
Adalbert of Bremen 35, 37
allegory in Scripture 88-92
animal emotions 147-50
anthropomorphic representations in Scripture 89
anti-Semitism 6, 25, 44, 61, 156, 159-60
Appuhn, Charles 7, 30, 78, 86
Arema, Isaac 73-4
Aristotelian science and philosophy 81-2
Aristotle 63, 77, 89-92, 106-7
Arnauld, Antoine 116-19, 148, 151
At Judaei manifesto 72, 79, 109, 141, 152
atheism 119
Augustine 103, 110-13, 117-19, 134-5, 148, 151
Auschwitz 49
Averroes 103

Badiou, Alain 80, 108, 126, 156, 160
baptism 112-13
bar Yohai, Shimon 100
ben Asher, Jacob 95
Benjamin, Walter 155
Bible, the 67, 69, 77, 145-7, 153
 translations of 145
 see also Genesis
Birman, Claude x-xi, 129-30
Bloch, Marc 3
Blyenbergh, Willem van 61, 64, 136, 139, 150

Boethius 103
Bosch, Hieronymus 113
bourgeois theorists 56, 67, 70, 80, 138, 156
Burman, Franz 3-4
Buxtof, Johannes 48

Caro, Joseph 95-7
Cartesianism 3, 82
Castiglione, Baldassare 35
Catholic Church 110
Cavaillès, Jean 3
Chinese peoples 27-33
chosen people, Hebrews as 14-15, 26-30
Christianity 70, 110
Cicero 103
circumcision 24-33, 37, 43, 79, 100, 155, 160
Clarke, Adam 145
Cohen, Hermann 4-6, 65, 67, 95-6, 99, 121, 123
commands as distinct from teaching 139
contradictory teachings of Spinoza 50-4
cosmology 69
creation of the world 69, 89-90
Cyprian of Carthage 109

Deleuze, Gilles 160
Descartes, René 3, 61, 82, 114-20, 148
divine Law 130-1

'dogmatic' method of interpreting Scripture 87-91

eating the fruit from the tree of knowledge 136-47, 150
'election' for the heavenly kingdom 14-17, 23, 27-33, 38-42, 45, 71-6, 111-12, 115, 121
Eliezer 96 *see also Mishnat Rabbi Eliezer*
Enelow, H. G. 97-100
Engels, Friedrich ix-x, 68, 125
Ethics (Spinoza) 14, 16, 49, 62, 65, 70, 76, 85-7, 126-8, 136, 146-8, 151
Euthyphron, the 106-8
Ezekiel 40-1, 71

faith in Christ 109, 115, 134-5
Al-Farah 103
Fathers of the Church 110-11
fear, empire of 127-8
Florence, council of (1442) 110
Francès, Madeleine 86
free men, politics of 127-8
Freud, Sigmund 5
Friedmann, Georges 3
Fulgentius of Ruspe 110

Genesis, Book of 69-70, 137, 140-3, 149
Gordin, Jacob 5
grace 111, 115-19
Graevius, J. G. 4
Greek philosophy 66-7
Grotius, Hugo 121
Gutmann, Michael 98-9

Haim ben Attar 145
Halevi, Juda 74, 76, 92, 104-5, 140-1
Hebrew grammar 143-5
Heidegger, Martin 65
heresy 112-13, 118

Hesiod 63
hidden meaning in Spinoza 13, 29, 33, 49, 155
'hidden opponent' of Spinoza 81-2, 153
historical materialism 156-7
Hobbes, Thomas 121-6, 129, 133-5, 142-5, 148, 151, 153
Hodie Judaei manifesto 11-14, 17-20, 23-7, 31-2, 38-45, 152
human nature 50-2, 55, 111-12, 124

Ibn Tibbon 89
idolatry 69-70
'indecency' 35-8
Islam 19-20, 66, 68, 101, 103
Israel, State of 43

Jeremiah 40-1, 71
Jerome 40, 103-4, 110
Jesuits 111
Jesus Christ ix, 83-93, 112, 119, 133-5, 150-1
  Gospel of 68
  resurrection of 88-91
  spirit of 91-3, 134-5, 155
  see also faith in Christ
Jews, the
  gentiles' resentment of 16-21, 23-4
  hostility towards 20-1, 156
  naming of ix-xi, 6-9, 11-13, 23-8, 36-8, 48-9, 80, 108-9, 156
  particularism and separateness of 11, 16-17, 20-1, 24
  persecution of 19-21, 23-4, 28, 36-8
  prejudice and polemics against 49-50, 92
  religious conversion of 17-21, 26-30, 37-8, 43-4, 53
Joshua 91
judgement, concept of 115

Kant, Immanuel 160
kingship 138
Kol Nidre prayer 48-9
Kuzari, the 104-8, 140

Lacan, Jacques 160
Lagrée, Jacquline 30, 39, 71, 78, 150
law
   of the state 124-31
   universality of 141
   see also Mosaic law; natural law; Noahic law; obedience to law
Leibniz, Gottfried 3-4
Levinas, Emmanuel 4-5
Lévy, Benny 4-5, 65, 67
libertinism 37
Limborch, Philippe van 4
Luther, Martin 92
Luzzato, Hayyim 74-6

Maimonides 66, 71-82, 87-92, 95-105, 109, 119, 123-6, 129, 133, 135, 140-1, 145, 148-53, 155
marriage 149
Martini, Martino 28-31
Marty, Éric 156
Marx, Karl ix-x, 68, 125
Menasseh ben Israel 73-4
Mersenne, Father 114-18
Meschonnic, Henri 143-4
Meyer, Lodewijk 82
Milner, Jean-Claude viii-xi, 5-9, 11-20, 23-32, 35-8, 42-4, 47-50, 53, 56, 65-8, 72, 80, 155-6
miracles 90-1
Mishnat Rabbi Eliezer 99-104
Misrahi, Robert 30, 78
monotheistic religions 102-3
Moreau, Pierre-François 30, 39, 71, 78, 82, 86
Mosaic law 68, 72, 76-9, 121-2, 140-1, 155

natural law 55, 122, 125-6, 130-1
Nazism 25, 37, 65, 67, 108
Nero 11-12, 44
Noahic law 77, 98-102, 123, 140-1

obedience to Law 124-9, 134-5
Oldenburg, Henry 84, 89, 91-2, 109, 119
Origen 109
original sin, doctrine of 111-13, 118, 139
Ottoman Empire 19-20, 26
'outlaw ethics' vii, 80, 105

parables 151-2
parental tutelage 129
Patriarchs, the 86-7, 146
Paul, St ix, 67-8, 78-9, 88-91, 134
Pelagius and Pelagianism 110-14, 118
Pharisees 39-42, 71-6, 79
philosophy 61-9, 105, 114-15, 136-7
'pious men' 97-101, 105, 123, 141
Plato 63, 103-7
Poliakov, Léon 6, 61
policing 160
Portugal, Jews in 16-17, 21
power relations 125 *see also* sovereign power
Preus, J. Samuel 81-2
promises, breaking of 47-56

Qu'ran, the 103

remission of sins 133
reparation 57
'resident foreigners' 77-9, 123
revelation 88, 92, 120

Sabbatai Zevi 20, 26-30, 44
Sade, Marquis de 160
salvation
   by faith 109

of non-believers 110
'sceptical' method of interpreting Scripture 87-8
schismatics 109-110
scholasticism 3, 114
Scripture 61-4
  interpretation of 87-90
  seditious views 47-55, 123
Sesboüé, Bernard 109-10
Socrates 105-6
sovereign power 123-6, 129
Spain, Jews in 16-21, 23-4, 28, 32-3
Spinoza, Baruch
  excommunication of 3, 5, 61
  followers of 9
  hostility towards 4-5
  modernity of 70
  and theologians 119-20
  see also At Judaei; contradictory teachings; *Ethics*; hidden meaning; 'hidden opponent'; *Hodie Judaei*; *Theological-Political Treatise*; *Treatise on the Improvement of Understanding*
Stalinism 159
'state of nature' 122-7, 136
Strauss, Leo 4-5, 13, 17-18, 24, 38, 42-5, 52-3, 66-70, 77-8, 95-6, 102-8, 135-8, 149-53, 159
Synopsis of the Meditations 117-18

Tacitus 11-12, 18, 44
Talmud, the 69, 72, 75, 81, 140-1, 152
Taubes, Jacob 68
Ten Commandments 140-1, 150
Theological-Political Treatise (*TTP*) 3, 11, 13, 17, 20, 31-2, 38-42, 45, 47, 52, 55-6, 61-4, 70-1, 76, 80-7, 92-3, 95, 113, 123, 125, 130, 147, 150-3
Thomas of Aquinas 121
Thomasius 3-4
Torah, the 74, 95-101, 108
Touati, Charles 104
Treatise of the Improvement of the Understanding 53, 147
t'shuvah concept 108

Vanini, Cesare 119

Walton, Brian 145
women, role and status of 149
worker theorists 56, 61, 70, 138, 156-7, 160

Zalman, Shlomo 97
Zephaniah 71
Zionism 27, 42-5
Zohar, the 100
Zosimus, pope 111